Arguing about the World

Arguing about the World

The Work and Legacy of Meghnad Desai

Edited by
Mary Kaldor and Polly Vizard

BLOOMSBURY ACADEMIC

First published in 2011 by

Bloomsbury Academic
an imprint of Bloomsbury Publishing Plc
50 Bedford Square, London WC1B 3DP, UK
and
175 Fifth Avenue, New York, NY 10010, USA

CIP records for this book are available from the British Library and the Library of Congress

ISBN 978-1-84966-521-6 (hardback)
ISBN 978-1-84966-544-5 (ebook)

This book is produced using paper that is made from wood grown in managed, sustainable
forests. It is natural, renewable and recyclable. The logging and manufacturing processes
conform to the environmental regulations of the country of origin.

Printed and bound in Great Britain by the MPG Books Group, Bodmin, Cornwall

Cover design: Sam Egarr

Contents

About the Contributors

Montek Singh Ahluwalia is currently the Deputy Chairman of the Planning Commission for India. He has been a key figure in India's economic reforms from the mid 1980s onwards and has held various senior positions, including Special Secretary to the Prime Minister, Commerce Secretary, Finance Secretary and Member of the Planning Commission. In 2001 he was appointed as the first Director of the newly established Independent Evaluation Office of the IMF and resigned from this position in 2004 to take up his present assignment.

Jagdish Bhagwati is University Professor, Economics and Law, at Columbia University and Senior Fellow in International Economics at the Council on Foreign Relations. He was recently Co-Chair of the High-Level Expert Group on Trade appointed by the Governments of Britain, Germany, Indonesia and Turkey. He has uniquely combined seminal scientific contributions to the postwar theory of commercial policy, strengthening greatly the case for Free Trade, with several bestselling books and op-ed essays in leading newspapers and magazines on current policy issues. He has been Economic Policy Advisor to the Director General, General Agreement on Tariffs and Trade (1991–93), Special Advisor to the UN on Globalization, and member of the Advisory Committee to UN Secretary General Kofi Annan on the United Nations New Partnership for Africa's Development. He was member of the World Trade Organization-appointed Expert Group on the Future of the WTO, and of the Eminent Persons Group appointed by the Director General of the United Nations Conference on Trade and Development on the future of UNCTAD. He is widely regarded as the intellectual father of the post-1991 reforms that have transformed India.

Jennifer L. Castle is an Official Fellow in Economics at Magdalen College, and a James Martin fellow at the Institute for New Economic Thinking at the Oxford Martin School, Oxford University. Previously, she was a British Academy postdoctoral research fellow at Nuffield College. Her research interests lie in the fields of model selection and forecasting, time-series econometrics and applied macro-economics. She has more than a dozen articles in journals and academic books published or forthcoming, including the *Journal of Econometrics, Journal of Forecasting, Journal of Time-Series Econometrics,* and *Journal of Macroeconomics.*

Charles Goodhart was born in London in 1936. He obtained the Bachelor of Arts Degree from Cambridge in 1960 and PhD in 1963 from Harvard University. Charles Goodhart, CBE, FBA is now Emeritus Professor, Director of the Financial Regulation Research Programme at the London School of

Economics and Political Science (LSE). Before joining LSE in 1985 as the Norman Sosnow Professor of Banking and Finance, he had lectured at the University of Cambridge and LSE, been an economic advisor in the Department for Economic affairs, and worked at the Bank of England for seventeen years as a monetary advisor, becoming a Chief Advisor in 1980. During 1986, Goodhart helped to found, with Professor Mervyn King, the Financial Markets Group at LSE, which began its operation at the start of 1987. In 1997, he was appointed one of the outside independent members of the Bank of England's new Monetary Policy Committee, serving until May 2000, and between 2002 and 2004 was an advisor on financial stability to the Governor of the Bank of England. Besides numerous articles and discussion papers, he has written several books on monetary history, and a graduate monetary textbook, *Money, Information and Uncertainty* (1989); and has published two collections of papers on monetary policy, *Monetary Theory and Practice* (1984) and *The Central Bank and The Financial System* (1995); and an institutional study of *The Evolution of Central Banks* revised and republished in 1988. His most recent book co-authored with Harald Benink and Jon Danielsson is *The Future of Banking Regulation: the Basel II Accord* (2009).

John Harriss, a social anthropologist, worked with Meghnad Desai as the first Programme Director in Development Studies at the LSE in the early 1990s. He retired from the LSE as Professor of Development Studies in 2006 and has subsequently worked as Director of the new School for International Studies at Simon Fraser University, Vancouver, Canada. His recent books include *Power Matters: Essays on Institutions, Politics and Society in India* (2006) and (edited, with Sanjay Ruparelia, Sanjay Reddy and Stuart Corbridge) *Understanding India's New Political Economy: A Great Transformation?* (2011).

David Held is the Graham Wallas Chair in Political Science, and was co-Director of LSE Global Governance, at the London School of Economics. Among his most recent publications are *Cosmopolitanism: Ideals and Realities* (2010), *Globalisation/Anti-Globalisation* (2007), *Models of Democracy* (2006), *Global Covenant* (2004), *Global Transformations: Politics, Economics and Culture* (1999), and *Democracy and the Global Order: From the Modern State to Cosmopolitan Governance* (1995). His main research interests include the study of globalisation, changing forms of democracy and the prospects of regional and global governance. He is a Director of Polity Press, which he co-founded in 1984, and General Editor of *Global Policy*.

David F. Hendry, Kt, is Professor of Economics, Fellow of Nuffield College, and Director, Institute for New Economic Thinking at the Oxford Martin School University of Oxford: previously Professor of Econometrics, London School of Economics. He was Knighted in 2009; is an Honorary Vice-President and past President, Royal Economic Society; Fellow, British Academy, Royal Society of

Edinburgh, and Econometric Society; Foreign Honorary Member, American Economic Association and American Academy of Arts and Sciences. He has been awarded seven Honorary Doctorates, as well as the Guy Medal in Bronze by the Royal Statistical Society. He is listed by the ISI as one of the world's 200 most cited economists, and has published more than 200 papers and fifteen books on econometric methods, theory, modelling, and history; numerical techniques; computing; empirical economics; and forecasting.

Mozaffar Qizilbash is Professor of Politics, Economics and Philosophy in the Department of Economics and Related Studies and the School of Politics, Economics and Philosophy at the University of York. His research has focused on a variety of interrelated topics in economics and philosophy, welfare and development economics.

Danny Quah is Professor of Economics at the LSE and was Co-Director of LSE Global Governance. He is also a Council Member on Malaysia's National Economic Advisory Council; a member of the World Economic Forum Global Agenda Council on Economic Imbalances; and serves on the Steering Committee of the Abu Dhabi Economics Research Agency (ADERA) and the Editorial Boards of East Asian Policy, Journal of Economic Growth, and Global Policy, and on the Advisory Board of OMFIF Education. Professor Quah is a Senior Fellow at LSE IDEAS, Senior Research Associate at the Centre for the Study of Human Rights, and Chair of the Board of the LSE-PKU Summer School. During 2010, he was the Tan Chin Tuan Visiting Professor in the Economics Department at the National University of Singapore, and visiting Professor of Economics at Tsinghua University, Beijing.

Purna Sen has worked for almost thirty years on issues of social justice, firstly with policy and practice work on race equality in education in the United Kingdom and later focused on gender equality and human rights. This has included research, publications and activism on violence against women, culture and human rights, particularly in relation to sexual violence, trafficking, civil society organizing against violence, crimes of 'honour', as well as social development issues. Her work has taken her to many countries outside the UK including Barbados, India, Indonesia, Jamaica, Jordan, Korea, Maldives, Mauritius, Morocco, Nepal, Nordic countries, Swaziland, Papua New Guinea, Philippines, Rwanda and Sri Lanka. For several years she taught Gender and Development at the Development Studies Institute at the London School of Economics and was Programme Director for Asia and the Pacific at Amnesty International prior to joining the Commonwealth Secretariat as Head of Human Rights. She has consulted with many organizations including Article 19, the International Institute for Environment and Development and the British Council and held a Visiting Senior Fellowship at LSE. Her PhD investigated women's resistance to domestic violence in Kolkata. Purna is Director of the Programme for African Leadership at the LSE. Her contribution to this volume is written in her capacity as an LSE Fellow.

Robert Skidelsky was born on 25 April 1939 in Harbin, Manchuria. He read history at Jesus College, Oxford, and was successively research student, senior student, and research fellow at Nuffield College, Oxford. In 1978, he was appointed Professor of International Studies at the University of Warwick, and then joined the Economics Department as Professor of Political Economy in 1990. He is currently Andrew D. White Professor-at-Large at Cornell University. Since 2002, he has been chairman of the Centre for Global Studies. In 2010, he joined the Advisory Board of the Institute for New Economic Thinking. In 1991, he was made a life peer. He joined the Conservatives and was made Chief Opposition Spokesman in the Lords, first for Culture, then for Treasury Affairs (1997–9). In 2001, he left the Conservative Party for the cross benches. He is currently a member of the All Party Parliamentary Group on Extraordinary Rendition.

Acknowledgements

Both the event celebrating Meghnad's work and legacy and the current collection would not have been possible without the generous support of Howard Davies and the LSE Annual Fund. We are also especially grateful to Frances Pinter, Emily Gibson, Fiona Cairns, Chloe Shuttlewood, Caroline Wintersgill and James Powell at Bloomsbury Academic, Chandramohan S. at Macmillan Solutions, and to Fiona Holland and Denise Mahon at LSE Global Governance, for their significant contributions to this project. A special thanks to Harriet Carter for pulling the whole project together and to Polly Vizard who was primarily responsible for the intellectual framing of this project and did the lion's share of work on the introduction and the interview.

Mary Kaldor

Introduction

Polly Vizard

On 28 October 2010 an event was held in the Old Theatre at London School of Economics (LSE) to celebrate the work and legacy of Professor Lord Meghnad Desai in the year of his 70th birthday. The gathering brought together lifelong colleagues from academia, politics, publishing, the press and media, students, friends and family from the United Kingdom, India and beyond, reflecting Meghnad's diverse work over the decades in economics and the social sciences and, outside academia, his broader contributions to political and intellectual life.

Mary Kaldor, Professor of Global Governance and then Co-Director of LSE Global Governance (which Meghnad founded), introduced the event. She suggested that it is hard to characterize Meghnad Desai's work given that he is so eclectic in both subject and views. However, perhaps one way to describe him is as the true 'globalizer'. Neoliberals tend to support the free market and free movements of capital but not the free movement of labour and/or human rights or the extension of international law. For the left, it may be the other way round. They want respect for human rights or the right to move freely but not free trade or free movements of capital. But Meghnad supports globalization in *all* its aspects. This is what has made it so appropriate that Meghnad founded the Centre for the Study of Global Governance (subsequently LSE Global Governance) – which focused on the challenges of globalization.

Professor (Emeritus) Charles Goodhart, Director of the Financial Regulation Research Programme at LSE, first arrived at LSE in the 1966/67 academic year, by which time Meghnad was already in the Economics Department. He spoke of Meghnad's dedication to the School and to their shared project of putting the 'political' back into political economy. He recollected Meghnad's propensity to file stacks of papers in heaps across his office floors – through which others could only wade at their peril! He also spoke of Meghnad's warmth, welcome, generosity – a veritable LSE Buddha!

Clare Short, former Labour MP and Secretary of State for International Development, spoke of Meghnad's 'loveable and admirable' character, his contribution to scholarship and wisdom, and to making the world a better place – all unusual and attractive qualities. She highlighted Meghnad's role in creating the Human Development Report – which became a document in taking forward universal values and human rights – as well as the broad sweep of scholarship and understanding of left-wing economic and political thinking captured and reflected in *Marx's Revenge* and Meghnad's honest engagement within the sometimes difficult and turbulent life of the Labour Party.

Dr Purna Sen, Head of Human Rights at the Commonwealth Secretariat and one of Meghnad's former students, highlighted Meghnad's broader intellectual contributions as well as his personal commitment and leadership on personal freedom and on issues around non-discrimination, gender equality and social justice. Meghnad's influence in these areas extends beyond the reach of economics and even the social sciences into history and literature, reflected in such different contributions such as Meghnad's recent novel and his biography of the Indian film star *Dilip Kumar*, which Meghnad often describes as his greatest achievement. Purna Sen also highlighted a shared interest with Meghnad in the Bengali novelist Sarat Chandra Chattopadhyay. She drew a number of parallels between Sarat Chandra's promotion of the cause of women and Meghnad's own personal commitment and stand on the issue of personal freedom.

Professor Amartya Sen, Nobel Prize Winner in Economics and friend for more than forty-five years, remembered meeting Meghnad when he arrived at the University of California at Berkeley in the mid-sixties where Meghnad was already established, and where student unrest was spreading on campus. He also told of staying at Meghnad's apartment when he came to London. He recalled the great influences on Meghnad's thinking, Marx and Hayek, and commented on the style of Meghnad's delivery – combining levity and wit on the one hand with facts and analysis on the other – a combination, he suggested, that Meghnad shared with another great friend, Ken Galbraith. Meghnad's direct and provocative style had broadened knowledge and understanding and shaken conventional wisdom. Economics as a discipline, he suggested, raises extraordinary questions and invites us to inform, annoy, analyse, provoke and entertain. The great thing about Meghnad is that he has done all of these!

Former colleagues and friends who were not able to attend on October 28th sent messages – and others left messages in a book. Howard Davies, former Director of LSE, noted Meghnad's continued energy and commitment towards the LSE even in retirement. Another message was from Nick Stern, who wrote:

> There are many very funny Meghnad stories associated with his wonderful quick wit and irreverence (and resemblance to Don King!). One of my favourites recently was when he was accused in the press of stabbing Gordon Brown in the back, after he had made some typically derogatory remark comparing him with his predecessor. When I asked Meghnad what he thought about such an accusation, he said with outrage, 'I didn't stab him in the back, I stabbed him in the front'.
>
> Of course Meghnad has given his friends so much intellectual stimulation over the decades and lots of good stories. But of special importance for me is his quite extraordinary humanity and emotional support. In particular, when I was very down after the death of my father eighteen years ago, Meghnad walked me to and fro across Waterloo bridge helping me to understand the notion of acceptance, and he helped me greatly by relaying how hard it had been for him when he had lost his own father. I did, of course, receive much kindness around

that time from many good friends but Meghnad was special. There is so much to celebrate about this extraordinary friend, human being and academic. I am very sorry I can't be with you on 28th, and wish you all the very best for the occasion.

Meghnad was born in Vadodara (formerly Baroda) in India in 1940 and was awarded a first degree from the University of Bombay in 1958 followed by a Master's Degree in 1960. Against all expectations, rather that entering the Indian Civil Service, he took up a scholarship at the University of Pennsylvania, where he completed a PhD in 1964. Following Pennsylvania, Meghnad took a job as an Associate Specialist at the University of California, Berkeley in the Department of Agricultural Economics – and where the student movements of the sixties erupted on the campus around him. He was appointed as a lecturer at LSE in 1965 where another student rebellion was soon to unfold. Meghnad became a Professor of Economics at LSE in 1983 and was Convener of the Economics Department 1987–1990. He was Head of the Development Studies Institute at LSE 1990–1995, Founder Director of the Study of Global Governance (now LSE Global Governance) 1992–2003 and is currently LSE Professor Emeritus of Economics.

Meghnad is the author of thirteen books and editor or co-editor of a further eight. His CV also lists more than seventy-five book chapters and sixty-eight contributions to journals. He has held numerous visiting professorships and fellowships and has undertaken consultancies for a wide range of organizations including the United Nations Food and Agriculture Organisation (UNFAO), the United Nations Conference on Trade and Development (UNCTAD), World Bank and the United Nations Development Programme (UNDP). He was co-editor of the *Journal of Applied Econometrics* 1984–1991 and a member of the editorial board of the *Journal of Economic Surveys, International Review of Applied Economics, Pakistan Journal of Applied Econometrics, Journal of Quantitative Economics* (India), *Journal of Economic Dynamics and Control, Ethnic and Racial Studies, Review of Economic Studies* and *Review of International Political Economy*. He was created Lord Desai of St Clement Danes in 1991 and holds honorary degrees from the Universities of Kingston, Middlesex, East London, London Guildhall and from Monash University Victoria, Australia. Other honors received include the Pravasi Bharatiya Puraskar 2004 (award for Distinguished Overseas Indian from the Government Of India), the Distinguished Indian Alumnus Wharton School of Finance and Commerce 2004, Fellow of the Royal Society for Arts 1991, Bharat Gaurav awarded by the Indian Merchants Chamber 2002, Honorary Fellow of the London School of Economics 2005, Founding Fellow of the Academy of Learned Societies in Social Sciences and Padma Bhushan (awarded by the President of India 2008).

Meghnad's research agenda over more than half a century has ranged from Marxian analysis and economic crisis; through applied econometrics and monetary economics; unemployment, poverty and famines; the role of private markets and the state; human development and alternative measures of wellbeing; liberalization and globalization; and Indian development and reform. His work has engaged with many of the great economics debates of the post-World War Two era – from socialist planning and the 'transformation problem'; through the dynamics of capitalist growth and the causes of depressions and cycles; Keynisanism and monetarism; structural adjustment and the opening up of markets; and the challenges of governance in a globalized world. His first books were *Marxian Economic Theory* (1974), *Applied Econometrics* (1976) and *Marxian Economics* (1979). *Testing Monetarism* (1981) highlighted the importance of developing rigorous empirical methodologies for testing the validity of economic theories. A collection of his many journal articles were published in the two volume collection *Macroeconomics and Monetary Theory* and *Poverty, Famine and Economic Development – The Selected Essays of Meghnad Desai* (1995). The renowned work *Marx's Revenge: The Resurgence of Capitalism and the Death of Statist Socialism* was published in 2002. This was followed by *Development and Nationhood: Essays in the Political Economy of South Asia* in 2004, *Rethinking Islamism* in 2006 and *The Rediscovery of India* (2009).

At LSE Meghnad taught on a wide variety of courses including economic principles, econometrics, Marxian economics and development. Members of successive cohorts of LSE students over the decades have strong memories of Meghnad's lectures. Professor Kaushak Basu, once a student at LSE, recollects Meghnad's economics course – the one that started with Sraffa. Other former students remember Meghnad's emphasis on challenging the underlying assumptions sometimes made in theoretical economic models (such as 'no involuntary employment' and 'trade independent security') and on subjecting such models to rigorous empirical testing. Still others were influenced by his use of the power of mathematics to capture complex economic ideas; the breadth and scope of his interdisciplinary knowledge and analysis; and his ability to do all of this in two hour lectures without notes. Meghnad was also famous amongst students for his participation in student parties – where he generally partied harder than the students! And he played an important role in negotiating between the students and the School both during the student movements of the sixties and years later during key campaigns (such as that around South African divestment).

Beyond academia, Meghnad has played an active role in political life. He was Chairman, Holloway Ward Labour Party of the Islington Central Constituency 1977–1980 and Chairman of the Islington South and Finsbury Constituency Labour Party followed by a period as President. He has undertaken a range of community activities and was a non-executive director of The Indian Film Company 2008–2010. Meghnad has also become a well-known and lively commentator on the Indian scene, with regular contributions to the columns of newspapers such as the *Indian Express*. In addition to the biography *Nehru's*

Hero: Dilip Kumar in the Life of India (2004), contributions to broader political and intellectual life include a book on Ezra Pound (2006) and a novel (*Dead on Time* (2009)). When Meghnad turned seventy the *Daily Mail* congratulated the 'wild-haired Labour peer and economist' – noting that his birthday would be followed by a debut in a film with a cast including Bollywood legend Om Puri.

The current volume follows on from the event to celebrate Meghnad's life and legacy last October. We have tried to bring together contributions that reflect Meghnad's broad research interests and engagement with economics and the social sciences over the decades. It includes contributions from a wide range of individuals whose own work relates to Meghnad's in a variety of different ways.

The collection begins with a chapter by Robert Skidelsky, who suggests that the strength of Desai's account in *Marx's Revenge* is that he is one of the few professional economists to take Marx's economic seriously. As Meghnad shows, what Marx established was that capitalism, uncorrected by state policy, was likely to experience deep business cycles. This was in itself an important finding and challenged the equilibrium reasoning of mainstream economics. However, whereas Marx's dialectics pointed to a 'final crisis', his economics did not. He failed to prove that capitalism would collapse or that the causes of crisis would be fatal. This, Skidelsky suggests, was Marx's Tragedy. Further, as Desai shows in the second volume of *Capital*, Marx devised a model in which capitalism results in stable growth, possibly for hundreds of years.

Meghnad's interest in monetary theory is reflected in the contribution by Professor Charles Goodhart, who highlights the need for new forms of financial regulation in the wake of the 2007 financial crisis. One lesson of the crisis is that prior methods of financial regulation were insufficient and the chapter discusses the need for, and forms of, macro-prudential supervision. The achievement of price stability does not guarantee financial stability and financial *in*stability can imperil macro-economic outcomes. Further, 'comfortable assumptions' about the behavior of banks fell apart after the summer of 2007 and a tougher regulatory regime is required. Yet central banks have traditionally only had at their disposal a single instrument – namely, the ability to control and vary the official short-term rate of interest. Goodhart addresses the search for a broader range of macro-prudential counter-cyclical instruments which could potentially be wielded by central banks. The main instruments, he suggests, are capital and liquidity ratios. These may be extended or adjusted in a variety of ways (e.g. Pigovian taxes).

Dr Jennifer Castle and Professor David Hendry contribute to the volume a chapter on econometric modelling. In the preface, Hendry recollects Meghnad being one of his mentors at LSE when he became a MSc student, and of interacting with Meghnad in the Quantitative Economics Seminar run by Denis Sargan and Bill Phillips. The chapter challenges conventional wisdom by questioning approaches to econometric modelling that are exclusively based on pre-specified theoretical economic models rather than model selection strategies. According to Castle and Hendry, the assumption that theory models are correct, complete and immutable is totally unrealistic – a type of economic 'folklore' that fails to recognize that such models can at best be incomplete, rough and evolving guides to some of the dependencies in economies – with many features of reality not covered. There is an important link here with Meghnad's own contributions to econometrics – including his insistence on the need for rigorous empirical testing of theoretical economic models.

Jagdish Bhagwati, Professor of Economics at Columbia University, turns to the subject of Indian reform. He contrasts two narratives on the Indian experience – the optimistic narrative, which highlights the successes of neoliberal reform and the potential for India's growth rate to overtake that of China; and the sceptical narrative, which asserts that economic growth has 'lacked a human face', increasing inequality and immiserizing the poor. Bhagwati supports the optimists. He discusses how from the early 1990s, under the forceful leadership of Prime Minister Manmohan Singh, the Indian economy was opened up and a programme of economic reform was implemented. Enhanced rates of economic growth have, he contends, reduced poverty whilst not increasing inequality on reasonable measures – as evidenced by polling data on the self-reported position of disadvantaged groups, studies of the economic outcomes of 'scheduled castes' and 'scheduled tribes' and analyses of inequality using the Theil Index.

Dr Purna Sen moves on from issues of human development to questions of individual freedom and human rights. At the event at LSE in October 2010, Purna Sen spoke of Meghnad's interest in and personal commitment to the principle of individual freedom. Purna takes up this subject in her contribution to the current volume, comparing evolving public policy frameworks in India and Nepal with a particular focus on sexuality. Struggles for personal freedom in the sphere of gender relations are compared and contrasted with struggles for respect and legitimacy in relation to gay, lesbian and transsexual lives.

Professor John Harriss, who worked with Meghnad Desai as the first Programme Director in Development Studies at the LSE in the early 1990s, also focuses on questions of Indian development. Harriss explores the nature and importance of a volume jointly co-edited by Desai, the eminent political scientist Susanne Hoeber Rudolph from the University of Chicago and the Bengali economist the late Ashok Rudra in 1984 (*Agrarian Power and Agricultural Productivity in South Asia*). He examines the ideas put forward in this book and evaluates their importance in light of the changed circumstances of the present after almost thirty years in which India has generally experienced higher rates of economic growth than before, and in which agriculture now accounts for less than 20 per cent of GDP. He concludes that although times have changed since *Agrarian Power and Agricultural Productivity in South Asia* was written – on the cusp of major transformations in the Indian economy which understandably it did not anticipate – its assessments of the trends in the agricultural economy at the time it was written, and of changes in agrarian relations, were in many ways remarkably prescient.

Professor Mozaffar Qizilbash's chapter begins by considering Meghnad's contribution to the human development paradigm. Desai's classic paper 'Human Development: Concept and Measurement' presented an initial formulation of the Human Development Index which has proven to be influential; whilst a paper on measuring freedom was another notable contribution. Qizilbash's particular concern in the chapter is, however, with the issue of disability. He suggests that the human development paradigm is a fruitful basis for examining issues relating to disability, because it does not simply characterise human beings as a means to higher levels of income growth and production. There are also advantages in the context of justice and the evaluation of the quality of life to thinking about disability in terms of the capability approach, which has connections with the social model of disability, but provides a more generalized framework for analysis.

Montek S. Ahluwalia, who is currently the Deputy Chairman of the Planning Commission, Government of India and also the Sherpa for India for the G20 Summits, turns to the subject of the G20 and its role in global governance. He begins by presenting assessment of the performance of the G20 in the first two years when it was dominantly concerned with managing the global crisis. The chapter then examines the challenges facing the G20 in undertaking a more holistic reform of the international monetary system. Other tasks before the G20 are discussed and some comments are made on the issue of the legitimacy of the G20 as a mechanism for improving global governance. Ahluwalia concludes that the G20 did fairly well in the first two years of its existence both in managing the crisis and in making progress on improving the structure of regulation in the financial sector and also in strengthening IFIs. However, its effectiveness in bringing about macro-economic coordination among sovereign countries through the MAP process has yet to be established. Something like the MAP is necessary for the effective functioning of what is now a highly inter-connected global economy but it will be a long haul and countries should prepare themselves for a rough ride.

Finally, the chapter by Held, Kaldor and Quah turns to the current challenges of global governance and expresses the thinking of the former Co-Directors of LSE Global Governance. It argues that contemporary crises, whether natural disasters, banking collapse, or war, are interlinked. They all have to do with the transformation of our social, economic and political relations in the last few decades and the failure of our governing institutions to adapt to this transformation. In particular national institutions are incapable of grappling with problems of global scope yet the emerging family of international institutions is highly fragmented and lacks mechanism of accountability.

We begin, however, with an interview with Meghnad about his work and life, at the House of Lords in February 2011.

Interview

Professor Lord Meghnad Desai
House of Lords, 16 February 2011

Mary Kaldor and Polly Vizard

PV: Did you always have broad inter-disciplinary interests? Was there something about your early education/experiences that inspired this?

MD: I could not understand from the very start why I should be narrow – although this hasn't always been a great career strategy. I grew up in a very middle class family. No-one ever made any money and no one felt for the lack of it. Going to school in India we were encouraged to read widely. Our career paths were fixed as becoming a civil servant. It was very much a kind of a sub-caste where people were either teachers or civil servants. Or maybe lawyers. They all were non-manual, brain-working kind of people. And urban. But the entrance exam (for the civil service) required a general knowledge test in which anything could be asked. So we read and read – thousands of irrelevant facts.

When I was in Bombay I did an arts degree – to the despair of my parents, since a science degree would have made me an engineer or a doctor. My older brother and parents were always in despair because I was not always reading course work but anything I could. The libraries were so good. I had morning classes because the same building was used for the science people in the afternoon. But I never went home after classes but got my lunch sent and spent all day in the library reading anything that came into my hands. If there was a book I'd never heard of before, I took it down and I read it. For example, one day I came across *The Journals of André Gide*. I didn't know what it was or how famous he was but it was fantastic to read it.

I only went to one year of primary school when I was six. But my education started when I was two and a half and I more or less knew the entire curriculum when I went to primary school. My mother and grandfather taught me at home. We're an educated family and when I was born the probability was that I would have at least one college degree. I had to.

And so that was the way it was. I don't remember when I could not read, let me put it this way.

MK: Did you do this all in English rather than Gujarati?

MD: No, I didn't do much Gujarati. But my grandfather, my mother's father, he used to live with us. In a fairly small place, two rooms, kitchen and sort of bathroom. But he would say to me after he had had his lunch, 'come sit down with me and we will talk in English'. So he would teach me how to speak English. And he would talk... the railway station, this and that, and all sorts of things and then there were all these books. And of course newspapers. I started reading the *Times of India* at a very young age. Sports pages. And in sports pages you had all the country cricket scores. So I knew what Middlesex, and Sussex and Essex were. And there would be photographs so you cut out the photographs of the cricketers.

English was always taught at school though by someone who spoke Gujarati as a first language. The further up you go the more you were taught in English and by the time I got to matriculation a lot of the subjects were taught in English. Not by people who had any kind of English education but they were all reasonably competent. I was told from early on by my older brothers and my parents that your teachers often don't know more than you know! Don't worry, teachers do not know everything. If you ask them a question and they don't give you an answer, come home and we will tell you what the answer is.

PV: Rather than going for an expected career path, you ended up doing a PhD in the US. How did that come about?

MD: What happened was, I finished my matriculation at fourteen and my BA at eighteen, since I was born in July, then my MA, and I couldn't take the civil service examination until after I was twenty-one. I was doing a PhD and then I applied for a fellowship to go to Pennsylvania. We had American professors sponsored by the Ford Foundation. It's all part of the Cold War, you know. There was a professor of money and banking from Pennsylvania. I must have been both arrogant and naïve – I only applied to one university. I took the GRE (the General Test) and although in my entire Indian career I'd never had a first, to the complete despair of my parents, I scored 99 percentile in the GRE. Everyone was astonished. So they gave me a fellowship – enough to have tuition which was fairly expensive. It was $1600 for tuition and $1800 for living expenses – $200 a month for nine months and in the summer you had to get a job.

I also finished my PhD in double quick time. I finished my coursework and my thesis in twenty-one months. The fellowship attached me to a supervisor, Lawrence Klein. And Lawrence Klein wanted to do certain models of commodities – that was what his programme was. Two or three of us were attached to him. I had no idea – no statistics, no mathematics. But I was actually fascinated.

I had been doing some work on international commodity agreements and I knew something about international tin agreements. I thought 'Tin, I'll take tin'. So then he said 'OK, here's the data, start drawing diagrams.' And I was too frightened to say 'How do I do this?' Every week he would come to me and my fellow people in the group, who were all busy with their coursework. I only had to worry about mathematical economics and econometrics. So I just plunged myself in. I started doing things on desk calculators and then got into computers which in those days had cards, punch cards. So I did the fastest learning of econometrics, doing my PhD with Klein. He never acknowledged that I did not know and I had no courage to tell him. He always gave me enough rope to kind of extend me without ever saying this would be difficult. And before I knew it, I'd done a beautiful piece of work.

PV: And what was it like arriving in Pennsylvania, as a young man from India?

MD: It was very strange because I think in some sense I mentally prepared myself through my undergraduate degree because I had a sense that I'd begun to abandon India. The day I left India, I remember saying to myself somewhat pompously 'that's the end of that'. I didn't know how I knew I was not going to go back. I don't know why. I just decided to go do something else. Ok, so it's very lonely and you know, you couldn't call home because my family didn't have a phone at that time – it was trunk calls only and letters took ages. And I didn't have any money to go back. And then the Cuban Missile Crisis happened. The question being asked was: Was it five minutes to twelve, four minutes to twelve or six minutes to twelve? Just how close were we to nuclear destruction? I remember listening to Kennedy live in a down town bar in Philadelphia saying that any attack by Cuba on any part of the Southern Hemisphere would be regarded as an attack by the Soviet Union on the United States of America and that the US would retaliate. There was no point in running away because there's nowhere you can run away if the whole world is going to be blown up. And what would my parents think if I went back without a degree? So I stayed.

MK: And then did Berkeley offer you a job?

MD: Because I finished my PhD I either needed to do another thesis (because I had a four-year fellowship) or I needed to get a job. So Klein pulled out a letter and I was hired and found myself in California. It was great fun – $9,500 when I was twenty-three! I was sort of, you know, footloose and fancy free – I had money to buy books and all sorts of things, went to the jazz in San Francisco. I knew I had to succeed in the problems that were put before me – which was to find out why California milk was higher priced than Oregon milk. I did an amazing computer simulation – one of the largest ones at that time, 200 farmers, a supply curve, an estimated demand curve and all that. Milk regulation meant that the price of milk would be fixed by what the producers said was the cost of production plus a profit margin. But 20 per cent more than what was required was being produced and the extra milk was being dumped on the market. The people in the market for ice cream were complaining because they were being priced out. So I was protecting the interests of those people producing cheaper milk. After I finished, the government changed and my report died a quick death.

Then of course there was the great student rebellion. I was staff so I couldn't actually take part and also my visa didn't allow that. It was an amazingly spontaneous student rebellion. But very laid back with none of the intensity of rebellions in the UK – with people getting into disputes over the Trotskyites. They were discovering spontaneity, self-determination and things like that. And of course it's California – you have sunshine and Joan Baez would come and sing for us. And I think one of the finest political orators I have known in my entire life, a young man called Mario Savio. You could imagine how someone like Lenin took over a meeting and controlled it. He did that – turned it around by speech. Absolutely amazing. And then I also saw the birth of the hippie movement. Hippies didn't believe in argument, they believed in magic and Puff the Magic Dragon. It made me fearless. Because, growing up in India, you are always kind of timid – very middle class, very career-oriented, not getting into trouble. And later on I was still – I don't know whether it's true or not – I was on FBI files because I stood bail bond for many of these people.

MK: This is what you hear from people in Tahrir Square – 'it's making us fearless.' And they also talk about self-determination and being able to be an agent of history.

MD: My colleagues were all rather conservative, rural republicans. They had no idea what I was up to and no sympathy. But they left me alone. And of course I got to know people in the economics department, did lots of learning, lots of maths courses, continued to read widely in Indian history, American history, bought lots of books. I could've got a green card and job offers but a green card made me eligible for the draft. Even though I wasn't a pacifist, I took the view that I was not going to get drafted to fight on America's side. I had no doubt America was on the wrong side. Not a doubt. Because already in India in the 1950s I had been reading about the French collapse, so I knew about the French collapse in Indo-China. So I didn't come to Vietnam knowing nothing – whereas millions of Americans did. But it was an amazing time of affirmation. Lots of ideas floating around, discovering, as it were, the Third World roots of Western Civilisation and things like that. All of this happened in the 1960s. Great fun.

PV: Did you regard yourself as a Marxist, in India growing up and later on in America?

MD: No, no, not in India at all. I became a Marxist or a Marxian in America. That made me different from all the Indian Marxists. In fact, I was quite right wing – Bombay was much more right wing than Calcutta. I read Marx of course – we all read Marx. I actually became a Marxist as a part of the Vietnam War. The issues were different in America – there was a different perspective, with an emphasis on class structure, race and all that. Whereas in the UK it was all doctrinal debates and five versions of Trotskysim and in India, there was more emphasis on imperialism and colonialism. I started reading much more seriously the economics of Marx than most people did and I began to analyze India as a *multi-national polity*. This was something that as a left-winger you were not allowed to do. You had to say that India was a single united country, you couldn't say that class relations were different in Bengal, compared with Punjab, compared with the Gujarat. I wrote an article in 1970 in *New Left Review* called the 'Vortex in India' saying that the Indian Communist Party didn't have a proper class perspective. I started doing that and that made me very different. I went to Delhi School of Economics for a year and they just couldn't understand it.

PV: And when did you come to the UK?

MD: I had two job offers. One in Birmingham and one in London. LSE didn't answer my letter but suddenly sent me a cable. Alan Walters sent me a very nice letter saying 'yes, we'll have you'. LSE just said 'You're Hired' – more or less. I didn't bargain for a salary, a high salary. I was completely naïve. So I went from $9,000 to £1,400 plus £60 London allowance for my annual salary. LSE needed lecturers in econometrics. That was the year after they got Denis Sargan from Leeds and they were hiring at the lower levels.

PV: Sargan says in his memories of LSE that you were in the Econometrics sub-department from the beginning.

MD: I was one of the three people hired. Later, others like Steve Nickel and David Hendry arrived. Before I accepted the LSE offer on the Berkeley campus I knew Dale Jorgenson who was the rising young star. I said 'listen, what should I do, go to LSE?' He told me that LSE was about to get Hahn and Gorman and to do something that no-one else would do – to hire two mathematical economists. People thought at that time that one was a luxury. So we knew that LSE was about to go through this amazing growth. And Harry Johnson was going to come. So in the second half of the sixties Hahn, Gorman, Sargan arrived and Bill Phillips was already there. Harry Johnson came. It was just amazing. And because I had come from the American side, I had no compunctions about publishing. I wanted to publish. By the time I arrived at LSE I had four publications already in international journals so I was kind of a much-published person. So I had no problem with tenure.

Of course, we had our own LSE student uprising. First in '67. I was one of the eight people who signed a letter defending the students; along with them was the father of the leader of the Labour party, Ralph Miliband and John Griffiths. I was the only economist on that list. Derry Irvine, who became Lord Chancellor, was on the list. I had absolutely no doubt which side I was on and the fact that I was a junior untenured lecturer never bothered me.

And then the next year – a much bigger thing. By that time I was an honorary president of the LSE student union. This was the time of the 'Rivers of Blood' speech and I had run a couple of huge seminars against that and so the students liked me and made me an honorary president. I ended up chairing the one big meeting with 1,400 students which passed a resolution to occupy the LSE. There was a national demonstration to march on the American Embassy. I chaired it and the motion passed for a majority of 698 to 692. So I basically stayed with the students and was politically active. But I never missed a single lecture.

MK: When did you write your book on Marxian economics?

MD: That happened because during 68–69 we started saying 'why are we not talking about Marxian economics?' LSE was shut down for a whole month, when the gates were smashed in and so on. So I thought 'ok, I will give voluntary lectures in Marxian economics'. So I started doing voluntary lectures. Then in the early seventies there was a man who got into this business of taping lectures and getting them published for cheap. Harry Johnson was so idealistic that he gave money to this man who published a couple of Harry Johnson's lectures. My book was published. It was about Marx's analytical economic theory.

PV: What is the distinction between Marxist and Marxian?

MD: I wanted to teach the economic theory of Marx for the strictly academic bits – economic theory, the transformation problem etc – these were my concerns. I was actually stopped once on the Strand by someone saying 'have you solved the transformation problem?' My answer was that it had been solved so many times, I don't know why people keep on asking! I was the first person to do 'three circuits of capitalism' (Volume 2). Value relations are non-observable – all that is observable is money relations. Therefore you have to do a mapping – and that's how the transformation problem comes about. Econometrics has a similar sort of problem relating to identification. I think after Sweezy's book, mine was the first to have analytical components of Marxism, in a very short form. Then later on, Miroshima and others made the analysis much more mathematical. I was keeping the mathematics to a very simple level because I wanted to teach people who wanted to learn. And the book was translated into lots of languages – Turkish, Spanish, Greek, Portuguese and so on. And then a larger edition called *Marxian Economics* was published in 1979, dealing with Marx's incomplete theory of dynamics.

PV: Does *Marx's Revenge* pick up on this?

MD: *Marx's Revenge* is when I had given up the hope of socialism. It was the late eighties, early nineties and I finally decided that it's not going to happen. In fact, Marx did not actually seriously work out a precise theory of when capitalism would decline. In Volume 1 there is the perpetual cycle; in Volume 2 there is balanced growth without cycles and the idea that capitalism could go on forever; and in Volume 3 the declining rate of profit. I did not agree with Engels when he said that Marx had discovered the laws of dynamics of capitalism. It just looked like he had. When Volume 2 came out (modelling the smooth growth of capitalism), all hell broke loose and then Lenin and Luxembourg intervened. But the whole Leninist programme was a bet on something that Marx had not actually said. People were waiting for something that had not been predicted. In the early 1990s I spent much time puzzling about this. I used to get up in the morning and ask two questions: Why is the Soviet Union not here and why is capitalism still here? And Marx had written the answer to those two questions. I wanted to show that you could go back to Marx and get out of him the prediction that capitalism is a cyclical process. Capitalist development is a crisis-ridden process and modes of production come to an end when they realise their full potential. But there is no precise end – and no terminal crisis. And that's *Marx's Revenge*.

PV: Is the objective then to make capitalism work better and markets work better?

MD: I joined the Labour Party in 1971. I thought that is all you could do – make markets work better. The thing is that when markets work badly, workers don't benefit. Workers gain power when they're in a boom. In a slump workers lose out. And it's not the kind of slump where there'll be a big general strike and workers will take over. That doesn't happen – it happens the other way around. Workers are weak in a slump. Making capitalism work better is not an anti-worker strategy.

PV: And what is the link with your interest in Hayek?

MD: I read Hayek in Bombay and did a lot of work on Hayek in the 1970s, thinking about the nineteenth-century idea that social organisms are self-organizing and therefore they may have crises but they cure their own crises. Hayek had a theory of crisis as Marx did, and they both had the idea that social organisms are self-organizing entities, dynamic, evolutionary entities. Marx had the idea that socio-economic organisms can self-reproduce through crisis. So a crisis is not actually a tragedy – it is capital renewing itself. I found an amazing confluence between their ideas – the links between Hayek and Marx. These ideas were not shared by Keynes.

PV: What about LSE, when you arrived. Was still Hayek in the ascendency?

MD: No, by the time I came, Hayek had declined at LSE. LSE had become a down-the-line neoclassical mathematical department, not passionate like Cambridge where people would always say 'what would Maynard say about this?' We were very neoclassical and much more technical. I was into modelling, empirical modelling and so on.

I began to write against monetarism in the 1970s. Labour lost the election in 1979. I had to consider the proposition that if monetarists were right, Keynes was completely wrong. I wanted to do a proper academic test of monetarism in a systematic, theoretical, econometric kind of way. *Testing Monetarism* was an attempt to say that there was nothing in the available literature, as far as I could see, which corroborated monetarist conclusions. And because the UK was about to embark on an experiment of monetarism, it was a sort of warning.

MK: Were your views always consistent?

MD: No, they kept on changing. The only consistency is that I thought I was on the side of progress and redistribution, ending poverty, all that. But the means kept on changing.

Losing elections is one thing that's fundamentally changed my life. The fact that we could lose '79, '83, '87. After the 1987 election defeat my views underwent a profound change. If you see my inaugural lecture *Men and Things* (Economica 1986) you will see the Old Meghnad. By the time of my 1990 lecture *Is Socialism Dead?* my views had transformed.

Another example. When Nigel Lawson made a complete mess of the economy, and there was rampant inflation, I became convinced that British Chancellors of the Exchequer need a straight jacket so they do not move out of certain parameters. There had been all of the sacrifice during the 1980s and there was a modicum of stable growth and this man was wrecking it. I became a balanced budget fanatic.

MK: So you went from Marxism to Keynsianism to free markets?

MD: I had Marxism and Keynsianism together in my 'satchel' as it were. Keynsianism was for managing the downturns and day-to-day economic policy – but there is no 'Marxist economic policy'. All the way through, cycle after cycle, we were trying to generate full employment programmes and so on. When we were out of power Neil Kinnock had given a promise of two million jobs and we had to come up with a way of achieving this. But by the 1990s anti-inflation had become part of the framework so you had to achieve full employment within certain constraints. In 1992 when we thought we were about to be elected we all said that we supported the ERM with a bit of devaluation if Labour came to power – even though it restricted how much you could use fiscal policy. The other problem was succeeding in getting re-elected.

Gordon Brown confirmed my suspicion that no British Chancellor could be trusted not to make a mess. It was exactly the same as with Nigel Lawson. Everything was going well – there was good growth and unemployment was much lower with Gordon Brown than with Nigel Lawson. But from 2004 onwards he wrecked the budget. I had to contain myself. After all, I am still a member of the Labour Party. I could not believe that any Chancellor could do what he did. And everyone thought what a great Chancellor he was!

PV: But what about Gordon Brown's response to the banking crisis? Do you agree that he played a pivotal role?

MD: Paul Krugman said that Gordon Brown may have saved capitalism. Okay, let me give him some credit for that. The point was the rescuing was being carried out in America already. And Alastair Darling and Mervyn King were key and should be given more credit. But yes he did have the good sense to recognize where we were. But I would not have rescued the banks he rescued – I am a Hayeckian in that sense.

PV: But you would have rescued some banks?

MD: No, I wouldn't rescue any bank. Protect the depositors, but let the banks go.

MK: So how would you have protected the depositors? Guarantee everybody?

MD: Well you know that's what they did with Northern Rock – we insured the deposits. I was muttering in the margins at the time that it was a great opportunity. The deposits should have been transferred to the Post Office. Northern Rock should have been shut down. When you save a bank you are saving the equity holders and the bond holders. Look at Ireland. Ireland has wrecked itself by saving totally irresponsible banks. So there should be no equity or bond guarantee – as in Ireland. But I do support a depositor's guarantee. In America you have depositors' insurance. Here we have a guarantee up to a maximum in a single account. When there is a depositor's guarantee nobody has to panic if a bank is failing.

The merger of HBOS and Lloyds Bank was a criminal act. It was done by by-passing the competition rules that we ourselves had passed. I was present when Mandleson moved the motion that the competition rules would be disregarded in relation to the HBOS merger. I think that the Bank rescue was very dubious. People say that I don't have an alternative and I haven't worked out how much damage there would be without the rescue. But look at how much damage there has already been *with* the banks rescued.

PV: So you don't agree that the banks are 'too big to be allowed to fail'?

MD: Everybody knew they were doing bad things – it's quite astonishing how much people knew six months before the collapse that Lehman Brothers was in trouble. I mean this is not a dark secret. You just had to read ordinary newspapers. This is when I became a Hayekian again. He said that if you give people a lot of cheap credit, people will go and do foolish things. There will be mal-investment. And mal-investment will lead eventually to a crash. And people had forgotten all of that – probably because Mary's father (Nicky Kaldor) had destroyed him (Hayek) analytically! But he kind of came back. I remember before it all happened – saying to people that I knew the boom was about to come to an end. But the longer the boom lasted the more people thought it would last forever. But capitalism grows through crisis. Unless you allow firms to fail it will be unhealthy. You have to allow the free market to operate. This is not the free market. Banks should be allowed to fail.

MK: Do you think that for the next phase of capitalism there is a need for a new model of finance?

MD: The old model is fine but let the old model work. But if people believe in the free market, let there be a free market. Banks should be allowed to fail. If you let General Motors fail, why can't you let banks fail? There again, the nineteenth-century view is that capitalism grows through crisis. Unless you have competition and allow firms to fail, capitalism is not healthy. What I want out of the regulatory reform is a guarantee that no bank will ever be saved. The conditions need to be set out under which banks would be abandoned. Some people think the banks ought to be broken up. But the key thing is that they shouldn't expect any rescue from the public purse. They should know they are on their own.

PV: What about the limits of liberalization in India? Can India grow its way out of poverty?

MD: Liberalization is not the problem. I think it's a good thing. What is the problem is the Indian State, in as such that even when they had no liberalization, and so called socialism prevailed, they failed to spend money on health and education. They went on building this ghastly machine tool factory – real Soviet style. Employment was not generated and poverty remained partly because far too many people stayed on the land in low productivity occupations so the majority of people were poor. In the early 1970s, something like 70–75 per cent were poor. Then in 1990 there was a switch. Growth speeded up. But the lack of health and education was not addressed and people were not taken off the land again. The forces of liberalization were not strong enough to get out of this trap and this continues to be the case. Last year in the budget, 36 per cent of revenue was spent on interest payments, 3 per cent on health and education. It's the shocking legacy of all those years – an immense burden on India. The way you cure poverty is with excellent industrial growth. You build large factories, take people off of the land, put them in factories and give them permanent jobs. That is the way. And then you spend much more on health and education. We had the debate about socialism v. liberalization – but nobody pointed out that health and education were neglected in India. It is true that some states in the South are better than the North. But overall, India is below sub-Saharan Africa levels.

PV: Are you against the Employment Guarantee scheme?

MD: I'm not against it. But it is designed to discourage mobility of labour. You keep people in the constituency in which they are and give them 40–100 days of work. It is elastoplast – not a cure – an electoral strategy. But who am I to begrudge some people getting employment?

PV: Is it helpful or harmful, in terms of growth?

MD: It's completely neutral because it doesn't do anything. It is a palliative, to people who need a palliative. And it has worked much better than I had feared. But it is preventing people from thinking in terms of more radical strategies which come through industrialization.

PV: What about child labour standards? Are they a break on growth?

MD: Many children work at home – there are craft families for example which train children. What do children miss if they are working? They miss education and their health may be harmed. Some people argue that children working depresses the adult wage. But if you remove children from work, there is no guarantee that you can give money to the parents. One strategy would be to lay aside time for on-employment-location teaching, health checks etc., without necessarily preventing them from working.

PV: The UK went through a period of adjustment in the nineteenth century when child labour was banned. This must have also been difficult for the families concerned at the time; for children in families working in Lancashire cotton mills, for example. Why doesn't this argument apply?

MD: That's true but even in the nineteenth century living standards here were higher than in India. And if you are going to ban child labour in a very poor country, much poorer than the UK ever was, what happens to those families? First, you have to implement the law properly – which in India is always a problem. Second you have to counteract the income shortfalls through transfers. They are not working for fun – they're working because the family needs the income. You can make it less exploitative, you can allow time for education, health, but if you suddenly stop it there will be a welfare loss. Ideally, yes, ban child labour completely. But I do worry about income compensation for the families concerned. And I do also think about the implementation problems.

PV: What are your main writings on India?

MD: My work on India has also been a lifetime programme.

I was writing about India from the late 1960s. I'd always thought of a very big project writing the big book, about how India is a multi-national polity with uneven development and how different sub-nations with different patterns of capitalist developments and different class relations emerge. The whole Indian nation and Indian nation-state is a result of global influences and western expansion. That's what my *Rediscovery of India* is about. My *Rediscovery of India* and *Development and Nationhood* books combined bring together my

India work. And then there's the Dilip Kumar book on Bollywood. That is also part of my India work.

PV: What do you remember about the early days of the Human Development Report?

MD: Just when I was losing hope with the radical transformation in society, I got into human development. It kept me in there. It was a great, great experience. The report proved to be a great intellectual adventure – we got into really interesting intellectual problems and there was a fantastic intellectual atmosphere. There was Amartya (Sen), Mary's sister Frances (Stewart) and others.

MK: And whose was the great idea? Who had it first?

MD: Following the Latin American Debt Crisis I had been working with the Latin Americans and had come up with a new welfare measure based on remaining years of life – 'potential lifetime'. Given your current age, how many years have you got to live? Just like income it's linear and it's additive and means something to each person. Then there was a meeting at the UNDP (United Nations Development Program) where I was invited. The idea was to find a new measure of social progress and development – an alternative to income. One afternoon we sat around and discussed possible alternative measures. Amartya said that my measure did not make the grade. He thought it was biased because if you take a younger population, with a similar age, then you get a higher measure than if you get an elderly static population. He had had an article in 1981, in the *Oxford Bulletin*, where he had the idea of development as the distance from 'where you are' to the top – and how well-off someone was depending on the distance. Sitting around the table that afternoon, the Human Development Index was established in terms of life expectancy, education and some measure of income. I remember Frances mentioned malnutrition and children's malnutrition. And there was somebody there doing the calculations as we went along. By the end of the day we had done it!

MK: Richard Jolly had worked with Frances on *Adjustment with a Human Face* – didn't that precede it?

MD: It preceded it but it didn't have a measure. And Mahbub ul Haq was the person who saw the potential for this. And he was great because of the emphasis he put on communication. We wrote a draft and he got it written up by a professional body. Then he went and sold it. The UNDP was completely flabbergasted. Practically every country had at least more than one newspaper that had a story about the Human Development Report. The impact was completely out of any of our expectations. The HDI was a group effort – not as good as my potential lifetime measure, but something that politicians understand. Anyone can. You can stand on a street corner and explain to people what it is. There are very few things in economics like that.

MK: Do you remember when Richard Jolly and Sakiko Fukuda-Parr came to see us because they were going to make human rights the theme of the HDR?

MD: Yes, this was later, in 2000. But before this when I looked at freedom and human rights performance all hell broke loose. India, China and Iran went to the Secretary General and said not that we were wrong, but that the UNDP had no mandate for human rights. So we could not publish my human rights index, except by regional averages which is a completely meaningless number. So I went out and published it on my own, as political freedom, in the *LSE on Freedom* collection.

PV: What about your retirement – you seem to have been especially busy since you arrived at the House of Lords – with books, novels and a film debut?

MD: The terrorism book *Rethinking Islamism* basically followed from 7 July 2005 and 9/11. I wanted to sit down and explain to people, it is not the religion, it is the ideology – Islamism. To understand that you have also to do something about the history of the Ottoman Empire and what happened in the twentieth century and what happened before that. You have to go back to Mohammad and try to explain the schisms in Islam. You have to distinguish between Islam and Islamism. Although I am not religious myself, and I know all religion has caused problems, you need to separate religion and ideology. The book does this. I also wrote a book about the political economy of Ezra Pound and *Dead on Time*, a novel about the murder of a prime minister. All the male characters are horrible and all the women are nice! Except my Rupert Murdoch character who is quite nice! My other book, about Dilip Kumar, takes me back to my youth again. In 1950s India one of the major things was cinema. This is where I got my ideas about love and romance and so on. The book is a study of cinema and politics together in a particular phase in India when I was growing up. As for a Bollywood film? Yes, it's called *Life Goes On*. It's about to be released in the West End in March. I was only in it two minutes but I enjoyed it!

MK: If somebody asked you what you think is your intellectual legacy – what do you think is your most important intellectual contribution?

MD: I think my contribution is making Marxian economics a living subject. I'm very proud of that. Those three books, *Marxian Economic Theory*, *Marxian Economics* and *Marx's Revenge* are one kind of theme. I took the idea, which is not really economics, that is something like globalization, with free capital movements, free labour movements, is actually an ideal system. It's not there yet. But I would like free capital movements, free labour movements *and* human rights. I think my second achievement is my writings on India. My third achievement has been to bring some intellectual inquiry into politics and to be an independent thinker though unfortunately not a good party person. The Labour Party changed its thinking from naive leftism to naive Keynesianism to sophisticated Keynesianism. In terms of the construction of a left-of-centre's party thinking about economics being modernized, I think I made a contribution. Through writing in *Tribune*, writing in *New Statesmen*, you know all sorts of engaged activities, I don't know how I got time to do all that but I got an enormous amount of work done for the Labour party concerning economics, particularly before John Smith died.

MK: That's right, at your event I said that 'you're the only true globalizer'. Neoliberals tend to support the free market and free movements of capital but not the free movement of labour and/or human rights or the extension of international law. For the left, it may be the other way round. But you support globalization in all its aspects – which is why it is so appropriate that you founded the Centre for Global Governance.

MD: This came from Marx. It doesn't come from Keynes. He is a very provocative economist.

1

Marx's Tragedy

Robert Skidelsky

The Marx problem

According to Marxist scripture it was capitalism which was supposed to collapse, not communism. So Marx had finally been proved wrong. Not at all, says Desai in his provocatively titled *Marx's Revenge* (Desai, 2002). Desai claimed that the 'resurgence of capitalism and the death of statist socialism' was a vindication, not refutation, of Marx's prophetic powers: Marx's revenge was on the Marxists who had tried to bring about the end of capitalism prematurely. They had forgotten that Marx expected capitalism to continue until it had exhausted its productive potential, which might clearly take a very long time (especially if one included the whole world, and not just its richer part). This implied that all attempts to overthrow capitalism before the due date, whenever that was, were doomed from inception.

Desai's interpretation makes it difficult to understand why Marx himself bothered with revolutionary politics. In fact his argument is less sweeping than his book's title. Marx hoped for the violent overthrow of capitalism, but failed to prove that it was bound to collapse because of its internal contradictions. The demise of the capitalist system was a requirement of his dialectic, not the conclusion of his economics, and the two were in fact contradictory. Thus stated, Desai's thesis loses most of its provocation and is in fact in line with other post-Soviet interpretations of Marx (Hobsbawm, 2011; Stedman-Jones, 2002). But it does open up a new question: what happens after capitalism has exhausted its 'productive potential'? Is the coming of socialism only delayed, or is it destined to remain a never-never land of wish fulfilment?

The strength of Desai's account lies in the fact that he is one of the few 'proper', that is, professional, economists to take Marx's economics seriously. One can think of a handful – Maurice Dobb, Paul Sweezy, Joseph Schumpeter – but these were from the early twentieth century. Others have tried to incorporate bits and pieces of Marx into orthodox economics. In the early 1970s, Andrew Glynn and Robert Sutcliffe set out to prove empirically that the rate of profit had fallen in Britain and the United States (Glynn and Sutcliffe, 1972).[1] Cost-push theories of inflation at least nod to Marx's theory of class struggle. But Marx as an economist has virtually disappeared. Contemporary Marxists – nearly all non-economists – prefer the young Marx. Orthodox economics makes no mention of him. It is Desai's respect for Marx as an economist which leads him to his reading of Marx's work. It also suggests a more exact title for his book: *Marx's Tragedy*. For Marx's tragedy was precisely that he could not square his conviction that capitalism was doomed with his economics.

This conviction had come to Marx before Marx came to economics. In fact he was not an intuitive economist at all. No one who starts economics at the age of forty ever is. There is too much other stuff in one's head. Economists have to start innocent of all distracting ideas. They have to have minds sufficiently empty to construct those axiomatic models of human behaviour which are their bread and butter. Late adolescence is the ideal time to start such a training.

Marx displayed a considerable gift of exclusion in constructing his 'model' of history based on class struggle. But when it came to economics, he could never separate technical analysis from history, morality, or simple thirst for vengeance. These were basic ingredients of his thought and could not be sloughed off to make way for a new-born innocence. Exploitation and surplus-value were moral categories which he tried to fill with economic content; his vision of the violent overthrow of capitalism owes more to the Apocalypse than to the dialectic and even less to economics. And yet he can rival Keynes, a much more successful economist, as the most brilliant non-economist who has ever devoted himself to the study of economics. But Keynes was born in 1883, the year Marx died, and by the time he came to reflect on the human condition much of the nineteenth-century intellectual scaffolding on which Marx relied, notably the Hegelian dialectic, had been swept away.

The Marx of the *Communist Manifesto*

Marx's critique of capitalism was fundamentally moral. It was, he thought, too hateful and unjust to survive. Not only did it rob the mass of people of their means of production, but it also appropriated the fruits of the robbery, as one expects robbers to do. At the same time, Marx could not help but understand that capitalism was an emancipatory force. He was after all a child of the Enlightenment and the Industrial Revolution. Capitalism was the first economic system to apply science and technology to the problem of extracting a living from nature. It was part of Reason's break from a purely static, or cyclical past, and as such, a dynamic force making for progress. Technology promised an unprecedented expansion of productive power, which would free most people for the first time from toil, poverty, and superstition. But at the same time, capitalism, which placed the ownership and use of this technology in the hands of a small class of owners, aborted its liberating potential, by substituting the dictatorship of capital for the dictatorship of kings and priests.

Marx was not alone in feeling morally ambivalent about capitalism. Albert Hirschman has written beautifully of the efforts of the founders of classical economics to make 'love of money' morally respectable, against its widespread condemnation as one of the deadliest of sins. Adam Smith's solution was to re-label avarice 'self-interest', and to make 'self-interest' the engine of material progress (Hirschman, 1977). At the same time, the concentration of capital ownership in a frugal and enterprising class of burghers was defended as removing the brake on progress of the feckless top and bottom of society: the aristocracy and peasantry.

The dialectic was the perfect intellectual instrument for expressing Marx's contradictory understanding of capitalism. He learned it from Hegel. In Hegel's philosophy, history is the story of the growth of reason. Each partial, incomplete stage of human consciousness produces its negation which is absorbed into a more complete, higher-level consciousness till the attainment of absolute reason, in which the whole of reality is determined by mind. Thus the Hegelian historical mission is 'fulfilled unconsciously, despite their crimes and passions, by particular nations or classes' (Kolakowski, 2005). Capitalism could thus be seen a necessary stage in the ascent of man.

Marx, influenced by his early political experiences which made him doubt Hegel's claim that the Prussian state was the embodiment of Reason, turned Hegel's clash of ideas into a clash of classes. History was the story of class conflict. Hegel's successive partial stages of reason were simply different phases of property relations, each of which gave rise to conflict. As Marx came to see it, religion, the great enemy for the thinkers of the Enlightenment, was simply the spiritual veil used by the propertied to blind the property-less to their true situation.

Marx only worked out one phase of his 'dialectical materialism', the transition from feudalism to capitalism (Hobsbawm, 2011, p. 147). In this story, the increasingly wealthy, but politically subordinate, 'burghers' of the towns become the class of 'bourgeoisie' which overturns the land-based manorial system. The bourgeoisie is the first class to exploit labour systematically, and use the extracted surplus for capital development rather than luxuries, wars, cathedrals, and so forth. But capitalist civilization, in turn, becomes a fetter on the further development of the productive forces. It is overthrown by the proletariat which it has created, which establishes the classless reign of communism.

The whole riddle of Marx is why he envisaged this particular end game. In a sense it was needed to 'complete' the dialectic. The economy was running out of productive sectors, and society out of classes. What further revolution in the productive forces could one imagine beyond that being brought about by science and technology? And what further class history was possible? The bourgeoisie was the only minority class left. It had created its last successor, the working class, or proletariat. This was the universal class – the material embodiment of Hegel's universal Reason – empirically because it was the vast majority of the population, but dialectically because it was the only class without property to defend. Thus its victory would simultaneously end class society, property *relations* and history itself, which was simply the story of class struggle. This may have been the conclusion of the dialectic, but the dialectic was an intellectual construction, a model, and its determinism was purely logical. Without its blinkers, one could easily envisage many new productive possibilities, new mixed forms of property relations, and a new role for the state, embodying Reason, as the mediator of these, as Hegel had proposed. This raises the interesting question of the relationship between the dialectic and the Apocalypse. It might seem that Marx set up his scheme of dialectical materialism to satisfy the demand of Judaic-Christian millenarianism, that the righteous shall inherit the earth.

The most coherent expression of Marx's dialectical approach *before he became an economist* is in the compressed, explosive prose of the *Communist Manifesto* of 1848. Its praise for capitalism is unrestrained: 'The bourgeoisie in its scarce one hundred years, has created more massive and more colossal productive forces than have all preceding generations together ... What earlier century had even a presentiment that such productive forces slumbered in the lap of social labour?' (Engels, 1888; Marx, 2002 (1848)).[2]

In an uncanny pre-figurement of today's globalization, Marx wrote:

> The bourgeoisie, by the rapid improvement of all instruments of production, by the immensely facilitated means of communication, draw all, even the most barbarous, nations into civilization. The cheap prices of its commodities are the heavy artillery with which it batters down all Chinese walls, with which it forces 'the barbarians'' intensely obstinate hatred of foreigners to capitulate. It compels all nations, on pain of extinction, to adopt the bourgeois mode of production; it compels them to introduce what it calls civilization into their midst, i.e. ... it creates a world after its own image. (Engels, 1888; Marx, 2002 (1848))

However, this achievement was purchased at a huge cost:

> All fixed, fast-frozen relations, with their train of ancient and venerable prejudices and opinions are swept away, all new-formed ones become antiquated before they can ossify. All that is solid melts into air, all that is holy is profaned, and man is at last compelled to face with sober senses, his real conditions of life, and his relations with his kind. (Engels, 1888; Marx, 2002 (1848))

Marx never doubted that capitalism was a necessary, progressive stage in the unlocking of human potential. In a much less well-known passage written five years after the *Communist Manifesto* he praises British rule in India for stirring up this stagnant society:

> Sickening as it must be to human feeling to witness those myriads of industrious, patriarchal and inoffensive social organizations, disorganized and dissolved

into their units, thrown into a sea of woes ... we must not forget that these idyllic village communities, inoffensive though they may appear, have always been the solid foundation of Oriental despotism; that they restrained the human mind within the smallest possible compass, making it the unresisting tool of superstition, enslaving it beneath traditional rules, depriving it of all grandeur and historical energies ... The question is, can mankind fulfil its historical destiny without a fundamental revolution in the social state of Asia? If not, whatever may have been the crimes of England she was the unconscious tool of history in bringing about that revolution. Then whatever bitterness the spectacle of the crumbling of an ancient world may have for our personal feelings, we have the right, in point of history, to exclaim with Goethe: 'Sollte diese Qual uns qualen/ Da sie unsre Luste verhmehrt?' [Should we be grieved by this pain that increases our pleasure?]. (Marx, 1853 as quoted in Kolakowski, 2005, p. 285)

From Marx's Olympian standpoint, all this unsettling was historically justified, because, by its brutality in unleashing human potential, the bourgeoisie was bringing into existence the weapons and the class which would destroy it. But at this point in the Manifesto the thread of argument snaps, and rhetoric takes its place.

The weapons which will destroy bourgeois rule are ever-deeper crises of overproduction; the class which will destroy it is the working class. A combination of immizeration, alienation, and the stripping of illusions and partial ties have brought into existence a new united class of avengers. Echoing Mary Shelley's *Frankenstein*, Marx likens capitalism, to 'the sorcerer, who is no longer able to control the powers of the nether world whom he has called up by his spells' (Engels, 1888; Marx, 2002 (1848)). 'What the bourgeoisie produces, above all, is its own grave-diggers. Its fall and the victory of the proletariat are equally inevitable' (Engels, 1888; Marx, 2002 (1848)).

The *Communist Manifesto* is testimony to the extraordinary persuasive power of dialectical reasoning allied to rhetorical brilliance, but it fails to establish even a presumption for Marx's conclusion. The proletarian uprising and communist end-game were not predicated on facts, but arose from a 'philosophical, indeed an eschatological, argument about human nature and destiny' (Hobsbawm, 2011, p. 116). The proletariat 'was needed to realize the aims of German [dialectical] philosophy' (Lichtheim, quoted in Hobsbawm, 2011, p. 116). Belief in the apocalyptic moment never left Marx, despite the repeated failure of history to live up to his expectations. Thus the famous passage in the first volume of *Das Kapital*, vol.1 (1867):

Along with the constantly diminishing number of magnates of capital, who usurp and monopolize all advantages of this process of transformation grows the mass of misery, oppression, slavery, degradation, exploitation: but with this too grows the revolt of the working-class, a class always increasing in numbers and disciplined, united, organized by the very mechanism of the process of capitalist production itself. The monopoly of capital becomes a fetter on the mode of production, which has sprung up and flourished along with it and under it. Centralization of the means of production and socialization of labour at last reach a point which become incompatible with their capitalist integument. The knell of capitalist private property sounds. The expropriators are expropriated. (pp. 714–5)

After Marx's death, Friedrich Engels, his life-long friend and intellectual comrade was left with the unenviable task of trying to tie up the loose ends. The motor of history would finally be broken, he wrote in his introduction to the 1888 English edition of the *Communist Manifesto*, because 'a stage has been reached where the exploited and oppressed class – the proletariat – cannot attain its emancipation from the sway of the exploiting and ruling class – the bourgeoisie – without, at the same time, and once and for all, emancipating society at large from all exploitation, oppression, class distinctions and class struggles' (Engels, 1888, preface). In other words, history stops when society runs out of classes. But under what circumstances will this come about?

Marx never succeeded in giving a compelling answer to the question: what would cause the apocalypse which would end the bourgeois phase of private property? His problem was that although the dialectic pointed to the final crisis, economics did not. This is the main point made by Meghnad Desai. All that Marx plausibly established, writes Desai, was that capitalism – uncorrected by state policy – was likely to experience deep business cycles. This challenged the equilibrium reasoning of mainstream economists. But there was nothing specifically Marxist about this, though Marx was a pioneer of business-cycle theory.

Marx's theory of capitalist crisis

The economic case for the collapse of capitalism rests on the exploitation theory, which Marx developed as a result of his mid-life confrontation with Ricardo. For Ricardo, the price of commodities was fixed by the number of hours worked. Marx argued that this applied only to the exchange value of labour. The amount of use-value the employer got from the worker's labour was higher than the exchange-value he had to pay for that amount of work: the difference was exploitation, or the 'surplus-value' he extracted from labour. Profits arise solely from the exploitation of labour. It was the robbery of part of the worker's labour power which was the root of the class struggle; this is what made the capitalist system economically unviable. There are two versions of its economic collapse: the 'crisis of profitability' and the crisis of 'realization' (Marx, 1981, pp. 349–355).

Meghnad Desai has succinctly summarized the first, from chapter 23 of *Capital*, vol.1:

Capitalists employ workers to make profits. But as they employ more workers, unemployment goes down. This puts pressure on real wages. As real wages, as well as employment, go up, the share of profit goes down, and there is a squeeze on the rate of profits. At this boom stage of the cycle, capitalists retaliate by investing in labour-saving technology. As unemployment increases, the pressure on real wages eases, and they may even go down. This is the slump. Profitability improves; this encourages capitalists to expand their business now, with the new technology, and the cycle continues its upward course. (Desai, 2002, p. 67)

The Marxist cycle thus exhibits the following features: (a) at full employment real wages encroach on profits, (b) this leads to depression in the short run as firms curtail production and lay off workers to restore profitability, (c) in the medium-run profitability is restored by labour-saving inventions and other mitigations. These will increase the 'organic composition' of capital, but new technology, and other offsets may raise the productivity of labour sufficiently to cancel this out and maintain a constant profit rate over the long term.

However useful this is as an explanation of some business-cycle phenomena (for example, it can helpfully be used to explain the crises of the 1970s, when powerful trade unions pushed wages ahead of productivity, and how these crises were overcome), it is not a theory of capitalist collapse. What Marx missed out was that technical change could reduce unit labour costs *even as* the organic composition of capital rose, thus allowing higher real wages to be paid in the long run without the rate of profit falling.

The *Communist Manifesto* hinted at another source of crisis: the 'crisis of realization'. In commercial crises 'a great part' of not just products but also of productive capacity is periodically destroyed ... because there is too much civilization, too much industry, too much commerce ... The conditions of bourgeois society are too narrow to comprise the wealth created by them' (Engels, 1888; Marx, 2002 (1848)). These inexact phrases point to a theory of underconsumption which was later developed by the English Liberal J.A. Hobson and the German Marxist Rosa Luxemburg. Contrary to much received wisdom, Marx did not predict that real wages would fall. But he had to assume that they could not rise proportionately to the increase in labour productivity. So Rosa Luxemburg asked: given the stagnation of real wages, how could the manual working class provide an adequate market for the ever-increasing volume of goods being turned out by the new machines? 'After all', she remarked, 'the only purpose of investment was to produce things which could be sold at a profit. And if things cannot be sold, why should capitalists keep investing?' (Luxemburg, quoted in Desai, 2002, p. 91).

This remains a pertinent question in the light of what happened in the first decade of this century, when real wages in western countries have fallen relative to the returns to capital.

Luxemburg argued that capitalism would try to overcome its crises of overproduction and underconsumption by using the state to open up foreign markets and build up armaments to absorb surplus capital. But again there was nothing here to indicate a final collapse. There are always new markets, new wars, actual or potential. And in addition to these, surplus capital can be dumped into financial instruments or absorbed in public consumption on health and education.

Marx failed to prove that either of these causes of crisis would be fatal. Both Lenin and Rosa Luxemburg were driven to invent theories of imperialism to explain capitalism's unexpected survival. Lenin argued that by opening up new labour supplies abroad for exploitation capitalism could afford to bribe domestic workers with higher wages. Luxemburg argued that imperialism was a way of opening up new investment opportunities for surplus capital. The less dramatic truth was that capitalism was a dynamic system capable of endlessly reinventing itself. As Desai writes: '*Capital* fails to come up with a single story about the dynamics of capitalism that in any way predicts – even with various conditions attached – its eventual downfall' (Desai, 2002, p. 79). Realization that his theories of crises failed to establish the apocalyptic moment is probably why Marx never finished the last two volumes of his magnum opus.

Then comes the nub of Desai's argument: in a famous passage from the preface to the *Contribution to the Critique of Political Economy*, Marx wrote: 'No social order ever disappears before all the productive forces for which there is room in it have been developed; and new higher relations of production never appear before the material conditions of their existence have matured in the womb of the old society itself. Therefore, mankind only sets itself such tasks as it can solve.' (Marx, quoted in Desai, 2002, p. 44). Yet generations of Marxist revolutionaries, inspired by Marx's dialectic – or more probably by his millenarianism – did set themselves 'tasks' which they could not 'solve', in both the Soviet Union and China at horrendous human cost. And for this Marx was responsible. He offered them, in effect, a false prospectus.

Life after capitalism?

'Will there be socialism after capitalism?' asks Desai. Not, it seems, via the established Marxist theories of crisis. But there is another route out of capitalism which does not rely on class struggle, 'final' crises, and revolution, but is simply a consequence of the fact that it has completed its historical mission. If the historic function of capitalism is to equip the world with a sufficient quantity of capital goods to supply all reasonable human needs, then the logic of continuing a system geared to the ever increasing accumulation of capital equipment will disappear. People will 'have enough'.

Marx wrote of the tendency of the rate of profit to fall over time. As Desai observed this was a 'standard piece of political economy' (Desai, 2002, p. 75).

Although Marx's argument depended on the replacement of labour (the source of profit) by machines, it can be put another way. The more plentiful capital equipment becomes, the lower will be the rate of return on each increment to capital. This tendency can be offset for a time but not indefinitely by the export of capital from capital abundant to capital-scarce parts of the world (imperialism), or by technological progress which continues to raise labour productivity sufficiently to cut the unit cost of labour. In 1930, Keynes argued that if capital grew at 2 per cent a year, and technical efficiency improved by 1 per cent a year, then in a hundred years capitalists would give up investing, and working people working, because the existing stock of capital and technology would be enough to satisfy all their wants at a small fraction of their historic work effort (Keynes, 1930, p. 325, 329). A capitalism in which the accumulation of capital no longer took place is a contradiction in terms. Whatever name one gave to the new dispensation it would not be capitalist.

What would an economic system which had moved beyond scarcity look like? Given the uncertainties surrounding his central prophecy, Marx was understandably unwilling to give any details of 'life beyond capitalism' which he thought would come with communism. Engels talked about a 'kingdom of freedom' which lay beyond the 'kingdom of necessity'. But like Marx he had little to say about what life in this 'kingdom of freedom' would be like.

Under communism, everyone would have 'enough'. But communism was more than just a rearrangement of property rights. It was the condition of a fuller life, in which the division of labour would be reduced to a minimum, and people would be free to choose what to do. The few words Marx had to say about life in the communist utopia resembles Goethe's ideal of *Vielfältigkeit* – many-sidedness:

> … nobody has one exclusive sphere of activity but each can become accomplished in any branch he wishes, society regulates the general production and thus makes it possible for me to do one thing today and another tomorrow, to hunt in the morning, fish in the afternoon, rear cattle in the evening, criticize after dinner, just as I have a mind, without ever becoming hunter, fisherman, shepherd or critic' (Marx, 1977, p. 169).

Patrick Coby remarks sardonically, '[i]t is safe to say that Marx's worker is an amateur for whom the freedom of his work is more important than its skillful execution' (Coby, 1986, p. 30).

The final paragraph from Trotsky's *Literature and Revolution* presents an equally utopian picture of life after capitalism:

> It is difficult to predict the extent of self-government which the man of the future may reach or the heights to which he may carry his technique. Social construction and psycho-physical self-education will become two aspects of one and the same process. All the arts – literature, drama, painting, music and architecture will lend this process beautiful form. More correctly, the shell in which the cultural construction and self-education of Communist man will be enclosed, will develop all the vital

elements of contemporary art to the highest point. Man will become immeasurably stronger, wiser and subtler; his body will become more harmonized, his movements more rhythmic, his voice more musical. The forms of life will become dynamically dramatic. The average human type will rise to the heights of an Aristotle, a Goethe, or a Marx. And above this ridge new peaks will rise. (1924, p. 209)

Both Marx and Keynes, then, thought that capitalism was destined to end in a 'stationary state' when its productive potential was exhausted. There are two main grounds for casting doubt on this. First, their simple model of machines replacing human labour ignored capitalism's ability to exploit still untapped human productive potential. In today's economy the source of profit is not physical but human capital – knowledge, technical skills, creativity. Investment in physical capital might cease, but as long as human capital can go on being improved, it can go on being bought and sold at a profit. Secondly, the Marx-Keynes model ignores the insatiability of wants. The sole purpose of production, wrote Adam Smith, is consumption. Provided consumption continues to rise in line with incomes, there is no reason why capitalism, which is unrivalled in its ability to produce consumption goods, and to stimulate new wants, should not go on indefinitely, with people working (perhaps for increasingly shorter hours) to obtain the consumption goods they want. Such a system may be insane, as well as morally bankrupt, but there is no *economic* reason why it should end.

It is fair to say that we have scarcely begun thinking seriously about what a transition to a more stationary state would entail, in terms of the distribution of jobs and the distribution of goods and services. At present our thoughts are rightly concentrated on regaining full employment after the Great Recession of 2008–9. But if capitalism can no longer guarantee full employment in the long run, we should start making preparations for life after capitalism. Marx at least points us in the direction.

Notes

1   The 1970s saw a revival of 'economic Marxism', which subsided when Reagan and Thatcher 'restored' capitalism.
2   Marx never talked about 'capitalism'. He used the word 'bourgeoisie' to emphasize the class-based character of the capitalist system. But capitalism can be substituted without loss of meaning. Pedantically, capitalism is a system in which the ownership of capital is concentrated in the hands of a single class – the bourgeoisie – which puts it to use for profit.

References

Coby, P., 1986. The utopian vision of Karl Marx. *Modern Age*, Winter.
Desai, M., 2002. *Marx's revenge: the resurgence of capitalism and the death of statist socialism*. London, New York: Verso, 2002.

Engels, F., 1888. *Communist manifesto*. English edition. London: Lawrence and Wishart.

Glyn, A. and Sutcliffe, R., 1972. *British capitalism, workers, and the profit squeeze*. Harmondsworth: Penguin.

Hirschman, A.O., 1977. *The passions and the interests: political arguments for capitalism before its triumph*. Princeton, NJ: Princeton University Press.

Hobsbawm, E., 2011. *How to change the world: tales of Marx and Marxism*. Boston: Little, Brown.

Keynes, J.M., 1930. The economic possibilities of our grandchildren. *Collected Writings of JM Keynes* (1973), Vol. IX. London: Macmillan for The Royal Economic Society.

Kolakowski, L., 2005. *Main currents of Marxism*. New York: W.W. Norton & Company.

Marx, K., 1974. *Capital*, vol.1. Student's edition. London: Lawrence and Wishart.

Marx, K., 1974. *The German ideology*. In Selected Writings, McLellan, ed. Oxford: Oxford University Press.

Marx, K., 1981. *Capital,* vol.3. (tr. Fernbach). Harmondsworth: Penguin.

Marx, K., 2002 (1848). The communist manifesto. G.S. Jones, ed. Harmondsworth: Penguin.

Trotsky, L., 1924. Literature and revolution. Keach ed. Chicago: Haymarket Books.

2

Macro-Prudential Supervision

Charles Goodhart

Preface

I first came to the London School of Economics in the academic year 1966/67, as a junior lecturer in Money and Banking, a specialist subject overseen by Professor Richard Sayers. Meghnad was already here, younger but already with a stronger academic record than me, and much more of a generalist, with an enthusiasm for almost all aspects of political economy. He had, and retains, boundless energy and infectious enthusiasm, inspiring both colleagues and students.

The calm of academic life at that time was then, however, disturbed by what became known as 'The Troubles' in early 1968 when LSE followed the example of Berkeley and the students in Paris. Meghnad gave a sympathetic ear to the students and helped to reconcile the various parties at a most difficult and precarious juncture.

These disruptions were a minor factor in my own decision to leave LSE to take up, first a temporary but then a more permanent, position at the Bank of England. When I eventually returned to LSE in 1985, Meghnad had transformed from being a young lecturer into a senior professor, indeed the Convenor of the Faculty of Economics. Yet more honours, notably in the guise of a life peerage would shortly follow. But, throughout, Meghnad has retained his infectious enthusiasm, his joy of life, his wide-ranging interests, his original viewpoints, his determination to find, enunciate, and abide by the truth (even if it cost him a position as spokesman in the Lords), and of course his idiosyncratic hairstyle and filing system (piles on the floor).

If anything, Meghnad has become even more of a generalist as he has grown older (global governance), while I have stuck to my narrower line of research. But even so we have often found ourselves together at seminars and conferences, to my great pleasure, since Meghnad is fun to be with and always a fount of both acute and entertaining commentary on events, theories and people.

One of Meghnad's many interests is monetary theory, and, of course, like all of us he has been fascinated by the financial crisis that started in 2007 and remains on-going. This crisis has taught us that our prior methods of financial regulation were insufficient. It is, therefore, with great pleasure that I put forward my paper on the need for, and forms of, macro-prudential supervision as a contribution to his Festschrift.

Why is macro-prudential supervision needed?

The experience of the last few years reveals, all too starkly, that the achievement of price stability, as evidenced for example by the successful conduct of inflation targets, does not guarantee financial stability. Initially there had been fears that the pursuit of price stability might lead to greater volatility in real output (Rogoff, 1985), but, at least during the Great Moderation (which we in Europe would date 1992–2007), the reverse was true. Output grew more steadily than in previous decades, prior to the collapse in 2008 Q4.

There may have been some, amongst officials, economists and commentators, who believed that such greater macro-economic stability, in inflation and output (and also in nominal interest rates and unemployment), would bring in its train greater stability in asset prices. If such macro-economic fundamentals were behaving more steadily, then surely asset prices would also do so? Yet, even if we exclude the latest crisis years, there is little evidence of greater asset price stability during the years 1992–2006 than in the previous equivalent period 1977–1991, with the exception of government bond prices.

Thus in Table 2.1, we take the standard deviation, around the trend as measured by an H-P filter applied from 1970 to end 2009, for a set of US variables.

There are reasons to explain the divergent behaviour of macro-economic fundamentals and asset price variability. One set of such reasons relates to the relationship between the time-varying risk aversion of agents operating in financial markets, and the macro-economic fundamentals. This was primarily developed by Minsky (1977, 1982 and 1986). When the macro-economic fundamentals appear to be set fair, risk aversion falls. Financial intermediaries both increase leverage and move along the risk curve, the more so as relatively riskless interest rates on public sector debt decline. To use Minsky's terminology, borrowers and lenders move from hedge assets/liabilities to more speculative assets/liabilities, and in some cases to Ponzi assets/liabilities. So when, after a period of successful steady expansion, an adverse shock occurs, it is likely to have a much more devastating effect on financial stability, than that same shock would have had during a period of greater macro-economic disturbance

Table 2.1[1] The Volatility of US Asset Prices

Standard Deviation around Trend	1977–1991	1992–2006
NYSE	1.255553	4.389932
US Housing Prices	0.838291	0.748006
$/Yen Exchange Rate*	0.000368	0.000515
$/£ Exchange Rate*	0.103489	0.066887
US 10 year T Bond	0.894748	0.492445

* For Exchange Rate data, the HP filter is from 1971 to 2009.

(Vardoulakis, *et al.*, 2010). The enhanced effect of such a shock, following a period of successful steady growth, may be all the greater if market participants have an exaggerated belief in the ability of the authorities to protect them from such tail events; a belief which became known as the 'Greenspan put'.

Be that as it may, the evidence is now clear that the achievement of price stability does not guarantee financial stability. Moreover, financial instability can imperil macro-economic outcomes. Although the objective of achieving financial stability was given something of a back seat in the years up till 2007, partly because responsibility for the financial supervision of individual institutions was hived off, in many countries such as Japan and the UK, to a separate Financial Services Authority, it was historically and traditionally the second core purpose of most central banks. Within the euro-zone there was also the complication that, whereas the conduct of monetary policy was transferred to the European Central Bank (ECB), prudential supervision remained nationally based. Now the need to achieve that objective has been re-affirmed and re-emphasized.

So there are now to be two separate targets for central banks to achieve. But central banks typically have a single instrument: the ability to control and vary the official short term rate of interest. This has led many, following Cecchetti *et al.* (2000), to argue that inflation targeting be amended to allow interest rates to 'lean against the wind' of asset price fluctuations.

There are gradations to this proposal. At a minimum there is a continuing need to reconsider how housing prices might best be included in the main inflation indices, since booms/busts in housing and property prices have been the most common accompaniment of episodes of financial instability. Housing price movements have been (so far) excluded altogether from the Harmonised Index of Consumer Prices, commonly used in Europe; and the way that they should be measured for the assessment of inflationary pressures remains contentious.

The use by the European Central Bank (ECB) of a second monetary pillar could also be viewed as an attempt to incorporate some such 'leaning'. Financial booms, and busts, are usually accompanied by major fluctuations in leverage and credit expansion, and these latter are likely (but not alas certain) to show up in monetary aggregate data – unless hidden in the 'shadow, or near, banking system'. Moreover, from a central banking viewpoint, such a second pillar has the virtue of relating policy to monetary aggregates, which, unlike housing or equity prices, are more clearly in the locus of monetary policy. Yet, particularly in the short run, the monetary variables are so hard to interpret that the ECB has, as far as can be assessed from the outside, made relatively little quantitative use, so far, of its 'second pillar' in setting official interest rates.

This is partly because of difficulties in assessing whether financial markets, and asset prices, have moved significantly away from equilibrium. There are always siren voices, often from eminent economists, to argue that the Dow Stock Exchange index at 15,000 or housing price/income ratios of 4 or 5, are perfectly consistent with equilibrium (given prospects of faster growth and lower real interest rates than in the past). In the face of such uncertainty, it takes a brave and determined central banker (and one whose political base is solid) to consciously aim to depress the real economy in order to mitigate a perceived, but uncertain, asset price boom.

Moreover, one of the key elements of an inflation targeting regime lies in the ability of a credible central bank, adopting such a regime, to stabilize inflation expectations. The successful dedication of the interest rate instrument to the medium-term stabilization of prices is a powerful instrument for that purpose. Blurring the focus of interest rate adjustment to incorporate two targets would, on this view, weaken both the accountability of the central bank *and* its ability to keep inflationary expectations anchored. At a time when many are fearful either of a future upsurge of inflation or of persistent deflation, or even of one followed by the other, the need is rather to reaffirm the focus of central banks in using macro monetary policy, i.e. interest rates (plus Quantitative Easing when the zero bound is hit), to hit the inflation target, rather than diluting that focus by adding a second objective.

But, if official interest rate adjustment is to continue to be dedicated to the macro-economic purpose of maintaining price stability, then how are central banks to achieve their concern with maintaining orderly financial conditions as a pre-condition for the maintenance of price stability, now that that role has become so prominent? At present, the powers of most central banks in this field are limited to 'delivering sermons and organizing burials' (King, 2009). So, the search is on, at least in some quarters, for a second (set of) instrument(s), macro-prudential counter-cyclical instruments, which may be wielded by central banks, alongside and independently of official interest rates. This would allow the Tinbergen principle, of two objectives and two instruments, to be achieved. But what form might such additional macro-prudential instruments take?

What macro-prudential instruments?

Counter-cyclical instruments

As noted in several Reports, e.g. Brunnermeier, *et al.* (2009), the focus of regulation/ supervision, in the decades up until 2007, has been on the individual bank, or financial intermediary, with insufficient attention being paid to systemic effects, spill-overs and externalities. This is now being corrected. A more systemic approach needs to be put in place. The formation of the European Systemic Risk Board (ESRB) is an example of this new approach. Although the (legal) power to enforce and to amend regulation remains with the individual nation state within the EU, the ability of the ESRB to issue warnings and to propose regulatory changes, and to require the relevant national authorities to comply with such proposals or to explain why not, could (depending on how the ESRB performs in practice) prove a powerful mechanism for initiating macro-prudential supervision[2] and control.

So the ESRB provides a procedural mechanism, wherein the macro-prudential instruments can be deployed. Turning now to the instruments themselves, there are two main such instruments, and a penumbra of less conventional, and perhaps more fundamental, possibilities. The two main instruments are capital and liquidity ratios. Let us turn to capital ratios first.

Capital ratios

Risk management is a complicated business, with many facets. The Basel Committee on Banking Supervision (BCBS) Capital Accord of 1988 only addressed credit risk. They turned next to the subject of Market Risk, comprising interest rate risk, liquidity risk, etc., in banks' trading books. When they circulated their early discussion drafts, they soon found that their heuristic, rule-of-thumb approach to assessing such risks was technically far behind the internal risk management approach of the large international banks, who had been developing internal risk management models based on finance theory, in particular the Value-at-Risk (VaR) Model. The BCBS recognized that they were comparatively deficient in risk modeling, and in effect adopted the commercial banks' internal modeling techniques, both for the Market Risk amendment to the Basel Accord (1996) and, more important, as the basis for Basel II. In a sense the BCBS had been intellectually captured.

Basel I had soon come under fire. Its risk 'buckets' were far too broad. Any loan to a private corporate had the same (100 per cent) weight whether to the largest/safest company or to some fly-by-night start-up. So the regulators were requiring too much regulatory capital to be placed against 'safe' loans, and too little against 'risky' loans. This led banks to sell off 'safe' loans (securitizations) to entities outside the regulatory net – including the emerging shadow banking system – and to hold onto their risky loans. So the regulation, intended to make banks safer, was instead making them riskier. The answer seemed to be to rely more on market risk assessment, either by credit rating agencies (CRAs), or, even better, by the banks themselves in either the Foundation or Advanced internal ratings based (IRB) approaches. The basic idea was to allow the regulators to piggy-back on the greater technical risk-management skills of the regulated, and one of the boasts of the authors of Basel II was that it aligned regulatory capital much more closely with the economic capital that the banks wanted to keep for their own sake.

This was, however, a misguided strategy. A commercial bank's concern is how to position itself under normal conditions, in which it can assume, even for large banks, that outside conditions will not be much affected by its own actions. If really extreme conditions do develop, the authorities will have to react. Moreover, such a bank is unconcerned with any externalities that its failure might cause. For such purposes tools such as VaRs, stress tests, etc., are well designed. But the regulators' concerns should have been quite different. Their concern should have been exclusively about externalities, since the banks' creditors should properly absorb internalized losses. They should have worried about the strength of the system, not so much that of the individual bank, about co-variances rather than variances, about inter-active self-amplifying mechanisms rather than about stress tests that assume a world invariant to the banks' own reactions (Brunnermeier, *et al.*, 2009).

Why did it all go so wrong? First there was often an implicit belief that, if one acted to make all the individual components (banks) of a (banking) system operate safely, then the system as a whole would be protected from harm (fallacy of composition). Second, there was a tendency among the regulators, and at the BCBS, to patch up the system incrementally in response to criticism (and to events) rather than to think about fundamental issues. Regulators, and supervisors, tend to be pragmatists rather than theorists – and they had little enough help from economists, many of whose main models abstracted from financial intermediation and/or default!

Be that as it may, the slow, and painful, advent of Basel II did nothing to mitigate the cycle of credit expansion and taking on extra leverage, up until August 2007, and its abrupt and destructive reversal thereafter. Defaults, volatility and risk premia were all reduced to low levels (2003–6), and ratings whether by CRAs, or internally, were high and rising. With profits, and capital, further enhanced by the application of mark-to-market accounting, all the risk models and powerful market pressures were encouraging banks and other financial intermediaries to take on ever more leverage, right until the bottom fell out of the market in July/August 2007.

The need is now to rethink the application of capital ratios. There are, at least, five issues that need to be considered, being:

1 The base to which the ratio should apply, notably whether this should just be a simple leverage ratio and/or risk-weighted, and its application to contingent calls on (bank) funding, e.g. off-balance sheet and unused credit lines, as well as on balance sheet items;

2 The definition of applicable capital for such purposes;

3 Whether the ratio should be constant, or time and state varying, and if the latter whether such variation be done by discretion or be done by some rule/formula;

4 The 'normal' level of such ratios; and

5 The sanctions to be imposed for transgressing that level.

There are now answers to some of these questions. In view of the ease with which either a risk-weighted, or a leverage ratio on its own can be manipulated (in the first case by levering up with assets whose risk-weighting is 'optimistic'; in the second case by holding riskier assets on balance sheet, while securitising/selling safer assets), the latest proposal of the BCBS is to go for both simultaneously. Again the treatment of contingent claims and off-balance sheet entities is being tightened up, but in view of the somewhat fuzzy nature of contingent commitments to extend loans (incomplete contracts) in future, this is likely to remain a grey area.

Similarly the definition of applicable capital is being narrowed. Various forms of hybrid or subordinate debt that were junior to deposits and so gave protection in the event of a default, but did not themselves provide much, if any, protection against that default, will no longer play a role as they used to do in Tier 2, and in some cases even in Tier 1. The focus now will be on Tier 1 capital, and within that on Tangible Core Equity, or TCE.

Next, the prospective required ratios of Tier 1 or TCE capital both to risk-weighted assets (RWA), or leverage, are being raised but with quite a long transition period, at least until 2012, in view of both the current recession, the weakened state of the banking system and the slow growth (or even decline) in bank lending to the private sector.

Issues where there has been less agreement relate to (3) whether the ratios should be constant or time-varying and (5) whether there should be a ladder of sanctions for transgressing the ratio. On issue (3) many central bank officials claim that the opportunity for time/state varying ratios was already available under Pillar 2 of the Basel II accord, in a discretionary mode, to supervisors; that this option remains and is all that is desirable. Against that, one can note that Pillar 2 of Basel II has rarely, if ever, been activated; that it is always going to be subject to the 'Level Playing Field' critique, and that its activation will almost invariably run directly contrary to market forces and pressures, and so would be (politically) very unpopular. On these latter grounds one can argue that some form of 'rule' or 'formula' based mechanism needs to be put in place in order to give regulators/supervisors the backbone and support ever to introduce time/state varying ratios. In response to the valid criticism that no set of rules/formulae can ever fully and properly take account of the infinite range of future possibilities, they could be applied on a 'comply or explain' basis.

The systemic concern that many academics have at the forefront of their minds is of a generalized asset price boom/bust within their (national/regional/sectoral) financial systems, which would be represented by a general expansion in (a) credit to the private sector, (b) leverage, and (c) asset price increases, especially in housing and property. On the other hand, the concern that more politicians/commentators have at the forefront of their minds is the contribution that individual financial institutions (banks) may make to the potential instability of the system as a whole. Thus 'systemic' financial intermediaries may be identified, perhaps on some (as yet undecided) combined criteria of size, activities and inter-connectedness, and regulated/supervised separately from the rest. Even within the set of 'systemic' financial intermediaries, the required capital ratio might, perhaps, vary depending on the assessed (but how measured) extent of that individual intermediary being systemic. Although the measurement of the extent of individual systemic weight is far less advanced than the measurement of overall cycles in leverage/credit expansion, etc., the momentum for varying such ratios for each individual 'systemic' institution has been, on this view, rather stronger.

In view of the difficulties of any mechanism of time/state varying capital ratios, other methods for achieving some counter-cyclical effects remain also under consideration. A leading example has been the Spanish dynamic pre-provisioning procedure. This, however, falls foul of accountants and tax authorities (who fear that it may be used to defer tax payments). In particular accountants dislike applying generalized probabilities rather than specific outcomes. However, considerable pressure is now being applied to accountants to accept generalized provisions, at least to assets in the 'hold to maturity' category, which provisions might be state varying. This approach, of course, has many overlapping characteristics with a state varying capital ratio, and the choice between the two could depend on which seemed more acceptable and 'do-able'. Cyclical movements in expected losses are, however, much smaller than cyclical movements in unexpected losses, so adjusting capital is much more important than adjusting provisions.[3] Ideally we should have both time/state varying capital ratios and dynamic pre-provisioning.

It is, perhaps, with the final issue, the applicable ladder of sanctions, that least progress has been achieved. This reflects an inherent weakness in the BCBS international procedures. Since laws and sanctions are a national prerogative, and the BCBS has no formal basis and acts as an advisory body, it has always refrained from suggesting any sanctions as a consequence of undershooting its proposed ratios. The untoward result of this has been that virtually all those involved, whether ratings agencies, market operators and commentators, or even the regulators themselves, have taken the BCBS proposed ratios as absolute minima which can never be infringed without serious reputational consequences.

But this, of course, destroys, indeed has destroyed, the potential buffering role of (required) capital, and has transformed the *usable buffer* into the shape of the much more exiguous margin above the required capital ratio. That has been a major draw-back of the whole BCBS approach to date. Despite the example of the FDIC Improvement Act (1991) in the USA, which established a sensible ladder of sanctions, the BCBS has still refrained from grasping this nettle. Of course, if the normal required ratio was set relatively low, with an expectation that there would be much more aggressive use of time/state varying counter-cyclical add-ons, it could amount to much the same in the end, but there is no evidence at all of this being likely. Instead the currently most probable outcome is for a large increase in the standard required ratio(s), after a transitional period, with little, or no, counter-cyclical additionality. If so, it behoves the BCBS to consider, and to suggest, how an appropriate ladder of sanctions might be introduced and applied. There is, alas, not much sign as yet that the BCBS are moving in this direction.

Liquidity ratios

The Basel Committee on Banking Supervision had failed in an earlier attempt to reach an Accord on Liquidity in the 1980s. Partly as a result, asset liquidity had subsequently been run down. The general hypothesis, shared alike by most bankers and most regulators, was that so long as banks had 'sufficient' capital, they could always access efficient wholesale money markets and thereby replace asset liquidity by funding liquidity. While these money market liabilities were short-term, compared to bank assets, the interest rate and credit risks generated by such a maturity mismatch could then be resolved by securitization and by hedging via derivatives. Finally the assumption was that adherence to Basel II would ensure 'sufficient' capital.

These comfortable assumptions fell apart in the summer of 2007. The actual, and prospective, losses on mortgage backed securities, especially on sub-primes, and the gaming of Basel II, especially by European banks, meant that adherence to the Basel II requirements was not enough to provide complete assurance on future solvency in many cases. Especially with the opacity of CDOs, the markets for securitization dried up, as did short-term wholesale markets, e.g. asset-backed commercial paper, and unsecured interbank term loan markets. This led to a liquidity crisis.

According to the prior set of assumptions, this could/should never have happened. It took everyone, including the central banks, largely by surprise. One response was that this pickle was largely the fault of the commercial banks' own business strategies (too few 'good' public sector assets, too much reliance on short-dated wholesale funds and securitization, too great a mismatch, etc.), so to help banks out of this hole would generate moral hazard. Perhaps, but the virulence of the collapse became so great that all the central banks were forced to expand their provision of liquidity over an ever-increasing range of maturities, collateral and institutions.

When it comes to designing specific liquidity ratios, many of the same considerations apply, such as:

1 The base, for example whether done on a simple leverage ratio basis, or assessed via a maturity mismatch (or a combination of both?). How to handle contingent claims on funding needs;

2 The definition of liquid assets for such purposes;

3 Whether the ratio should be constant, or time/state varying, and if the latter whether such variation should be done by discretion or by some rule/formulae;

4 The 'normal' level of such ratios; and

5 The sanctions, if any, imposed on transgressions of the normal level.

Many of these involve the same issues as were already reviewed for the application of capital ratios, and do not need to be repeated here. But, whereas virtually everyone accepts the need for capital ratio requirements, not everyone, notably not Buiter

(2008), sees a need for imposed liquidity ratios. In part such disagreement relates to the definition of liquid assets (2 above), and, deriving from that discussion, a deeper analysis of exactly what is the purpose of liquidity ratios in the first place.

The point at issue here is that a central bank can, if it so chooses, buy, or more usually lend against the collateral of, virtually any asset. Moreover, during the recent crisis, central banks both lent against a wider range of collateral assets, or, when they sought to maintain the strict nature of their lending terms, they agreed to a swap, under some Special Lending Scheme, of non-acceptable assets (e.g. various kinds of mortgages) for acceptable assets (e.g. public sector debt). Willem Buiter has simply taken this logic to its extreme. Thus a central bank can, in principle, liquefy any asset – though it will be hesitant to do so if there is no stable market price for that asset, since it puts excessive risk on its books. Any asset that can be transformed into cash by borrowing from a central bank is liquid. Hence all assets are, in principle, liquid; so all commercial banks are, at all times, fully liquid, and there is no need to require banks to hold some sub-set of particular (usually low-yielding, public sector) assets. It is just a tax on banks and a subsidy to the government.

What, if anything, is wrong with that argument? There are, in my view, at least two inter-related counter-arguments. The first relates to time. If a bank holds only relatively illiquid private sector debt, it will find it hard to raise cash quickly by selling such assets on the private market, at least without generating a sizeable reduction in the prices of such assets, and thereby amplifying the crisis (an externality). So such a commercial bank would be forced to turn to the central bank for liquidity support at a very early stage in the crisis. The problem with that is that, in a crisis, time is short and of the essence. Time is always needed, and rarely sufficient, to discover the facts and to assess how best to resolve the issue. Moreover, the stigma issue, whereby a bank requesting liquidity support from the central bank is perceived by the market as, *ipso facto*, less creditworthy, has not yet been resolved. So greater reliance on the central bank for liquidity support enhances the potential conflict between transparency and policy effectiveness (n.b. the political row over the secrecy surrounding the Bank of England's loans to the Royal Bank of Scotland (RBS) and to Lloyds Bank in the autumn of 2008).

The second issue relates to the discount, the terms on which the central bank should lend to commercial banks. This issue has been muddled by the common, but misguided, claim that the central bank should only lend at a penal rate, relative to the market. The basic error of this position becomes clear by realising that, if the central bank is only to lend on worse terms than the market, it would never be asked to lend at all! The truth, however, is often that the assets which a commercial bank can pledge, or sell, are sufficiently illiquid that that action could reduce their value considerably. If these are all that a commercial bank has available, then the central bank faces a serious problem. Either it will be prepared to lend at such a large discount to the current market that it protects its own position, but provides little, if any, assistance to the borrowing bank, and may thereby provoke further (mark-to-market) falls in such asset prices; or it will lend on relatively generous terms, thereby supporting the borrowing bank and the market, but by so doing put its own balance sheet, and by inference taxpayers, at risk. It is essentially this same conundrum that put the TARP exercise in difficulties; too low a price, and it does not help the banks; too high a price, and taxpayers may be subsidising banks.

So, even when a central bank may be put under pressure ultimately to lend against any asset that a commercial bank may have available to offer, the existence of a liquid asset ratio provides protection for a central bank from having to do so. It not only provides time for the authorities to resolve the crisis, but also greatly reduces the difficulty of being able to decide on the appropriate terms for doing so. Once, however, one recognizes that the purpose of a liquid asset ratio is essentially to provide protection to the central bank, from being forced quickly into a position of making markets in illiquid assets, it provides at least an initial guide to thinking about both the composition and the normal amount (ratio) to be required of such assets. In particular, private sector markets, especially for mortgage-based assets, can rapidly become illiquid, and wholesale funding markets also can dry up. This suggests that liquid assets, for this purpose, should consist primarily of public sector debt, and also be sufficient to meet liquidity needs for a sufficiently long period, say 10 weeks, that could enable a central bank to respond to a generalized liquidity drought.[4]

Other, somewhat less conventional, proposals

The core of most macro-prudential proposals consists of a reinforcement of capital/liquidity ratios. Such proposals may be extended, or adjusted, in a variety of ways:

1 Pigovian taxes

2 Application to a wider base of systemic intermediaries

3 Extended margining

Pigovian taxes

In so far as capital/liquidity ratios force banks to reorient their portfolios in a way that they would not do voluntarily anyhow (in which case the regulation is superfluous), they represent an added cost to the bank involved. An alternative way of seeking to make banks behave in a systemically safer way is to impose taxes on such facets of their behaviour as could lead to systemic failure and the use of taxpayer money[5], such as increasing taxes on size, inter-connectedness and certain prescribed activities (e.g. prop desks). The obvious advantage of this is that it would be an attempt to make the banks pay, up front, for such systemic cost that may have to be borne later by the taxpayer. In this respect it has much in common with the various (American) schemes for insurance, to be discussed later.

There would, however, be great difficulties in estimating such Pigovian taxes fairly and efficiently. Most proposals for such ex ante levies simply involve either a pro rata, or a progressive, levy related to some measure of size, with no serious attempt to assess systemic risk. There could be an obvious likelihood that such levies would just deteriorate into being a populist means of raising revenues at the expense of banks. Unless such a tax was applied world-wide, it, like the Tobin tax, would be massively avoided by migration.

Whereas those subject to capital/liquidity ratios can, and do, appreciate the rationale for such requirements, a levy, that was perforce broad-brush, rather than closely tailored to systemic externalities, would just be perceived by those paying as a penal attack on banks (and other institutions) subject to it. It would, therefore, likely to be even more subject to massive avoidance schemes, whether by transferring financial intermediation geographically or within each country across the border to non-taxed intermediaries.

In the current climate of popular anti-bank opinion, however, and now that President Obama has called in January 2010 for an ex post tax on US banks, which relied heavily on wholesale markets, the (world-wide) introduction of such a tax seems virtually assured. At a time of stretched public sector financing, with banks being deeply unpopular, the attractions of a tax which could also be justified on the grounds of being a pay-back for past, taxpayer funded, crises, or a protection against the need for similar future taxpayer funding, seem overwhelming. Besides the USA, Sweden has already introduced such a tax; Germany and the UK are planning to do so; and the IMF will be proposing, in April 2010, ways of doing so. The question now is not whether such a tax will be introduced, since it will be, but rather the form that it will take, and the consequences of its introduction. These latter issues have still to be determined.

Application to a wider base of systemic intermediaries

The aim of introducing reinforced capital/liquidity ratios on banks is to reduce systemic risk, of the kind recently suffered. But the failure of financial intermediaries, other than banks, can have systemic implications. Indeed, the main problems in the USA arose amongst *non-banks*, e.g. the broker/dealer investment houses, such as Lehman Bros and Bear Stearns (though the two remaining such houses have now become banks), insurance companies, such as AIG, monolines, the GSEs, Fannie and Freddie, and money market mutual funds (such as Reserve Primary Fund after the Lehman default).

One approach, perhaps more explicit in the USA than in Europe, with Secretary of the Treasury, Tim Geithner's plan and Barney Frank's House Bill is to designate a set of financial intermediaries as systemic, and to extend macro-prudential regulation to them too. But just how does one define, or calibrate, which institutions are systemic, and would not the set of systemic institutions be subject to continuous change, depending on conditions, innovation, etc? But at least the line of analysis in the USA is rational, whereas in Europe proposals to extend (macro-prudential) regulation beyond the banking system seem to relate more to the political popularity of the institutions involved rather than to their capacity to set off systemic financial collapse. Thus the main thrust in Europe has been towards extending regulatory controls over hedge funds and private equity, whose capacity for causing systemic failure is limited (pace LTCM), whereas there has been much less concern about insurance (and reinsurance) companies and mutual funds.

Extended margining

In a sense both capital and liquidity ratios represent a version of margining. As the bank increases the size of its portfolio, it has to hold additional margins of both capital and liquidity. This concept of margining can be extended to other financial sectors. For example, and particularly, in the housing market one could apply maximum, or even time/state varying, Loan to Value (LTV) ratios, or Loan to Income (LTI) ratios. The same approach can be applied to the financing of equity positions, and, in principle, to a wide range of financial markets.

A general problem, for such additional margining, is that money and finance are fungible, so that there are usually several alternative methods of achieving a desired financial position, e.g. by switching finance to an uncontrolled (possibly foreign) lender. Of course if the main purpose of the exercise is to protect the domestic lender, not the domestic borrower, from taking up a, supposedly dangerous, position, the ability of the borrower to refinance from an uncontrolled source may not be such a worry. If the main aim is to protect the borrower from getting over-extended, then the usual support mechanism is to remove legal protection against default for a lender who has not abided by the margin regulations.

Besides such proposals for extensions of capital/liquidity ratios, there are a number of more radical ideas for changing the structure in which banks, and perhaps other financial intermediaries, operate and to do so in such a way as to aim to make them less subject to systemic collapse. Such proposals include:

1   The removal, or the reduction, of the tax allowance (the tax wedge) on interest rates – as was done for household mortgage interest payments in the UK. This proposal was apparently once favourably received by the Chancellor, George Osborne, in the UK, but would be difficult to introduce unilaterally without raising international cross-country competitiveness concerns, and has not, I believe, been widely promoted outside the UK.

2   The amendment, or adjustment, of limited liability for certain financial operations, or certain financial agents. For example, certain types of intermediation, such as hedge funds, or prop desk activity, could only be undertaken under a partnership arrangement. Alternatively certain classes of financial officials, e.g. directors and senior officials of banks for example, might have an additional liability for n times the par value of a share in their own company, which liability would continue for j years after they had left that bank. There was a proposal, by Neil Record in the Op. Ed. pages of the Financial Times (6 January 2010),

to make all bonus payments to highly-paid bankers subject to claw-back. Again the (legal) complexity of such an exercise, alongside other problems, has been such that there has been little support for such an approach, though there are arguments in its favour.

3 Various methods of controlling, and limiting, officials' remuneration (e.g. the Walker Report, 2009). This issue, however, gets so caught up in so many other political and populist matters, and is, perhaps, so tangential to the wider issue of macro-prudential regulation, that it will not be further pursued here.

Generic problems with such macro-prudential regulations

There are major problems of measurement (primarily of systemic risk) and of calibration (of the macro-prudential instruments). It is extremely difficult to assess the risk of a systemic collapse at any time. Most early warning systems soon become relatively useless out of sample, because in so far as a systemic problem *can* be predicted, market agents will take steps to offset, and hence prevent, it occurring. Almost by definition, financial crises are only predicted by a small minority of commentators. In my view the best work on pre-conditions for a financial crisis has been done by Claudio Borio, and colleagues (2002, 2004 and 2009) at the BIS, who have focussed on two main factors, being unusually rapid expansion of (bank) credit and unusually high levels, and growth rates, of housing and property prices.

Having (dimly) assessed the uncertain probability of either an individual default, or a systemic collapse, what then is the (marginal) effect of requiring either higher capital, or liquidity ratios, in averting such an outcome? On capital, some work has now started on this, examining tail events, and the 'marginal expected shortfall', as developed by Acharya, *et al.* (2009) of New York University (NYU), but such work remains at a nascent level. As Hellwig reminds us (Blum and Hellwig, 1995; Hellwig, 2008), there has been no proper analysis of the appropriate quantitative requirement for capital; and the analysis of the need for liquidity (see earlier section) is, if possible, even more rudimentary.

In such circumstances required ratios are usually chosen by some rough rule of thumb, e.g. to equal the ratios held already on average, or by those banks whose performance has seemed best. Moreover, little, or no, attention is given to the fact that the effect of imposing a 'required' ratio depends sensitively on the (ladder of) sanctions imposed for transgressing that requirement. Given the (usually) arbitrary number chosen, getting the pattern of sanctions roughly right may be the most important feature of the regulatory exercise, but one that is all too rarely attempted.

Be that as it may, in the aftermath of the worst financial crisis for 75 years, and with little analytical help from economists, the general cry from regulators is that capital and liquidity ratios should be raised, and considerably so, especially in certain areas such as the capital requirements for trading books.

The effect of this will be to raise the cost of bank intermediation. The supposed (Modigliani-Miller) offset via lower debt costs (as credit risk declines) will not work in so far as depositors were already fully insured. And where they were not so insured this effect may well be matched by an enhanced reassessment of the inherent riskiness of banks. The idea that tougher regulation would bring down risk premia on bank wholesale funding significantly in the near future is, in my view, improbable. Of course, such tougher regulation is to be introduced over a transitional period, but bankers are forward-looking, and such proposed regulations will cast their shadow forward.

The, almost inevitable, result will be higher spreads between deposit rates and loan rates (the spread being a measure of the cost of intermediation), and a significantly smaller share of bank intermediation within overall financial intermediation. After all, one of the aims of such tightened regulation is to cut an overly-large, some would say bloated, banking system down to size, and to make the diminished remainder safer (and duller) as well as smaller.

Will it be good, or bad, to shrink the banking sector as a proportion of the overall financial system? The truth is that we do not know; we have barely begun to ask that question. It is unlikely to matter much for the public sector, or for large private sector corporations, since they both can access capital market directly. It will probably have a less serious effect on Anglo-Saxon countries, where capital markets are more advanced, than in Euro-zone countries which rely more on relationship banking. It is ironic that much of the pressure for much tougher regulation comes from just those same Euro-zone countries, since it may have a more adverse impact on their own systems. Perhaps the marked current decline (as of early 2010) in Euro-zone bank lending and deposit base is a precursor of a long-lasting effect.

The main concern relates to the financial (borrowing) opportunity for households and SMEs. Most of mortgage finance and of lending to SMEs has been originated by banks, and most used to remain in bank portfolios (hold to maturity). The faster growth of credit expansion than of the growth of the retail deposit base in recent years led both to the expansion of bank wholesale funding (including off-balance-sheet SPVs) and securitization (originate to distribute (OTD)). Both such channels have recently gone into reverse. If these, particularly securitization, cannot be revived, then limiting the availability of household and SME finance to what can be provided from the natural growth of retail deposits (with deposit rates held down to sustain bank profitability) may be quite problematical. How this concern may play out, and be resolved perhaps, is just not knowable at present.

Another possible feature of the toughened regulatory regime may be enhanced counter-cyclical add-ons during boom periods. The intention is that these should be relaxed during downturns. But many bankers are sceptical whether effective ratios can be significantly reduced during a crisis, or a bust. A severe downturn raises risk aversion, and perceptions of risk. Even if the regulators should reduce *required* ratios at such a moment, would the market, the credit rating agencies, etc., be willing to countenance banks taking advantage of that to lower actual ratios? So many bankers doubt whether supposed counter-cyclical, time/state varying regulations would actually work that way in practice. They see such proposals as a method of jacking up such ratios in the good times, while market forces keep actual ratios at this elevated level in the bad times. So they suspect that so-called counter-cyclical measures will just in practice be another way of raising capital and liquidity ratios throughout the cycle.

Such generalized regulatory tightening will, also of course, exacerbate the border problem between the regulated and the unregulated. The more rigorous are the constraints on the regulated, the greater the incentive to jump over the border and undertake unregulated business. The greater the focus on the banks, and the more constrained their activities (e.g. narrow banking), the greater the likelihood of encouraging intermediation elsewhere and the greater the probability that the next crisis will centre in the, artificially promoted, unregulated sector.

Of course there is then a temptation to extend regulation even further through the financial system. But where does one draw the line? Since the main objective is to prevent systemic collapse, the answer presumably is to include within the regulatory net all those financial institutions (including market infrastructure institutions, such as Centralised Clearing Houses) whose failure could have systemic consequences. Indeed the current general idea now is to have a separate regulatory system for systemic institutions, and a lighter regime for the non-systemic.

But, although such proposals are widely set forth and endorsed, there is little enough analysis of how to measure the extent to which an institution may be systemic. About the best that can be done is to assess how far a change in one bank's market position has a contemporaneous effect on other banks' positions; this branch of analysis includes Acharya and Richardson (2009), Acharya, *et al.* (2010), Adrian and Brunnermeier (2009), Brunnermeier and Pedersen (2009), Segoviano (2006, 2010) and Segoviano and Goodhart (2009). Also see the International Monetary Fund (IMF) 'Global Financial Stability Report' (April 2009, Chapter 3).

Moreover, the extent to which an institution may have a systemic effect is not constant, but will vary over time, and dependent on the state of the economy. Perhaps one of the greatest weaknesses of present regulatory proposals is that such proposals often depend on the ability to distinguish a set of 'systemic financial institutions'. Yet there is no present ability to define such a set, nor even to outline in any detail the characteristic (factors) that should be the basis of such a definition. Nor is the set of systemic financial institutions likely to be constant over time, or invariant to the conjuncture.

Of course one can reasonably identify the extremes, i.e. those institutions which are so large, so central and so interconnected that their failure would cause havoc elsewhere, and those equally so small, idiosyncratic and special that their failure would be almost unnoticed. But there will be a large (and changeable) grey area in between. How will the line be set in this grey area? With such an arbitrary dividing line, how can one justify different regulatory regimes that depend on accidents in setting this line? If the division between the systemic and non-systemic, and the criteria for making this division, is reported, it is likely to set up incentives for re-jigging the business to be on one side, or the other, of the line (whichever side is felt to be preferable). If the treatment, on either side of the dividing line, was to be different, could the authorities keep the listing, and the criteria for that listing, secret? Given the general advantages of transparency, and the need for accountability, should they wish, or be allowed, to go for secrecy in any case?

All the above regulatory issues maintain an implicit assumption of a closed economy with a single government and legal structure, though possibly with several regulatory and supervisory bodies, subject to some kinds of coordinating mechanism. The most intractable regulatory problem, however, is that almost all systemic institutions will have a significant cross-border presence. Such institutions are 'international in operation, but national in death'. The legal systems, notably insolvency proceedings and bankruptcy laws, differ from country to country. This greatly complicates crisis resolution for such cross-border international systemic institutions; the Lehman Bros bankruptcy was a case in point. But this is a large subject, and both I and Richard Herring have written on this topic recently, to suggest a way forward (Avgouleas, Goodhart and Schoenmaker, 2010; Herring, 2010); so I shall skip over this subject here.

Even when we side-step the international cross-border issue, the range of generic problems confronting macro-prudential regulatory proposals remains formidable. And this is to discount, almost entirely, the generalized dislike of government intervention and regulation that pervades many (American) circles. 'Regulation is static, whereas markets are dynamic'. It takes an inordinate time to agree and to introduce regulation. By the time that they are ready for introduction, the regulated will have found ways to avoid them. Regulators and supervisors are, by comparison to market agents, relatively poorly-paid bureaucrats, out of immediate touch with current market practices and realities. Any attempt to differentiate the imposition of regulation between countries, for example for counter-cyclical purposes, is likely to run up against the 'level playing field' challenge, that the country-specific requirement will simply shift intermediation abroad, though there may be ways to mitigate this.

Conclusion

The introduction of counter-cyclical macro-prudential instruments should be done. Nevertheless the exercise will be difficult and success is far from assured. At least the BCBS, and to a lesser extent the EC, are now headed in the right direction. Let us hope that they, and the ESRB, will significantly improve the achievement of financial stability.

Notes

1 Sources: FED St Louis – US Housing Prices, Exchange Rates and US 10 year T Bond IFS(IMF) – NYSE S&P 500.

2 It may be worthwhile to reiterate the distinction between regulation, which involves setting the rules of conduct, and supervision, which concerns monitoring adherence to such rules and enforcing compliance with them.

3 Rafael Repullo pointed this out to me.

4 A subsidiary issue is whether there should be a limit on the maturity/duration of the public sector debt that could be counted as liquid. My view is that no such limit is needed for the following reasons:

   a All such debt is liquid in the sense of (almost always) being tradeable in large volumes at low bid-ask spreads without changing prices much against the trader.

   b While interest rate risk does increase with duration, that risk can be specifically hedged via swaps. What matters is the interest rate risk of the bank's portfolio as a whole, not that of any individual item within it.

   c Once there is confidence in future price stability, as in the nineteenth century, long yields tend to move very little in response to changes in short rates. In the nineteenth century in the United Kingdom Consols were widely regarded as the most liquid asset, beyond cash, that a bank could hold.

   d Any line drawn, above which such debt would not be treated as liquid, would not only be arbitrary, but would also cause market distortions.

5 Note that the imposition of ex post, i.e. after the crisis, levies on surviving banks will not have such a beneficial effect and will have other disadvantages as well.

References

Acharya, V., Pedersen, L.H., Philippon, T. and Richardson, M., 2010. *Measuring systemic risk*. Stern School of Business, New York University. (Work in progress.)

Acharya, V. and Richardson, M., eds., 2009. *Restoring financial stability: how to repair a failed system*. NJ: John Wiley & Sons, Inc.

Adrian, T. and Brunnermeier, M.K., 2009. *CoVaR*. Federal Reserve Bank of New York staff reports 348.

Avgouleas, E., Goodhart, C. and Schoenmaker, D., 2010. *Living wills as a catalyst for action*. (Work in progress.) Available through Dirk Schoenmaker: dirk.schoenmaker@duisenbergschooloffinance.com.

Blum, J. and Hellwig, M., 1995. The macroeconomic implications of capital adequacy requirements for banks. *European Economic Review*, 39, pp. 739–749.

Borio, C. and Drehmann, M., 2009. *Towards an operational framework for financial stability: "fuzzy" measurement and its consequences*. BIS working paper 284.

Borio, C. and Lowe, P., 2002. *Asset prices, financial and monetary stability: exploring the nexus*. BIS working paper 114.

Borio, C. and Lowe, P., 2004. *Securing sustainable price stability: should credit come back from the wilderness?* BIS working paper 157.

Brunnermeier, M., Crockett, A., Goodhart, C., Persaud, A.D. and Shin, H., 2009. The fundamental principles of financial regulation. *Geneva reports on the world economy*, 11. Geneva: International Center for Monetary and Banking Studies, ICMB, and Centre for Economic Policy Research, CEPR.

Brunnermeier, M.K. and Pedersen, L.H., 2009. Market liquidity and funding liquidity. *Review of Financial Stability*, 22(6).

Buiter, W.H., 2008. Central banks and financial crises. *Financial markets group*. Discussion paper 619. London: London School of Economics and Political Science.

Cecchetti, S.G., Genberg, H., Lipsky, J. and Wadhwani, S., 2000. Asset prices and central bank policy. *Geneva reports on the world economy*. International Center for Monetary and Banking Studies and Centre for Economic Policy Research, 2.

Hellwig, M., 2008. *Systemic risk in the financial sector: an analysis of the subprime-mortgage financial crisis*. Max Planck Institute for Research on Collective Goods. November.

Herring, R.J., 2010. *Wind-down plans as an alternative to bailouts: the cross-border challenge* [online]. University of Pennsylvania: Wharton Financial Institutions Center, The Wharton School. Available at http://fic.wharton.upenn.edu/fic/papers/10/10-08.pdf.

International Monetary Fund, 2009. Responding to the financial crisis and measuring systemic risks. *Global financial stability report*. April.

King, M., 2009. [speech]. Lord Mayor's Banquet. London: Mansion House. 17 June, 2009.

Minsky, H.P., 1977. A theory of systemic fragility. In: E.I. Altman and A.W. Sametz, eds. *Financial crises*. New York: Wiley.

Minsky, H.P., 1982. *Can "it" happen again? Essays on instability and finance*. Armonk, NY: M.E. Sharpe, Inc.

Minsky, H.P., 1986. *Stabilizing an unstable economy*. New Haven: Yale University Press.

Record, N., 2010. How to make the bankers share the losses. *Financial Times*, 6 January.

Rogoff, K., 1985. The optimal degree of commitment to an intermediate monetary target. *The Quarterly Journal of Economics*. MIT Press, 100(4), pp. 1169–89.

Segoviano, M., 2006. *Consistent information multivariate density optimizing methodology*. Financial markets group discussion paper no. 557. London: London School of Economics.

Segoviano, M., 2010. *The CIMDO-copula. robust estimation of default dependence under data restrictions*. IMF working paper. Washington: International Monetary Fund.

Segoviano, M. and Goodhart, C., 2009. *Banking stability measures*. IMF working paper 09/04, Washington: International Monetary Fund.

Vardoulakis, A.P., Goodhart, C.A.E. and Tsomocos, D.P., 2010. *Minsky's financial instability hypothesis revisited*. Financial markets group working paper. London: London School of Economics. Available at http://papers.ssrn.com/sol3/papers.cfm?abstract_id=1773946.

Walker, D., 2009. *A review of corporate governance in UK banks and other financial industry entities – Final recommendations* [online]. Available at: http://www.hm-treasury.gov.uk/d/walker_review_261109.pdf.

3

A Tale of Three Cities: Model Selection in Over-, Exact, and Under-specified Equations

Jennifer L. Castle and David F. Hendry[*]

Preface by David F. Hendry

It is a great pleasure to contribute a chapter on econometric modelling to a Festschrift in honour of Professor Lord Meghnad Desai. Meg was one of my mentors at LSE in 1966 when I first became an MSc student, and was closer in spirit to the students than the faculty, although he was already a lecturer. We interacted most in the Quantitative Economics Seminar run by Denis Sargan and Bill Phillips whose sometimes arcane debates Meg helped translate into operational terms. We both lived in Islington or nearby for most of the 1970s, then a lively area of North London yet relatively close to the School. We also became close companions in the LSE faculty cricket team, and discussed econometrics on the train journeys to and from the ground at Berrylands, as well as statistics, philosophy of science and economic history with other team members. This was consistent with Meg's eclectic interests, spanning all aspects of econometric modelling, empirical analyses, macro-economics and money, Marxian economics and the history of economic thought, later including globalization and global governance, all well-reflected in the contents of this volume. In an era when specialization has been a dominant force, his many and diverse contributions are a welcome beacon of genuine multi-disciplinarity, and a leading indicator of a recent recognition of the benefits of drawing on a range of skills and knowledge.

When I wrote *Autoreg*, the computer system for econometric modelling which included the precursor to *PcGive*, he was an avid and enthusiastic user, fostering its development, albeit describing it as an engine for destroying economic hypotheses. For example, Desai and Weber (1988) explicitly adopts both a general-to-specific (*Gets*) strategy and rigorous testing of the selected models for mis-specification and predictive failure. Although we worked on

*This research was supported in part by grants from the Open Society Institute and the Oxford Martin School.

similar applied topics, we somehow never managed to be co-authors, perhaps reflecting our substitutability in empirical modelling rather than Meg's complementarity to almost all his colleagues. The methodology of empirical econometric modelling was inchoate in the early days, mainly fitting economic theory-derived specifications to time-series data and puzzling over the many test rejections such models tended to accrue. But group discussions, visitors and many seminars and workshops helped clarify the key issues, leading to the advances recorded in Mizon (1995) and Hendry (2003). In these, John Denis Sargan played a pivotal role, and Meg's editing of Sargan (1998) has ensured some of his main contributions have been recorded (also see Maasoumi, 1988, for reprints of many of Sargan's papers). Our contribution here is to describe developments since the late 1990s: Campos, Ericsson and Hendry (2005) provide a comprehensive review prior to then, together with reprints of many of the most important papers on model selection and econometric modelling.

Introduction

Model selection from a general unrestricted model (GUM) can potentially confront three very different environments, where the GUM may be an over-, exact, or under-specification of the data generation process (DGP). In the first, and most studied setting, the DGP is nested in the GUM, and the main role of selection is to eliminate the irrelevant variables while retaining the relevant. In an exact specification, the theory formulation is precisely correct, but is embedded in a broader model to check for possible omitted variables, non-linearities, breaks or data contamination. The most realistic case is where some aspects of the relevant DGP are correctly included, some irrelevant variables are also included in the GUM, but some relevant variables are omitted, leading to both over- and under-specification. We review the analysis of model selection procedures which allow for many relevant effects as well as irrelevant variables being included in the GUM, and exploit the ability of such procedures to handle perfect collinearity and more candidate variables, N, than observations, T. Reviewing all of the possibilities, where it is not known in advance which one obtains, reveals that model selection can excel relative to just fitting a prior specification, yet has very low costs when an exact specification was indeed correctly postulated initially.

In economics, it is essentially impossible to specify any model that nests the DGP: the high dimensionality, non-stationarity, and unknown non-linearity of economies entail large, complicated and evolving DGPs. Rather, empirical investigations consider small subsets of variables, $\{x_i\}$ say, suggested by theoretical analyses, which represent reductions of the DGP. For every choice of x_t, there exists a local DGP, denoted LDGP, which is the joint density over the available sample, $D_x(x_1 \ldots x_T \mid \theta_T^1)$, where $\theta_T^1 (= \theta_1, \ldots, \theta_T)$ is its parametrization: see e.g., Hendry (2009) for a recent discussion. Such LDGPs can be close to, or far from, the process that actually generated $\{x_t\}$ depending on the reductions needed to map from the DGP to the resulting LDGP. Good theoretical analyses hopefully guide empirical studies towards LDGPs that are useful for their intended purposes, be those modelling data to understand its properties, testing theories, forecasting, or policy advice. Thus, the choice of which set of variables to analyze is fundamental to the success of a study. Unfortunately, there cannot be generic advice on how to achieve a good initial formulation, as that depends on the unknown DGP, and hence on the unknown reductions implicit in postulating the LDGP through the choice of $\{x_t\}$.

Even given a good choice of the set $\{x_t\}$, there remains the key issue of modelling $D_x(x_1 \ldots x_T \mid \theta_T^1)$, since however excellent an economic theory may be, many aspects must be data based. First, a functional form may be suggested by theory, but usually only over a wide class (e.g., monotonically non-decreasing; or embodying relative risk aversion; or not linear, etc.). Secondly, the time period of decisions can rarely be specified theoretically: a one-period lag may be a minute, day, week, month or year, and so on, and whatever it is, need not match the available frequency of observations (e.g., quarterly). Thirdly, the theory usually requires–often unstated–*ceteris paribus* conditions on effects not included in the analysis: but the wide-sense non-stationary nature of economic data make such conditions vacuous in practice. This is especially true of the neglect of special events that cause shifts in DGPs, which theories perforce ignore. Further, macro-economic theories rarely address the heterogeneity of behaviour across agents, although varying endowment distributions can make aggregate parametrizations non-constant. Next, assumptions about the exogeneity of some of the 'givens' also cannot be based on prior reasoning alone. Finally, though this list is illustrative rather than exhaustive, the data may be inaccurately measured or even contaminated over sub-periods. Thus, even if a brilliant theory delivered a 'correct' specification of the LDGP–thereby conflating the DGP and LDGP for $\{x_t\}$ – that is only the start: a major modelling exercise inevitably remains in jointly addressing the main issues in empirical model specification of the complete set of determining variables, their dynamics, functional forms, and parameter constancies.

To highlight recent progress, we will consider three cases. First, an *exact specification* defined by a theory-based joint density $D_x(x_1 \ldots x_T \mid \theta_T^1)$ that is indeed the DGP, where the specified model correctly represents that joint density. We outline an approach such that the theory variables are always retained, despite commencing from a much larger GUM within which it is nested, yet the theory specification is not imposed. This is designed to check the validity and completeness of the theory. Secondly, we will consider a setting where an investigator correctly includes all the relevant variables in $\{x_t\}$, and also many irrelevant variables, not knowing which elements are relevant and which irrelevant. Thus, the GUM is over-specified, but still nests the DGP. Since which variables are relevant empirically is unknown, the theory variables cannot be forced to be retained in this setting, differentiating it importantly from the first. Finally, we consider the case where only some of the determinants of the DGP are included in the LDGP. Thus, other substantive effects are inadvertently omitted, leading to an under-specified model which does not nest the DGP, but also contains variables that would be irrelevant were the DGP correctly nested in the GUM. This seems the most likely scenario empirically, especially as many outliers, breaks and data mistakes will not be known in advance.

Our objective is to examine the role of automatic model selection in each setting, and contrast its performance with that of simply estimating a pre-specified theory model. We will show that:

(a) when the theory model is the DGP and is forced to be retained within a much larger initial model, which could even have more candidate variables that observations, *selection has no effect on the estimated parameter distributions*, so these are the same as directly estimating the correct and complete theory model;

(b) when the GUM is an under-specification of the DGP, selection can deliver estimates with smaller mean-square errors (MSEs) around their DGP values compared to just estimating a theory-model that is an under-specification of the DGP;

(c) when the GUM nests the DGP, but it is not known which variables are relevant and which irrelevant, the costs of selection are small.

Thus, in all three settings, spanning the range of possibilities in empirical research, selection either dominates, or is equivalent to, estimation of a theory-based specification.

Such a finding runs counter to widespread folklore about model selection, which is usually deemed at best to be a necessary evil and at worst, a pernicious practice that distorts parameter estimates. Criticisms include pre-test bias (see e.g., Judge and Bock, 1978), over-fitting by data mining (see e.g., Lovell, 1983), repeated testing that undermines the validity of inferences (see e.g., Leamer, 1974, 1983), with results that are dependent on the path searched (see e.g., Pagan, 1987), and constitute 'measurement without theory' (see e.g., Koopmans, 1947), so have a high probability of delivering garbage. Hendry (2000) discusses the origins of these beliefs, and shows that they lack substance as generic claims. Nevertheless, some model selection algorithms do have such properties: indeed, the most common empirical approach of fitting many models (often covertly) and picking the 'best' one has all these problems in spadefulls, compounded by it being impossible to assess the true uncertainty about the reported choice. Recent developments of automatic model selection algorithms based on the 'LSE methodology' of general-to-specific (*Gets*) modelling, after testing for a congruent initial GUM, ensure that all are avoided: bias correction after selection can be based on the known properties of the selection procedure (see e.g., Hendry and Krolzig, 2005); the selection provides a near unbiased estimate of fit measured by the equation standard error, so there is no over-fitting (see Hendry and Krolzig, 2005); repeated testing difficulties are avoided by only selecting variables, and not models as in some approaches, setting the significance level to control retention of chance significant irrelevant variables at the desired rate (see e.g., Castle, Doornik and Hendry, 2011a); path dependence is avoided by exploring all feasible simplifications (see e.g., Hoover and Perez, 1999, and Doornik, 2009); theory models are embedded in the selection to be retained if they are valid (see e.g., Hendry and Johansen 2010); so selection will not deliver garbage, and yet will retain the relevant variables with almost the same probabilities as if the DGP had been the initial specification (see e.g., Hendry and Krolzig, 2005 and Castle *et al.*, 2011a).

The reason we refer to the above eminent authorities' claims as folklore is not just that massive improvements in the theory and practice of automatic model selection have rendered their analyses otiose (but unfortunately not forgotten), they all implicitly presume that the initial theory model is correct, complete and immutable, which is totally unrealistic. Once it is admitted that theory models are at best incomplete, rough and evolving guides to some of the dependencies in economies, and many features of reality are not covered by any theories, it becomes obvious that selection is inevitable. Consequently, it is essential to analyze the many extant approaches, from imposing theory models on data, through covertly running 'hundreds of regressions' and only reporting a few that the investigator 'liked', to using other selection devices (such as AIC from Akaike, 1973, or SIC from Schwarz, 1978, or the LASSO from Tibshirani, 1996). Without a structured and controlled approach based on congruent and encompassing models, inferences are hazardous. Indeed approaches that do not commence from a formulation that nests the DGP (or even the LDGP) are bound to end with an incorrect specification; those that use expanding (rather than contracting) searches can miss key combinations of variables; those that do not search comprehensively for breaks will often conclude with non-constant relationships; those that do not specify congruent encompassing models cannot rely on their inferences; and those without a theory analysis cannot interpret their findings. Thus, all the ingredients of our approach seem essential.

Our review focuses on the linear regression context, although most of the results can be generalized to non-linear equations (see Castle and Hendry, 2011), or to systems (sketched in Hendry and Krolzig, 2005). We explicitly confront the problems posed by omitted variables interacting with structural breaks, specifically location shifts where previous unconditional means change at some points in the sample, as in Castle, Doornik and Hendry (2011b). The resulting procedures invariably lead to more candidate variables, N, than observations, T, so that issue is also addressed, based on Hendry, Johansen and Santos (2008) and Johansen and Nielsen (2009) as implemented in *Autometrics* (see Doornik, 2009, and Hendry and Doornik, 2009). Such an approach seeks to locate the DGP for the chosen set of variables, building on Hoover and Perez (1999) and Hendry and Krolzig (2005): its properties are documented in Castle *et al.* (2011a) and Castle and Hendry (2011) *inter alia*.

The various cases are illustrated using an extension of the original *PcGive* artificial data set of 159 observations (mimicking quarterly data, 1953(3)–1992(3): see e.g., Doornik and Hendry, 1994), designed in 1984 to simulate the impact of the 1970 Oil Crisis on a 'DHSY' consumption function (as in Davidson, Hendry, Srba and Yeo, 1978: for a recent update, see Hendry, 2010). The four variables involved are consumers' expenditure c, income i, inflation Δp and aggregate output q, where the Oil Crisis induced a sharp unanticipated rise in inflation and a concomitant fall in output following a location shift in 1973(3). The consumption function in fact related c_t, to i_t, Δp_t, c_{t-1}, and i_{t-1}. The database has since been extended by Jurgen Doornik adding 20 irrelevant variables, denoted $z_{0,t}, \ldots, z_{19,t}$, the lags of which are also irrelevant, enabling all three settings to be illustrated. Figure 3.1 shows time-series plots of the DGP variables in the four panels labelled a, b, c, d.

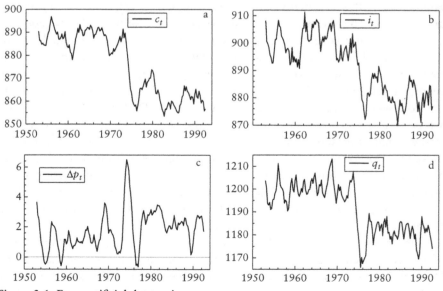

Figure 3.1 Four artificial data series

The structure of the chapter is as follows. We first consider the case where the model is an over-specification of the DGP, allowing for some substantively relevant variables, as well as many irrelevant effects. Next, we draw on Hendry and Johansen (2010) who show that when the theory model is precisely correct and is 'forced', selection leaves the distribution of the estimated parameters of interest unchanged relative to simply fitting the DGP. Then we use results in Castle and Hendry (2010b) to highlight the manifest advantages of selection from a GUM relative to fitting an incorrect equation, even though the former omits the same subset of relevant variables. Finally, we conclude.

Over-specification

We consider two canonical cases. First, we discuss the null model where all the variables under consideration are irrelevant. This serves to establish that even in such an extreme case, which nevertheless satisfies the assumption that the GUM nests the DGP, when setting significance levels appropriate to the problem under analysis there is only a small chance of retaining several irrelevant variables whose coefficient estimates are adventitiously significant. Many of the issues about model selection questioned in the literature, as noted above, can be resolved in this setting. For example, it is obvious that selecting a model by goodness of fit will not recover the DGP, and that tighter significance levels raise the probability of locating the correct specification of the null model.

In the second case, there are some relevant and many irrelevant variables, which extends the previous section by including some non-zero parameters in the DGP. Now the key difficulty, so to speak, is sorting the wheat from the chaff. All estimated coefficients have sampling distributions, so some relevant variables (those with non-zero parameters) may be insignificant by chance, and some irrelevant significant by chance. Now there is a trade off between ensuring retention of relevant variables and elimination of irrelevant as the significance level changes. To clarify concepts, we define the *gauge* as the average retention frequency of irrelevant variables, and the *potency* as the average retention frequency of relevant variables. While close to size and power respectively, the concepts differ importantly as we also require models to be congruent so variables can be retained when they are insignificant to offset what might otherwise be a failure on a mis-specification test. False retention of insignificant irrelevant variables can occur under the null of no mis-specification: see Castle *et al.* (2011a).

The aim of selection is to choose a final specification that is as close to the DGP commencing from the GUM as would be found commencing from the DGP itself, using the same decision rules. When that can be achieved, the costs of search (selection) are clearly small. However, the DGP itself may be retained rarely even when commencing from it if some relevant variables' estimated parameters would have small t-statistics in the available sample. The costs of inference–not keeping relevant effects–apply even when the DGP specification is correctly postulated, but, absent omniscience, the model is not known to be the DGP, so inference must be conducted to determine what variables are significant. Part of the confusion in earlier analyses of model selection was failing to draw this crucial distinction between the costs of inference—which are inevitable and unavoidable in any non-exact science—and the costs of search, which are additional due to commencing from a GUM which nests, but is larger than, the DGP. Thus, a failure by a search algorithm to locate the DGP may simply reflect that the DGP would not be retained even if it were the initial model.

The null model

The first canonical case is one in which all N variables are irrelevant, so potential 'over-fitting' is the main problem. Consider a constant-parameter linear regression with $N<<T$ mutually orthogonal but irrelevant regressors for $t = 1,...,T$:

$$y_t = \sum_{i=1}^{N} \beta_i z_{i,t} + \varepsilon_t \quad \text{where} \quad \varepsilon_t \sim \text{IN}\left[0, \sigma_\varepsilon^2\right] \tag{1}$$

where $T^{-1}\sum_{t=1}^{T} z_{i,t} z_{j,t} = \lambda_i \delta_{i,j} \; \forall i, j$, where $\delta_{i,j} = 1$ if $i = j$ and is zero otherwise, with $\{\varepsilon_t\}$ independent of all $\{z_{i,t}\}$, when $T >> N$. In the GUM given by (1), all aspects of its specification are correct and known to be correct, except it is not known that all regressors have $\beta_i = 0$. Full-sample least-squares estimation of the GUM is feasible here as $N < T$, and yields $(\hat{\beta}_1 ... \hat{\beta}_N)$, all of which are unbiased estimators (of zero), and from orthogonality and normality:

$$\hat{\beta}_i \sim \text{N}\left[0, \sigma_\varepsilon^2 \left(\sum_{t=1}^{T} z_{i,t}^2\right)^{-1}\right] \tag{2}$$

Also, the squared residual standard deviation $\hat{\sigma}_\varepsilon^2$ provides an unbiased estimate of the squared equation standard error σ_ε^2, a useful baseline to monitor for possible over-fitting. Then:

$$t_{\hat{\beta}_i} = \frac{\hat{\beta}_i}{\hat{\sigma}_{\hat{\beta}_i}} \quad \text{where} \quad \hat{\sigma}_{\hat{\beta}_i} = \hat{\sigma}_\varepsilon \left(\sum_{t=1}^{T} z_{i,t}^2\right)^{-1/2}.$$

When t-testing for the significance of each regressor at significance level α, corresponding to a critical value c_α, a decision to retain the ith regressor is made if $|t_{\hat{\beta}_i}| > c_\alpha$. The complete set of well-known probabilities of rejections and non-rejections under the null for (1) are shown in equation (3).

event	probability	number retained
$P\left(\left|t_i\right| < c_\alpha, \forall i = 1,\dots N\right)$	$(1-\alpha)^N$	0
$P\left(\left|t_i\right| \geq c_\alpha \left\|t_j\right\| < c_\alpha, \forall j \neq i\right)$	$N\alpha(1-\alpha)^{N-1}$	1
$\vdots$	$\vdots$	$\vdots$
$P\left(\left|t_i\right| < c_\alpha \left\|t_j\right\| \geq c_\alpha, \forall i \neq j\right)$	$N\alpha^{(N-1)}(1-\alpha)$	$N-1$
$P\left(\left|t_i\right| \geq c_\alpha, \forall i = 1,\dots N\right)$	α^N	N

$$(3)$$

Then, the average number of null variables retained from equation (3) is given by the binomial sum:

$$m = \sum_{i=0}^{N} i \frac{N!}{i!(N-i)!} \alpha^i (1-\alpha)^{N-i} = N\alpha. \tag{4}$$

The key determinants, when the tests are indeed independent and distributed as t, are N and α, so in principle any value of m is possible. However, sensible decision rules must link these two decision variables, and one simple rule is $\alpha = k/N$ for a small integer $k = 1, 2, 3$ say. Thus, when $N = 100$, which is 'large' relative to most time-series models, then for $k = 1$, one would set $\alpha = 0.01$ which yields $m = 1$. Consequently, 99 out of the 100 irrelevant regressors would be eliminated on average, and just one retained. A great deal is learned about what does not matter, effecting a massive reduction from an initial 100 candidate regressors to one or a few 'spuriously significant' variables that are adventitiously retained, although the conventional measure of the 'size' of the procedure is:

$$1 - (1-\alpha)^N = 1 - (1-0.01)^{100} \simeq 0.63,$$

suggesting such a procedure is not useful. The conventional significance level of 5 per cent is fine for a single, or 1-off, test, but is not helpful once multiple tests are required. The cost of shifting to a tighter significance level like 1 per cent is that c_α increases, making it harder to retain relevant variables when they are present in a large set of irrelevance.

Illustrating regressions with no relevant variables

Using the extended *PcGive* artificial data set, we formulated a GUM for one of the irrelevant variables, $z_{0,t}$, dependent on its first 2 lags, a constant and on current and 2 lags of $z_{1,t},\dots,z_{19,t}$, which made 60 variables for the remaining 157 observations. Selecting by Autometrics at $\alpha = 0.01$, so $m = 0.6$, duly delivered the null model, which matched the null DGP. Thus, over-fitting did not occur despite $N = 60$ irrelevant regressors in the GUM.

However, before considering cases with relevant variables there are seven important considerations: congruence, normality, bias corrections, different significance levels for different groups of decisions, 'forcing' retention of variables, goodness of fit, and selecting variables, not models. We take these in turn.

Congruence

First, inferences based on conventional statistics and critical values are valid only if the GUM is congruent, which here requires a constant-parameter linear regression with no omitted relevant variables, accurate data, and errors ε_t that are distributed as $\text{IN}[0, \sigma_\varepsilon^2]$ independently of the regressors. Any violations of congruence can induce false selections, which cannot necessarily be rectified by heteroskedastic-autocorrelation consistent estimators of parameter standard errors (HACSEs, as in e.g., White 1980, and Andrews, 1991), both because these do not reflect the selection decisions made *en route* to the chosen specification, and because they rely on the untested *non sequitur* that the problem manifest in the residuals is due to the assumed solution for the errors. For example, residual autocorrelation could be due to an unmodelled break, and HACSEs will not 'correct' that. Thus, for an estimable GUM, the first step is to test for congruence, which if it is accepted, then there exists a simplification path to a congruent final model (which may be the GUM if there are no valid reductions). In *Autometrics*, five such tests are standard, namely autocorrelation, heteroskedasticity, non-normality, non-linearity, non-constancy, close to the set used in *Autoreg* (see Hendry and Srba 1980, and e.g., Desai and Weber, 1988): these are delineated below. To control the overall null rejection frequency, determined by any one mis-specification test rejecting, we set $\delta = 0.01$ for each test, yielding $1 - (1 - 0.01)^5$ from Equation 3, or about 5 per cent overall.

Normality

Secondly, although normality is an aspect of congruence, it also plays a separate role. When the distributions of tests are close to the normal, with what Denis Sargan called 'thin tails' in Sargan (2001), critical values increase slowly with decreases in α in the tails. Equation 5 records these changes, rounded.

$$
\begin{array}{cccccc}
\alpha & 0.05 & 0.01 & 0.005 & 0.0025 & 0.001 \\
c_\alpha & 2.0 & 2.6 & 2.8 & 3.0 & 3.3
\end{array}
\tag{5}
$$

For example, even at 0.25 per cent, $c_{0.0025} = 3.0$, just requiring a t-value of 3.0, rather than the famous 2.0, to reject the null. Yet, if 0.25 per cent is applied to (4), $m = 100 \times 0.0025 = 0.25$ so only one irrelevant variable out of 100 would be retained once every four trials, with none retained on average on the remaining three trials. While ts of 2 are conventional, moving to values around 3 (at $\alpha = 0.0025$) would entail almost never retaining irrelevant variables even after starting with $N = 100$ candidates. Of course, such an analysis places a premium on having approximate normality. Indeed, the next consideration also requires approximate normality, making it doubly important.

Bias corrections

Thirdly, bias corrections were developed in Hendry and Krolzig (2005) and analyzed by Castle *et al.* (2011a). As only 'significant' estimates are retained, this corresponds to a decision rule where:

$$\tilde{\beta}_i = \hat{\beta}_i \quad \left| t_{\hat{\beta}_i} \right| > c_\alpha$$
$$\tilde{\beta}_i = 0 \quad \left| t_{\hat{\beta}_i} \right| \le c_\alpha \tag{6}$$

when the final retained estimates are denoted $\tilde{\beta}_i$. The distribution of $\tilde{\beta}_i$ for only those regressors that are retained by $|t_{\hat{\beta}_i}| > c_\alpha$ is called the conditional distribution; the complete, or unconditional, distribution also includes all the zero values assigned by (6). Selection by $|t_{\hat{\beta}_i}| > c_\alpha$ induces a doubly-truncated t distribution where the central part, namely values between $\pm c_\alpha$, is discarded, and only the tails are retained. It is convenient to approximate this by a doubly-truncated normal distribution where all the formulae are well known (see e.g., Johnson, Kotz and Balakrishnan, 1994).

When $\beta_i = 0$, the resulting estimates are unbiased, as $E[\hat{\beta}_i] = 0$, but for $\beta_i \ne 0$, the retained $\tilde{\beta}_i$ need to be corrected for selection, since from (6) only significant estimates are retained, so:

$$E\left[\tilde{\beta}_i \, \middle| \, \left| t_{\hat{\beta}_i} \right| > c_\alpha\right] \ne \beta_i. \tag{7}$$

However, the truncation point c_α is known, so one can correct $\tilde{\beta}_i$ after selection, denoted $\tilde{\tilde{\beta}}_i$, such that:

$$E\left[\tilde{\tilde{\beta}}_i \, \middle| \, \left| t_{\hat{\beta}_i} \right| > c_\alpha\right] \simeq \beta_i. \tag{8}$$

Bias correction as in (8) leads to some increase in the mean-square errors (MSEs) of the estimated coefficients of relevant variables, namely where $\beta_i \ne 0$, and exacerbates the downward bias in the unconditional estimates due to setting some $\tilde{\beta}_i = 0$. There is no impact on the bias of estimated parameters of irrelevant variables, as their $\beta_i = 0$, but there is a marked *decrease* in their MSEs—essentially a 'free lunch'—since most bias correction occurs for $|t_{\hat{\beta}_i}|$ near c_α, and that is the most likely outcome under the null, driving the resulting $\tilde{\tilde{\beta}}_i$ near to zero. This result applies at loose α, so even if many irrelevant variables were retained, their estimated parameters would be small on average after bias correction, suggesting a possible approach when selecting forecasting models, providing estimates of the equation standard error were also bias corrected.

Significance levels differing by decisions

The fourth consideration is to use different significance levels for different groups of decisions, which will lead into the fifth, namely 'forcing' the retention of some variables. If a subset of variables is deemed substantively important, then it could be selected at a loose significance level, say 25 per cent, whereas other variables that are thought to be less important, but still may be relevant, are selected at a much tighter level such as 0.5 per cent, so need strong evidence for their retention. In particular, selection and mis-specification testing are often conducted at different significance levels, as are linear and non-linear reactions.

'Forcing' retention of variables

The fifth consideration is 'forcing', which relates to always retaining some variables, while others are subject to selection. In effect, the first set uses a 100 per cent significance level: that is what retaining the GUM entails, of course. 'Forcing' allows a theory model to be embedded in a GUM where only the additional variables are selected. While this guarantees that the theory-based variables are retained, they may not be significant nor have their anticipated signs, and other variables may transpire to be the important determinants of the dependent variable. It is often advisable to force retention of the intercept, as it can be insignificant early in a simplification yet highly significant in the final model. We return to the distributional properties of parameter estimates for forced variables below.

Goodness of fit

The crucial aspect about goodness of fit is that it was *not* considered by the decision rule. For a known model where all regressors are relevant, choosing parameters by goodness of fit (or maximum likelihood) has important justifications. For selecting which variables to include, goodness of fit has no justification, and is most unlikely to choose a model that is a close approximation to the DGP. Implicitly, the selection of α affects the resulting goodness of fit, as measured by $\tilde{\sigma}_\varepsilon$ in the chosen representation, but that information is not directly used to select. Nevertheless, while such a result only holds in the present null model setting, the probability of selecting the DGP *rises* here as the significance level becomes tighter–the worst fitting model, namely one with no variables, matches the DGP.

Selecting variables not models

The final issue is that the calculations in equation 3 are based on selecting variables commencing from a congruent GUM, not selecting models. There are N variables, but 2^N models, one of which must certainly maximize goodness of fit, or 'penalized' versions thereof (like AIC). There are so many sub-models within the set of 2^N that many will be non-congruent, and most will not be useful approximations to the DGP. For the above example of $N = 100$, $2^{100} \simeq 10^{30}$, some of which will surely be 'garbage'. Indeed, it is difficult to imagine usable values of α such that the retention of spurious models from 2^N could be controlled unless N was very small. To understand the difference between selecting models and selecting variables, consider a procedure that not only tested the relevance of each regressor in (1), but also tested all possible pairs, all triples, etc., right up to all combinations of $N - 1$. That would augment equation 3 with a vast array of probabilities of rejecting on F-tests for every possible combination. There are bound to be many combinations 'significant' by chance.

We conclude from the above analysis that eliminating irrelevant variables is not a fundamental difficulty for variable selection–even when there is a large number of potential candidate regressors. Despite its many special characteristics, and the fact that the complete null model is not an empirically relevant case in economics, it is important to know that when significance levels are set sensibly, over-fitting holds few terrors. We now need to explore the impact of selecting when there are relevant variables in (1), then extend the analysis to selecting in realistic economic settings with collinearity, breaks, non-normality, dynamics, omitted variables, non-linearity and probably measurement errors, perhaps leading to $N > T$.

Regressions with relevant variables

We next consider (1) when some of the $\beta_i \neq 0$, where some $\beta_i = 0$ as before, but it is not known for certain which regressors are relevant. In an orthogonal case like (1), Castle et al. (2011a) show that the selection decision can be made in '1-cut': rank every $|t_{\hat{\beta}_i}|$ and retain (discard) those which exceed (are smaller than) c_α. Thus, there is no repeated testing even when $N = 1000$ (say, which is the case they consider). The probability of retaining relevant variables depends on the non-centrality, ψ_i, of their $|t_{\beta_i}|$, where $\psi_i = 0$ when $\beta_i = 0$. Naturally, this probability falls as c_α increases, and in any case is quite low even for conventional significance levels, as (say) $p[t_{\beta_i} > 2 \,|\, \psi_i = 2] \simeq 0.5$, but rises exponentially as ψ_i increases, so that $p[t_{\beta_i} > 3 \,|\, \psi_i = 6] > 0.99$.

Castle et al. (2011a) also show that *Autometrics* applied to the same setting as '1-cut' tends to outperform it in MSEs, and they also present supporting Monte Carlo simulation evidence on the performance of *Autometrics* for a range of autoregressive-distributed lag models.

Perfect collinearity

Consider as a simple example the DGP:

$$y_t = \beta_1 x_{1,t} + \beta_2 x_{2,t} + \varepsilon_t \tag{9}$$

where in fact $\beta_1 = -\beta_2$, but that is not known. When the GUM is specified as

$$y_t = \gamma_1 x_{1,t} + \gamma_2 x_{2,t} + \gamma_3 (x_{1,t} - x_{2,t}) + v_t \tag{10}$$

using a comprehensive multi-path search, then one path will delete $(x_{1,t} - x_{2,t})$ and (for sufficiently large test non-centralities) retain $x_{1,t}$ and $x_{2,t}$; a second path will eliminate $x_{2,t}$ and should retain $(x_{1,t} - x_{2,t})$ but also drop $x_{1,t}$ as now insignificant; and similarly for the third path commencing from first dropping $x_{1,t}$. Thus, an advantage of such procedures in dynamic specification searches is that they allow many forms of possible lag response to be included, such as $x_{1,t}$, $x_{1,t-1}$, $\Delta x_{1,t}(= x_{1,t} - x_{1,t-1})$, $(x_{1,t} + x_{1,t-1})$ and so on, where the relevant subset is retained. Campos and Ericsson (1999) discuss the importance of the choice of the initial linear transformations of the regressors in the GUM for the final selection when testing is only for null hypotheses like $\gamma_i = 0$.

The potential cost of doubling the number of variables by perfect collinearity is that the procedure will now retain approximately $2\alpha n$ irrelevant regressors. On the one hand, it could be argued that should not occur because there are still only n separate regressors, hence null retentions will be unchanged. On the other hand, many linear combinations of variables are being included and in a t-test based approach, such combinations could be significant (still under the null) even when the components would not be. For example, $x_{1,t}$ and $x_{1,t-1}$ might have t-test values less than c_α, yet $(x_{1,t} + x_{1,t-1})$ have a significant coefficient and so be retained by chance.

Given the difficult analytic nature of trying to establish which of the two arguments holds, we have undertaken a number of Monte Carlo simulation studies. The simplest is close to the model in (10). The DGP is:

$$y_t = \varepsilon_t \quad \text{where} \quad \varepsilon_t \sim \text{IN}[0, \sigma_\varepsilon^2] \tag{11}$$

for $t = 1, \ldots, T = 100$ where:

$$x_t \sim \text{IN}_2[0, \mathbf{I}] \tag{12}$$

We first consider a case with no collinearity. The GUM has the form in (13) as a baseline to check that the gauge $g \simeq \alpha$ with 5 irrelevant regressors:

$$y_t = \beta_0 + \beta_1 x_{1,t} + \beta_2 x_{2,t} + \beta_3 x_{1,t-1} + \beta_4 x_{2,t-1} + \varepsilon_t \tag{13}$$

Setting $\alpha = 0.01$, with diagnostic tests for congruence also at 1 per cent, $M = 10000$ replications delivered $g = 0.014$ which is a little 'over-gauged' as anticipated from conducting diagnostic tests. Thus, on average $5g = 5 \times 0.014 = 0.07$ irrelevant variables were retained per replication. Without diagnostic checking, $g = 0.0098$ so the algorithm is calibrated to deliver the correct significance level under the null when there are no diagnostic checks.

If we now include perfectly collinear variables, repeating these simulations, but with the GUM specified as:

$$y_t = \gamma_0 + \gamma_1 x_{1,t} + \gamma_2 x_{2,t} + \gamma_3 \left(x_{1,t} - x_{2,t}\right) + \gamma_4 x_{1,t-1} + \gamma_5 x_{2,t-1}$$
$$+ \gamma_6 \left(x_{1,t-1} - x_{2,t-1}\right) + \gamma_7 \Delta x_{1,t} + \gamma_8 \Delta x_{2,t} + v_t \tag{14}$$

where (14) has 9 irrelevant regressors with four collinearities, again at $\alpha = 0.01$, now $M = 10000$ replications delivered $g = 0.0057$ so that

$9g = 9 \times 0.0057 = 0.05$ irrelevant variables were retained per replication. This is actually slightly smaller than anticipated, but is consistent with the argument that adding perfectly collinear variables does not increase the retention rate.

Finally we examine the case where $N >> T$ and there is perfect collinearity. We augment (14) with $\sum_{j=1}^{100} \delta_j u_{j,t}$ where:

$$\mathbf{u}_t \sim \text{IN}_{100}[\mathbf{0}, \mathbf{I}] \tag{15}$$

resulting in 109 regressors for 100 observations. Selection at $\alpha = 0.01$ with $M = 10000$ replications delivered $g = 0.0105$, so $109g = 1.14$ irrelevant variables were retained per replication despite including over 100 irrelevant variables. Undertaking selection at $\alpha = 0.005$ yields 0.44 variables retained per replication, demonstrating that inclusion of many irrelevant variables does not lead to over-fitting.

However, since much of the analysis depends on having approximate normality, we now turn to how that might be obtained, and also address the issues of multiple structural breaks, outliers, and data contamination, leading to a special case where $N > T$.

Impulse-indicator saturation

One of the simplest cases where more candidate variables than observations occurs is adding an impulse indicator for every observation to the set of possible explanatory variables, a procedure called impulse-indicator saturation and denoted IIS below (see Hendry et al., 2008, and Johansen and Nielsen, 2009). When $N > 0$, using IIS creates $N + T > T$. At first sight, such a setting seems quite problematic, but it is not. As shown by Salkever (1976), the Chow (1960) test includes an indicator variable for every observation in the forecast period, and tests for them being significantly different from zero. Recursive estimation can be interpreted as having an impulse indicator for every observation in the later period, sequentially removing them one by one. Rolling windows put in blocks, first in the future and then in both the future and the past when moving through the sample. Consequently, many existing methods can be interpreted as using indicators for every observation, but in different ways. Indeed, reversing recursive estimation involves implicitly entering more indicators than data points.

In the simplest IIS theory in Hendry et al. (2008) and Johansen and Nielsen (2009), indicators are added in two blocks of $T/2$, significant outcomes in each block being recorded then that block omitted while the other is included, again recording significant outcomes, then the two sets of significant indicators are added together in the final specification. Unequal and multiple splits are also analyzed, and Autometrics uses a general block algorithm, and searches across many such splits: no matter how many splits are tried, an outlier will only be found to match an indicator if it is there.

Under the null that there are no outliers, IIS will retain αT indicators by chance: thus, for example, when $T = 100$ and $\alpha = 0.01$, one indicator will be significant by chance, in effect reducing the available sample from 100 to 99 as an observation is 'dummied out'. Viewed as a robust estimator, therefore, IIS is 99 per cent efficient. Of course, there is little point in using IIS when the null is true. Rather, the aim of IIS is to check at every observation whether there has been an outlier, same-signed contiguous blocks of outliers which would reveal a location shift or data contamination in a subsample. Castle *et al.* (2011b) conduct an extensive Monte Carlo simulation study of IIS under the alternative for many break forms including multiple breaks.

Here, α must be the appropriate significance level for the underlying distribution, the form of which is rarely known. In practice, α is usually chosen for the normal, so the question arises as what happens when IIS is applied to a non-normal distribution. Castle *et al.* (2011b) consider a Student-t distribution with 3 degrees of freedom, denoted t_3, and show that impulse indicators capture much of the non-normality in this fat-tailed distribution. Many indicators are retained, of course. Despite the critical value, c_α, used for selection being incorrect, after IIS the resulting distribution is sufficiently near normal that the null retention frequency of other irrelevant variables is close to, but slightly larger than, α. The retention of relevant variables is improved relative to ignoring the fat-tail problem.

Thus, IIS enables normality to be a reasonable assumption for inference and bias correction. Selection for non-linearity depends on near normality to avoid spurious outcomes. Moreover, the form of analysis showing that IIS can be feasible—despite more indicators plus regressors than observations—applies to cases with $N > T$ due to more candidate regressor variables than observations, as we now discuss.

Illustrating regressions with no relevant variables using IIS

Repeating the exercise above with IIS, which creates $N + T = 217$, and now selecting at $\alpha = 0.0025$, so $m \simeq 0.5$, again delivered the null model. In both illustrations, there was a probability of just under a half of locating the null DGP, and the second demonstrates the practical implementation of $N > T$ using block searches. The crucial issue, however, is whether the original non-null DGP can be located.

Illustrating regressions with relevant variables using IIS

The *PcGive* artificial DGP for the consumption equation is:

$$c_t = 0.85c_{t-1} + 0.5i_t - 0.35i_{t-1} - \Delta p_t \qquad (16)$$

and direct estimation yields:

$$c_t = \underset{(0.022)}{0.84}\, c_{t-1} + \underset{(0.027)}{0.49}\, i_t - \underset{(0.032)}{0.33}\, i_{t-1} - \underset{(0.085)}{0.95}\, \Delta p_t$$

$$\hat{\sigma} = 1.10 \quad F_{ar}(5,148) = 1.09 \quad F_{arch}(4,149) = 0.78$$

$$\chi^2_{nd}(2) = 0.48 \quad F_{het}(8,148) = 1.05 \quad F_{reset}(2,151) = 3.67^* \qquad (17)$$

R^2 is the squared multiple correlation, and $\hat{\sigma}$ is the residual standard deviation, with coefficient standard errors shown in parentheses. The diagnostic tests are of the form $F_j(k, T - l)$ which denotes an approximate F-test against the alternative hypothesis j for: k^{th}-order serial correlation (F_{ar}: see Godfrey, 1978), k^{th}-order autoregressive conditional heteroskedasticity (F_{arch}: see Engle, 1982), heteroskedasticity (F_{het}: see White, 1980); the RESET test (F_{reset}: see Ramsey, 1969); and a chi-square test for normality ($\chi^2_{nd}(2)$: see Doornik and Hansen, 2008).

Including all four DGP variables and the 20 irrelevant $z_{01,t}, \ldots, z_{19,t}$, plus an intercept, with the same lag length of 2 as before and current-dated regressors, then $N = 72$, and $T = 157$ after creating the 2 lags. Applying IIS and setting $\alpha = 0.0025$, then $\alpha(N + T) = 0.5725$ so again the probability of retaining one adventitiously-significant irrelevant variable is just over a half, with a negligible probability of retaining more than one irrelevant variable or indicator. *Autometrics* finds the DGP equation plus one indicator with an estimate of 3.39 (1.08); that the relevant variables were retained follows from their large non-centralities seen in (17). When $\alpha = 0.001$, the DGP equation (17) is found precisely.

More candidate regressor variables than observations

First consider the case where $N = T$, so that a split-half approach–as with IIS–is feasible. The same logic applies, but now αN irrelevant variables will be retained under the null, each of which costs a degree of freedom, rather than a data point, spreading the 'cost' over the whole sample. For $N > T$, multiple blocks are needed to handle all the searches.

However, such block searches require expanding as well as contracting searches, so are no longer strictly general-to-specific. A key aspect is to use large blocks. Early selection algorithms, such as stepwise, added variables one at a time, so their significance could be masked by not jointly including other variables with the opposite net effect on the regressor (e.g., negatively when the current candidate has a positive effect). As shown in Castle *et al.* (2011a), the MSEs of *Autometrics* estimated parameters of relevant variables then increase linearly as N increases from $N \ll T$, through $N = T$ to $N \gg T$, so there is no 'jump' in the neighbourhood of $N = T$.

Illustrating regressions with relevant variables when $N > T$

To take a relatively extreme case, we will use a lag length of 20, so including an intercept and current-dated regressors $N = 504$, with $T = 139$ after creating 20 lags, but no IIS. Setting $\alpha = 0.001$, then $\alpha N = 0.504$ and again the probability of retaining one adventitiously-significant irrelevant variable is just over a half. Indeed, here *Autometrics* finds the exact DGP equation starting from almost any over-specified candidate set, with up to 20 lags, and without or with also undertaking IIS (there are no substantial outliers or breaks in the conditional model although there are in the DGP).

Including IIS makes $N + T = 643$, so a large excess of variables over observations has to be confronted, yet *Autometrics* again delivers the DGP equation (17) at $\alpha = 0.001$. The probability of retaining no irrelevant variables was just 0.36, so the outcome that none were retained was slightly 'lucky'. Importantly, such calculations are feasible prior to selection, and tend to be borne out by both simulations and artificial data modelling.

Models with non-linear variables

Castle and Hendry (2010a) test for non-linearity by forming the principal components w_t, say, of the original n regressors x_t, and use second and third powers and exponentials of the $w_{i,t}$. Since the w_t are generally linear combinations of all the x_t, their powers include many squares, cubics and up to triple interactions between the $x_{i,t}$. Their approach still applies when N would exceed T from adding up to cubic polynomials in the x_t (even without IIS), such that $N = n + n(n+1)(2n+4)/6 > T$ although $n << T$, since there would only be $4n$ variables in total. Applying that test to (17) yields $F(12,141) = 1.05$, so does not reject. A 'complete' test of all those non-linear functions in the $x_{i,t}$ would have added 48 variables even for $n = 4$.

When the test rejects and apparently entails a non-linear specification, it is essential to also apply IIS to avoid a spurious match between outliers and some of the non-linear terms as discussed in Castle and Hendry (2011). With $n = 23$ regressors excluding the dependent variable, we generate the demeaned squares and cubics of the corresponding principal components, $w_{i,t}$ and augment the GUM outlined above with $\sum_{j=0}^{2} \sum_{i=1}^{23} w_{i,t-j}^{k}$ for $k = 1, 2, 3$, resulting in $N = 279$ with a further $T = 157$ indicators from IIS. Although there are many perfectly collinear relationships, undertaking expanding and contracting path searches enables a non-singular representation to be obtained. Applying selection at $\alpha = 0.001$ results in the exact DGP specification being retained, so augmenting the GUM with many additional non-linear terms does not result in over-fitting: we would expect to retain 0.44 of a variable on average under the null of 436 irrelevant variables, regardless of whether the variables are standard regressors, principal components, or non-linear factors.

Exact-specification

Hendry and Johansen (2010) show that forcing retention of a correct theory-based set of variables (distinct from imposing their coefficient values) leaves unchanged the distributions of the parameter estimates in a GUM with many irrelevant variables as compared to direct estimation of the theory model. That result also holds for models with endogenous variables when there are adequate instrumental variables to viably estimate the GUM, and even when $N > T$.

While perhaps astonishing at first sight that selection has no impact on estimator distributions in such a procedure, the explanation is that the irrelevant variables can be orthogonalized relative to the correct theory variables, which does not alter the theory parameters, and it is well known that the inclusion or omission of orthogonal variables does not alter estimator distributions. Nevertheless, that result should profoundly alter attitudes towards model selection – it has no effect when the theory model is correct, and as we now show, can be hugely beneficial when the theory is incomplete or incorrect.

Forcing the correct specification

To demonstrate assume that the correct specification (16) were known and therefore embedded in a GUM with 2 lags of all variables and IIS by forcing c_{t-1}, i_t, i_{t-1} and Δp_t to be retained in selection. As with selection for relevant variables using IIS there are $N + T = 229$ regressors, 4 of which are forced, and $\alpha = 0.0025$. The resulting selected model is identical to the case where the theory variables are not forced, with one additional indicator retained. As the theory variables are highly significant, they would have been retained even if selected over and so forcing has no effect here. Likewise, if a subset of the relevant variables had been forced, the selected model would have been the same.

Forcing an incorrect specification

If we assume that the postulated theory consists of c_{t-1}, q_t, q_{t-1} and Δp_t rather than i_t and i_{t-1}, and hence irrelevant variables are forced in selection, again commencing with $N + T = 229$ regressors for $T = 157$ observations results in:

$$c_t = \underset{(0.022)}{0.84}\, c_{t-1} + \underset{(0.031)}{0.51}\, i_t - \underset{(0.032)}{0.32}\, i_{t-1} - \underset{(0.093)}{0.94}\, \Delta p_t - \underset{(0.029)}{0.01}\, q_t - \underset{(0.032)}{0.01}\, q_{t-1}$$

$$\hat{\sigma} = 1.09 \quad F_{ar}(5,146) = 1.02 \quad F_{arch}(4,149) = 1.20$$

$$\chi^2_{nd}(2) = 0.75 \quad F_{het}(12,144) = 1.18 \quad F_{reset}(2,149) = 1.83 \tag{18}$$

Both q_t and q_{t-1} are forced to be retained in the final selected model but both are insignificant. Including i_t and i_{t-1} in the regressor set resulted in them being retained through selection, so the final model is a close approximation to the DGP despite forcing irrelevant variables. The one indicator found previously is no longer retained as q_t and q_{t-1} could be picking up the outlier. Forcing theory variables does not guarantee that they will be significant or have the correct sign, but it is relatively costless as long the GUM nests the DGP variables. We now turn to the case where this doesn't hold.

Under-specification

If relevant variables are omitted from the GUM any resulting selected model will face the classical omitted variable bias problem. Selection cannot mitigate that, and motivates commencing from sufficiently general models to minimize the chance of excluding potentially relevant variables: the costs of commencing from an under-specified model by far outweigh the costs of commencing from an over-specified model. However, selection can be very beneficial even in under-specified models, particularly when the omitted variables are subject to breaks. Castle and Hendry (2010b) show that augmented general-to-specific model selection strategies using IIS can excel in mitigating most of the adverse effects of breaks in equations due to omitting relevant variables that suffer location shifts. To illustrate their analysis, first consider leaving inflation out of the GUM, while maintaining one lag and not selecting, which leads to:

$$c_t = \underset{(11.4)}{2.5} + \underset{(0.03)}{0.99}c_{t-1} + \underset{(0.04)}{0.50}i_t - \underset{(0.04)}{0.49}i_{t-1} \tag{19}$$

$$R^2 = 0.988 \quad \hat{\sigma} = 1.48 \quad \chi^2_{nd}(2) = 7.65^* \quad F_{ar}(5,149) = 7.82^{**}$$

$$F_{arch}(4,150) = 6.28^{**} \quad F_{reset}(2,152) = 2.98 \quad F_{het}(6,151) = 1.09$$

Three of the mis-specification tests reject. Figure 3.2 shows the resulting non-constancy using recursive estimation of (19).

Further, the omission of the breaking variable, Δp_t, leads to the fitted model being essentially in first differences, and suggests the absence of any long run. Implementing that idea:

$$\Delta c_t = \underset{(0.05)}{0.23}\Delta c_{t-1} + \underset{(0.03)}{0.50}\Delta i_t \tag{20}$$

$$\hat{\sigma} = 1.42 \quad \chi^2_{nd}(2) = 1.86 \quad F_{ar}(5,142) = 3.19^{**}$$

$$F_{arch}(4,141) = 2.25 \quad F_{reset}(2,145) = 0.15 \quad F_{het}(5,143) = 2.46^*$$

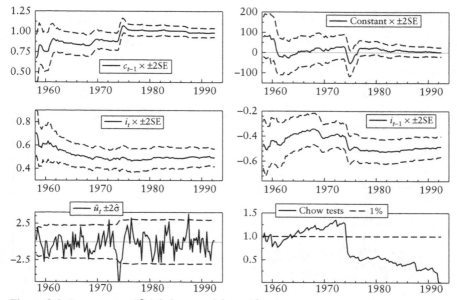

Figure 3.2 Incorrect artificial-data model specification

However, several mis-specification tests still reject, and the entailed solution in first differences suggests that c only responds 2/3rds to i (although the DGP has a 1–1 response).

Model selection with IIS

Now consider selection using IIS at $\alpha = 0.001$, commencing from a GUM with 2 lags, which delivers:

$$c_t = \underset{(0.05)}{1.15} c_{t-1} - \underset{(0.05)}{0.17} c_{t-2} + \underset{(0.03)}{0.51} i_t - \underset{(0.03)}{0.49} i_{t-1}$$

$$- \underset{(1.34)}{4.30} \, 1_{1974(1)} - \underset{(1.35)}{4.44} \, 1_{1974(2)} \tag{21}$$

$$\hat{\sigma} = 1.32 \quad \chi^2_{nd}(2) = 0.22 \quad F_{ar}(5,146) = 2.05$$

$$F_{arch}(4,149) = 0.91 \quad F_{reset}(2,149) = 0.55 \quad F_{het}(14,140) = 0.85$$

Indicators at the 'oil-crisis dates' 1974(1) and 1974(2) and the longer lag of c proxy the omission of Δp_t. That is a key benefit of *Autometrics* over conventional modelling, even when the basic set is substantively incomplete–picking up the break effects of an omitted variable that shifts is very advantageous relative to having a non-constant model. The break is only partly modelled by the dummy, and the rest by a near unit root (a typical outcome), which helps in forecasting, but misleads in policy reactions and latencies. However, no diagnostics are now

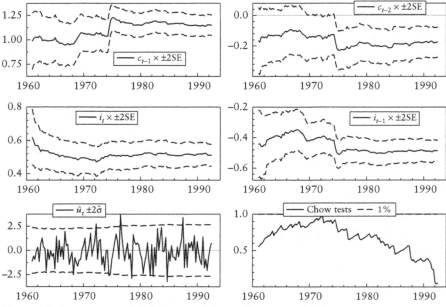

Figure 3.3 Incorrect artificial-data model specification with IIS

significant, and the fit is closer to that of the DGP ($\sigma = 1$), as well as the solved static long-run equation for c on i having a coefficient of 0.98, albeit that a unit root cannot be rejected. The theoretical and simulation analyses in Castle and Hendry (2010b) explain such outcomes. Figure 3.3 shows the resulting improvement in constancy for recursive estimation of (21). The Chow test does not reject anywhere, and the large outliers in 1974 have been eliminated.

Conclusion

Recent developments in automatic model selection enable the real complexities of economic data modelling to be tackled, jointly addressing many candidate variables, some of which matter whereas others do not, long lag lengths, non-linearity, multiple location shifts and data contamination. The intercorrelations between economic variables, their non-stationarity, and high dimensionality necessitate handling all of these together if sustainable models are to result.

The chapter has discussed the application of such methods to the three central states of nature, where the initial model is over-specified relative to the data generation process, exactly specified and under-specified. In the first setting, the key issue is eliminating irrelevant variables while retaining relevant, and even large numbers of candidate variables hold few terrors. In the second, selection over non-theory variables is costless when the theory variables are retained. In the third, a mis-specified outcome is bound to occur, but selection can mitigate some of the problems due to location shifts in the unknowingly omitted variables. Thus, selection from a much larger initial general unrestricted model is generally beneficial relative to fitting a pre-specified equation, reversing the widely-held folklore of the economics profession that model selection is a pernicious, if unfortunately necessary, activity.

References

Akaike, H., 1973. Information theory and an extension of the maximum likelihood principle. In: B.N. Petrov and F. Csaki, eds. *Second international symposium on information theory*. Budapest: Akademia Kiado, pp. 267–81.

Andrews, W.K., 1991. Heteroskedasticity and autocorrelation consistent covariance matrix estimation. *Econometrica*, 59, pp. 817–58.

Campos, J. and Ericsson, N.R., 1999. Constructive data mining: modelling consumers' expenditure in Venezuela. *Econometrics Journal*, 2, pp. 226–40.

Campos, J., Ericson, N.R., and Hendry, D.F., 2005. Editor's introduction. In: J. Campos, N.R. Ericsson and D.F. Henry, eds. *Readings on general-to-specific modelling*. Cheltenham: Edward Elgar, pp. 1–81.

Castle, J.L., Doornik, J.A. and Hendry, D.F., 2009. Model selection where there are multiple breaks. Working paper 472, Economics Department, University of Oxford.

Castle, J.L., Doornik, J.A. and Hendry, D.F., 2010. Evaluating automatic model selection. *Journal of Time Series Econometrics* 3(1), DOI: 10.2202/1941-1928.1097.

Castle, J.L. and Hendry, D.F., 2010a. Automatic selection of non-linear models. In: L. Wang, H. Garnier and T. Jackman, eds. *System identification, environmental modelling and control* (forthcoming). New York: Springer.

Castle, J.L. and Hendry, D.F., 2010b. A low-dimension, portmanteau test for non-linearity. *Journal of Econometrics*, 158, pp. 231–45.

Castle, J.L. and Hendry, D.F., 2010c. Model selection in under-specified equations with breaks. Discussion paper 509, Economics Department, Oxford University.

Castle, J.L. and Shepard, N., eds., 2009. *The methodology and practice of econometrics*. Oxford: Oxford University Press.

Chow, C.G., 1960. Tests of equality between sets of coefficients in two linear regressions. *Econometrica*, 28, pp. 591–605.

Davidson, J.E.H., Hendry, D.F., Srba, F., and Yeo, J.S., 1978. Econometric modelling of the aggregate time-series relationship between consumers' expenditure and income in the United Kingdom. *Economic Journal*, 88, pp. 661–92.

Desai, M.J. and Weber, G., 1988. A Keynesian macro-econometric model of the UK: 1955–1984. *Journal of Applied Econometrics*, 3, pp.1–33.

Doornik, J.A., 2009. Autometrics. In: Castle and Shephard, eds. 2009. *The methodology and practice of econometrics*, pp. 88–121. Oxford: Oxford University Press.

Doornik, J.A. and Hansen, H., 2008. An omnibus test for univariate and multivariate normality. *Oxford Bulletin of Economics and Statistics*, 70, pp. 927–39.

Doornik, J.A. and Hendry, D.F., 1994. *PcGive 8: an interactive econometric modelling system*. London: International Thomson Publishing; Belmont, CA: Duxbury Press.

Engle, R.F., 1982. Autoregressive conditional heteroscedasticity, with estimates of the variance of United Kingdom inflation. *Econometrica*, 50, pp. 987–1007.

Godfrey, L.G., 1978. Testing for higher order serial correlation in regression equations when the regressors include lagged dependent variables. *Econometrica*, 46, pp. 1303–13.

Hendry, D.F., 2000. *Econometrics: alchemy or science?* New edition. Oxford: Oxford University Press.

Hendry, D.F., 2003. J. Denis Sargan and the origins of LSE econometric methodology. *Econometric Theory*, 19, pp. 457–80.

Hendry, D.F., 2009. The methodology of empirical econometric modelling: applied econometrics through the looking-glass. In: T.C. Mills and K.D., Patterson, eds. *Palgrave handbook of econometrics*. Basingstoke: Palgrave Macmillan, pp. 3–67.

Hendry, D.F., 2010. Revisiting UK consumers' expenditure: cointegration, breaks and robust forecasts. *Applied Financial Economics*, 21, pp. 19–32.

Hendry, D.F. and Doornik, J.A., 2009. *Empirical econometric modelling using PcGive: volume I*. London: Timberlake Consultants Press.

Hendry, D.F. and Johansen, S., 2010. Model selection when forcing retention of theory variables. Economics Department, University of Oxford (unpublished paper).

Hendry, D.F., Johansen, S. and Santos, C., 2008. Automatic selection of indicators in a fully saturated regression. *Computational Statistics*, 33, pp. 317–35. Erratum, pp. 337–39.

Hendry, D.F. and Krolzig, H.-M., 2005. The properties of automatic Gets modelling. *Economic Journal*, 115, pp. C32–61.

Hendry, D.F. and Srba, F., 1980. AUTOREG: a computer program library for dynamic econometric models with autoregressive errors. *Journal of Econometrics*, 12, pp. 85–102.

Hoover, K.D. and Perez, S.J., 1999. Data mining reconsidered: encompassing and the general-to-specific approach to specification search. *Econometrics Journal*, 2, pp. 167–91.

Johansen, S. and Nielsen, B., 2009. An analysis of the indicator saturation estimator as a robust regression estimator. In: Castle and Shepherd, eds. 2009. *The methodology and practice of econometrics*, pp. 1–36.

Johnson, N.L., Kotz, S. and Balakrishnan, N., 1994. *Continuous univariate distributions – 1*. 2ⁿᵈ ed. New York: John Wiley.

Judge, G.G. and Bock, M.E., 1978. *The statistical implications of pre-test and Stein-rule estimators in econometrics*. Amsterdam: North Holland Publishing Company.

Koopmans, T.C., 1947. Measurement without theory. *Review of Economics and Statistics*, 29, pp. 161–79.

Leamer, E.E., 1974. False models and post-data model construction. *Journal of the American Statistical Association*, 69, pp. 122–31.

Leamer, E.E., 1983. Let's take the con out of econometrics. *American Economic Review*, 73, pp. 31–43.

Lovell, M.C., 1983. Data mining. *Review of Economics and Statistics*, 65, pp. 1–12.

Maasoumi, E., ed., 1988. *Contributions to econometrics: John Denis Sargan*. Cambridge: Cambridge University Press.

Mizon, G.E., 1995. Progressive modelling of macroeconomic time series: the LSE methodology. In: K.D. Hoover, ed. *Macroeconomics: developments, tensions and prospects*. Dordrecht: Kluwer Academic Press, pp. 107–69.

Pagan, A.R., 1987. Three econometric methodologies: a critical appraisal. *Journal of Economic Surveys*, 1, pp. 3–24.

Ramsey, J.B., 1969. Tests for specification errors in classical linear least squares regression analysis. *Journal of the Royal Statistical Society B*, 31, pp. 350–71.

Salkever, D.S., 1976. The use of dummy variables to compute predictions, prediction errors and confidence intervals. *Journal of Econometrics*, 4, pp. 393–97.

Sargan, J.D., 2001. Model building and data mining. *Econometric Reviews*, 20, pp. 159–70.

Sargan, J.D., 1988. Lectures on advanced econometric theory. In: M. Desai, ed. *Lectures on advanced econometrics by Denis Sargan*. Oxford: Basil Blackwell.

Schwartz, G., 1978. Estimating the dimension of a model. *Annals of Statistics*, 6, pp. 461–64.

Tibshirani, R., 1996. Regression shrinkage and selection via the lasso. *Journal of the Royal Statistical Society, B*, 58, pp. 267–88.

White, H., 1980. A heteroskedastic-consistent covariance matrix estimator and a direct test for heteroskedasticity. *Econometrica*, 48, pp. 817–38.

4

Indian Reforms

Jagdish Bhagwati

Perhaps the most appropriate way to start my tribute to Meghnad Desai, who has been in the forefront of discussions on Indian public policy for many years, is to discuss Indian reforms.

Today, there are two contrasting 'narratives' about India's reforms: one superlative and dramatically congratulatory, the other apocalyptic and hypercritical.

Perhaps the most dramatic, optimistic view of India has come from the once skeptical magazine, *The Economist*, which famously wrote nearly twenty years ago that India was a tiger that had been crouched for a long time but was unable to leap; the danger was that *rigor mortis* had set in. But the magazine wrote a raving cover page story 10 September 2010, abandoning its reservations and arguing that India's steadily accelerating growth rate since the 1991 pro-market, liberal (or 'neoliberal' if you wish to make them sound sinister) reforms was not a flash in the pan. Apparently throwing caution to the wind, it speculated that India's growth rate 'could overtake China's by 2013, if not before'.

But then, the naysayers, among them the socialists in the currently ruling Congress Party, have rejected the 'miracle' produced by the reforms by asserting darkly that the growth 'lacks a human face', that it is not 'inclusive', that the gains have accrued to the rich while the poor have been immiserized, that inequality has increased, and that India stands condemned before the world. Perhaps the most articulate critics are the 'progressive' novelists of India, chief among them Pankaj Mishra whom the op-ed page editors of *The New York Times* regularly and almost exclusively invite to write about the Indian economy, a privilege they do not seem to extend symmetrically to American novelists to give us their profound thoughts on the US economy.

Mishra's latest *Times* op-ed 2 October 2010, writes of the 'alarmingly deep and growing inequalities of income and resources in India', 'the waves of suicides of tens of thousands of overburdened farmers over the last two decades', 'a full-blown insurgency … in central India' to defend tribals against depredations by multinationals, 'the pitiless exploitations of the new business-minded India', and much else that is allegedly wrong with India.

While economic analysis can often produce a yawning indifference, and Mishra's narrative is by contrast eloquent and captivating, the latter is really fiction masquerading as non-fiction. The fact is that several analyses show that the enhanced growth rate has been good for reducing poverty while, measured meaningfully, it has not increased inequality and that large majorities of virtually all underprivileged groups polled say that their financial situation has not worsened and significant numbers say that it has improved.

Abysmal growth prior to reforms

The enhanced, and increasing, growth rate since the reforms followed a period of abysmal growth rates in the range of 3.5 to 4.0 per cent annually for over a quarter of a century, starting in the 1960s. The cause of the low growth had to do, not with our efforts at raising our investment rate, but with the fact that we got very little out of the investment we undertook. The reason was that we had a counterproductive policy framework whose principal elements were:

1 Knee-jerk intervention by the government through a maze of Kafkaesque licensing and regulations concerning investment, production and imports, prompting the witticism that Adam Smith's Invisible Hand was nowhere to be seen;

2 Massive expansion of the public sector into many areas other than utilities, with occasional monopoly granted to public enterprises by excluding entry by the private sector, with predictable inefficiencies that multiplied through the economy; and

3 Autarky in trade and inflow of equity investment which was so extreme that the Indian share of trade to GNP had fallen while it had increased in most countries, whereas the inward flow of equity investment had been reduced to minuscule levels.

This policy framework had been questioned, and its total overhaul advocated, by me and Padma Desai in writings through the late 1960s which culminated in our book, *India: Planning for Industrialization* (Bhagwati and Desai, 1970) with a huge blowback at the time from virtually all the other leading economists and policymakers who were unable to think outside the box. In the end, our views prevailed and the changes which would transform the economy began, after an external payments crisis in 1991, under the forceful leadership of Prime Minister Manmohan Singh who was the Finance Minister at the time.

It is often suggested by populist anti-reformers in India and their ideological friends abroad (such as my colleague Joseph Stiglitz), that the policy changes were imposed from outside, reflecting what has come to be known as the

Washington Consensus – a phrase that has the advantage of harnessing anti-Americanism in your cause – in favour of liberal reforms at the Bretton Woods institutions. But that is no more true than to argue that the Soviet *perestroika* under President Gorbachev and the Chinese economic reforms starting in the late 1970s were imposed by Washington. In all three cases, the driving force was endogenous, a realization by the leadership that the old, counterproductive policy model had run their economies into the ground and that a change of course had to be undertaken. In fact, if the contention of the populists was correct, one would have expected the reforms to be reversed once the 1991 payments crisis was over. Instead, successive governments have only intensified the reforms: no serious analyst wanted to turn the clock back and back into the future, embracing a failed policy model.

The early reforms were primarily focused on dismantling the licensing regime (known popularly as the 'permit Raj') which freed up the animal spirits of the private sector. The economy was also steadily opened up: the average import tariff on manufactures, at virtually 113 per cent in 1990–91, was reduced steadily, avoiding the folly of 'shock therapy', and now stands at 12 per cent. While privatization would prove politically difficult, its intended effects in terms of efficiency of management were sometimes achieved by opening up entry by private firms into the sectors that had been reserved for public sector enterprises: the entry of these firms, plus unwillingness to provide ever more subsidies to absorb losses, was like a pincer movement that meant 'shape up or ship out'.

The old policy architecture could not be demolished in one fell swoop. The leadership had to negotiate minefields of ideological opposition, bureaucratic intransigence, and the lobbies (called 'interests' by political scientists) that had fattened on the rents (i.e. monopoly profits) attending sheltered markets that they were earning. The 'three Is' – ideas, institutions and interests – of the old regime had to be confronted. Then, again, the post-1991 reformers felt that their task was akin to cleaning up after a tsunami. Hastening slowly was their only choice.

Substantially enhanced growth after the reforms

Still, as the reforms gathered steam, the effects on the growth rate were palpable. The growth rate, rising to roughly 6 per cent, nearly doubled in the 1990s, increased still further in the following decade and has recently been close to 9 per cent. The sense that India was now an 'emerging superpower' was a heady experience for Indian elites who had seen their country marginalized by policies that had become a laughing stock in the world while smaller nations in the Far East had emerged as the much-admired star performers.

The poor and the underprivileged have also benefited

But are the opponents of the reforms right to complain that the reformers have been focused on growth to the neglect of the underprivileged; and that the latter have been bypassed or immiserized?

It has become fashionable to say that this must be so because the Human Development Index, produced by the United Nations Development Program (UNDP), put India at the bottom, in 135th place, in 1994. But this is a nonsensical index which reduces, without scientifically plausible weights, several non-commensurate elements like literacy and diverse health measures to a single number. It is a fine example of how bad science gains traction as a result of endless repetition by the media: it must be dismissed as rubbish. There is no substitute for hard, scientific answers to the questions concerning what has happened, during the period of reforms and enhanced growth, to the poor and the underprivileged: and these answers, as I will presently sketch, are more benign.

To begin with, however, let me remind you that the common criticism that Indian policy was interested in growth for growth's sake is not even true if we go back to the early 1950s when planning took formal shape. In fact, my first job in the Indian Planning Commission half a century ago was to devise a strategy to bring the bottom 30 per cent of India's poor above the poverty line so they would enjoy a 'minimum standard of living'; and I came to the view, often expressed by the leaders of the Independence movement, that we had to grow the pie to do so: redistributing wealth in a country with 'many exploited and few exploiters' as the visiting Marxist economist Kalecki put it graphically to me in 1962, was not a strategy that could produce sustained impact on poverty. Growth was therefore regarded as a principal 'instrument', a strategy, for pulling the poor out of poverty through gainful employment, not as an end in itself. Growth was seen as what I have called an activist, radical 'pull up' strategy to reduce poverty. In no way was it viewed as a passive, conservative 'trickle down' strategy to reduce poverty, as illustrated by the film *Robin Hood* where the Earl of Nottingham and his vassals are eating legs of lamb and venison at the high table and crumbs fall below to the dogs and serfs underneath the table.

The growth strategy of pulling the poor up from poverty however did not work because growth itself did not materialize because of the counterproductive policy framework that I sketched above. But now that growth has actually been produced by the post-1991 reforms, what can we say about the wisdom of the growth strategy? Let me sketch some of the studies that seem to affirm it.

After a considerable debate, it is now generally accepted that the enhanced growth over nearly twenty-five years was associated with lifting nearly 200 million of the extreme poor above the poverty line. In contrast, and consistent with commonsense, the abysmal growth rate of the preceding quarter century saw no perceptible, beneficial impact on poverty. At a narrower level, the political scientist Devesh Kapur and associates have studied the fortune of the *Dalits* (untouchables) in India's most populous state, Uttar Pradesh, between 1990 and 2008, to find that 61 per cent of those surveyed in the east and 38 per cent in the west said that their food and clothing situation was 'much better' (Kapur, Prasad, Pritchett and Babu, 2010).

Most striking is the finding of the political scientist Al Stepan, drawing on polling data produced by the Center for the Study of Developing Societies in Delhi, that for every disadvantaged group including women, the response to the question 'Has your financial situation improved, worsened, or has remained the same' posed in 1996 and again in 2004, shows that every group has overwhelmingly remained the same or improved: those who claim to have worsened are invariably less than 25 per cent of the respondents (Stepan, 2011).

As for the relative economic outcomes of the disadvantaged groups, the economist Amartya Lahiri and associates have studied India's 'scheduled castes' and 'scheduled tribes', two particularly disadvantaged categories, and conclude that the last twenty years of major reforms 'have seen a sharp improvement in [their] relative economic fortunes'. Then again, using household expenditure data for 1988 and 2004, the Johns Hopkins economists Pravin Krishna and Guru Sethupathy conclude that inequality, using a well-known measure invented by the Dutch econometrician Henri Theil, while showing an initial rise, had fallen by 2004 back to the 1988 levels: a straight rise in inequality cannot be asserted (Krishna and Sethupathy, 2011).

I should also add that many reforms help the poor more than the rich because the rich can cope with the results of inefficient policies better than the poor. If the public sector generation and distribution of electricity is inefficient, and the electricity goes off in the middle of the night in Delhi's summer, the rich turn on their private generators and their air-conditioners continue working. But the poor man on his charpoy swelters as his small Usha fan is not working. Those who object to letting in Coke and Pepsi forget that the common man derives his caffeine from these drinks while the well-off critics get theirs from the Espresso and Cappuccino coffee in the cafes.

The most interesting political implication of the success in finally denting poverty significantly, though nowhere near enough, is that poverty is now seen by India's poor and underprivileged as erradicable. India is witness finally to what I have called the 'Revolution of Perceived Possibilities'. Aroused economic aspirations for betterment have led to political demands for the politicians to deliver yet more. This suggests, as my Columbia University colleague Arvind Panagariya and I have hypothesized, that voters will look to vote for the politicians who can deliver growth, and we would expect growth before the vote to be correlated with vote now. In an important paper, Poonam Gupta and Panagariya have recently tested this hypothesis and indeed found that it works (Gupta and Panagariya, 2011). Politicians should, therefore, be looking to augment reforms, not reverse them as misguided anti-reform critics urge. In fact, the recent dramatic success of Chief Minister Nitish Kumar, who had successfully delivered on prosperity, only underlines the lesson that the electorate will reward the politicians who have delivered and therefore are credible when they promise more.

So, politicians would do well to strengthen the conventional reforms, which I call Stage 1 reforms, by extending them to the unfinished reform agenda of the early 1990s. In particular, further liberalization of trade in all sectors, substantial freeing up of the retail sector, and virtually all labour market reforms are still pending. Such intensification and broadening of Stage 1 reforms can only add to the good that these reforms do for the poor and the underprivileged.

But these conventional reforms have also generated revenues which can finally be spent on targeted health and education so as to *additionally* improve the well-being of the poor: these are what I call Stage 2 reforms which were, let me remind you, in the minds of our earliest planners (as demonstrated by their inclusion in our Five Year Plans since 1951 and Programme Evaluation reports at the time) but have been handicapped principally by revenue constraints. When 'progressive' critics argue that Stage 2 reforms must replace Stage 1 reforms, because they appear superficially to be more pro-poor, they forget that Stage 2 reforms have been made possible only because Stage 1 reforms have been undertaken and have produced the necessary revenues.

This response applies equally to distinguished economists like Amartya Sen, whose policy prescriptions implicitly or explicitly supported the disastrous pre-reforms policies, and who is often quoted as saying about the post-reform policies that it is wrong to celebrate high growth rates when there is so much nutritional deprivation. Does he have a magic wand that would have improved living standards and increased nutritional intake without the high growth rates? Talking about hunger is different from providing policy prescriptions that will reduce it: talk is cheap but it also costs dearly in a country such as India where it is often mistaken for effective action.

How to get the most bang for your buck from programmes under Stage 2 reforms is where we also need to be turning our attention. Stage 2 reforms tend to involve 'social engineering' and are, therefore, inherently more difficult than Stage 1 reforms. If you want to reduce trade barriers, except for political difficulties, it's easy: you just slash them. But if you want to improve education, for example, you have to worry about the best classroom size, the issue of teacher absenteeism, the question of how to get poor children to the school when their parents might want to have them work instead, whether you should be using school vouchers, and so on. There is little doubt however that, once we have put our minds to work and our shoulders to the wheel, we will move ahead on both Stage 1 and Stage 2 reforms.

References

Bhagwati, Jagdish and Padma Desai, 1970. *India: Planning for Industrialization*. London: Oxford University Press, for the Development Centre of the Organization for Economic Cooperation and Development, Paris, 1970.

Bhagwati, Jagdish and Arvind Panagariya. Great Expectations. *Wall Street Journal*. May 24, 2004.

Crooks, Clive. Small World. *The Economist*. May 4, 1991. Issue 7750. special section p. 3–6. India's surprising economic miracle. *The Economist*. September 30, 2010. Volume 397. Issue number 8702. p. 11.

Economist, The. India's surprising economic miracle. *The Economist*. September 30, 2010. Volume 397. Issue number 8702. p. 11.

Kapur, Devesh, Chandra Bhan Prasad, Lant Pritchett, and D Shyam Babu. Rethinking Inequality: Dalits in Uttar Pradesh in the Market Reform Era. *Economic and Political Weekly*. August 28, 2010. Vol. XLV No. 35.

Gupta, Poonam and Arvind Panagariya. India: Election Outcomes and Economic Performance. Columbia Program on Indian Economic Policies Working Paper No. 2011–4.

Krishna, Pravin and Guru Sethupathy. Trade and Inequality in India. Columbia Program on Indian Economic Policies Working Paper No. 2011–5.

Mishra, Panka. Games India Isn't Ready to Play. *The New York Times*. October 2, 2010.

Mukim, Megha and Arvind Panagariya. Growth, Openness and the Socially Disadvantaged. Columbia Program on Indian Economic Policies Working Paper No. 2011–6.

Stepan, Alfred. Views from the Indian Electorate: Satisfactions and Dissatisfactions with Democracy, Politics and the Economy. Columbia Program on Indian Economic Policies Working Paper No. 2011–2.

5

Transgressing Heterosexual Norms

Some Observations on Recent Events in India and Nepal

Purna Sen

Introduction

In 2009 widespread celebrations greeted a historic Indian High Court judgement that ruled that the criminalization of homosexual acts contravened fundamental rights including the right to equality as enshrined in the Constitution. 2008–9 saw the advancement of Lesbian, Gay, Bisexual and Transgender (LGBT) rights in Nepal too, a development acknowledged and greeted with hope in and beyond the country. There was a sense of optimism that conservative attitudes to sexuality were loosening their grip on the lives of Indians and Nepalis.

In contrast, in 2010 the media reported case after case of 'honour killings' in northern India, mostly related to young people choosing marital partners and often perpetrated by the family of the woman concerned. These two threads, apparently contradictory, speak to the nature of change and resistance in the arena of sexual choice and sexuality. Conclusions may yet be premature but there are some interesting indications about the spaces in which sexual straightjackets will continue to be challenged.

Sexual rules and power dynamics enable or constrain individual lives, impacting on health and indicating the state of individual rights, freedoms, and opportunities. The HIV epidemic has enabled, or perhaps forced, attention onto the nature of, and the negotiation around, hetero-, homosexual and MSM[1] activity. Gender and development discourse has also tackled this taboo, asking us to look into the institutions of marriage and the household which shape 'normal' sexual relations. A recent interest in violence against women has further pushed us to problematize the construction of female sexuality and efforts to control it, and has promoted the links between these concerns and development agendas.

This chapter considers two aspects of sexuality considered 'unauthorized' or non-standard: the first in the context of husband-wife heterosexual partnerships; the second, homosexual relationships. I look at events in

India and Nepal, neighbouring countries where there appear to have been important shifts in the community policing of heterosexual relations (in India) and steps towards acceptance of homosexuality (in both India and Nepal). At first these dynamics seem to be at odds with each other – one moving in a progressive direction and the other conservative. But I conclude that they do not constitute a single site of struggle over sexuality. Rather, the control of male sexual access to women takes a course that is different and possibly distinct from the struggles for respect and legitimacy for gay, lesbian and trans lives.

This chapter does not attempt to give a comprehensive overview of these two arenas but draws attention to some contemporary dynamics in the battles over sexuality in the two countries concerned.

The problematic of marriage

Arranged marriage has a long history in India and it continues to thrive as a widely practiced means through which coupledom serves the interests of a group. Arrangements tie families together through the bodies of two people who are committed by others to spending their lives together, and having sex and children together. For many Indians the pairing is devoid of privacy, and sexual intimacy is furtive and not necessarily pleasurable; crowded living conditions result in the 'promiscuity of touch' (Kakar, 1990, p. 33) yet there may well be an absence of sensual or enjoyable intimacy (Kakar, 1990; Sen, 1998). A series of predictable phases that may never result in companionship or affection are captured succinctly by Singh as 'physical acquaintance, discovery of each others' minds and personalities, and possibly bonds of companionship'. But 'in most cases, [the spouses] suffer each other till the end of their days' (Singh, 1992, p. 47).

The institution of marriage is formidable in India. Divorce rates are low though they appear to have started to rise in recent years (e.g. *Telegraph*, 2005). The notion of the couple as indissoluble is strong and for some this makes death/suicide the only exit route (Kakar, 1990, p. 84).

The possibility of both spouses agreeing to their marriage appears not have found much purchase in South Asia. One indicator of this is the acceptance or otherwise, of international standards on marriage – in particular the Convention on Consent to Marriage (1964). This instrument has only three substantive articles requiring: the free and full consent of both parties, the identification of a minimum age for marriage and the official registration of all marriages. That marriage remains a deeply difficult institution to address is indicated by the fact that the Convention has been ratified by a mere fifty-five states including only two states in South Asia. Bangladesh ratified the Convention in 1998 though with reservations against articles 1 and 2. Sri Lanka has signed the Convention but has not yet ratified it. Neither India nor Nepal has ratified.

There are many reasons why some states have yet to accept such international norms: it may be that they are moving towards ratification of a long list of treaties; it may be that they feel their own provisions are strong enough and need no interference from outside; it may be that the State is not in agreement with the content of the proposed standard or it may be that the provisions of the treaty are too difficult or sensitive to implement. In terms of marriage in South Asia the political commitment to enforce the three not-unreasonable articles of the Convention has not yet been demonstrated. The issue of choice in marriage remains violently contested and possibly increasingly so. Caste and religious boundaries still constrain marriage alliances and it may be too costly a political price to pay for those who rely on such loyalties. Perhaps those with influence share popular notions as to where rightful control of access to women's sexuality should reside.

That the institutional arrangements of marriage can militate against pleasure or intimacy does not mean either that it always does so or that Indians, especially Indian women, somehow prefer to live without them. I have spoken in the course of research (Sen, 1998) and at other times to many women about their sexual lives and heard their frustrations either at the nature of their marital sexual relations, their distress at forced sex, nightly copulation or the use of condoms; some women find sex-less marriages deeply upsetting and long for something more personal or meaningful in their lives. Marriage rights, and the individual's control of their own sexuality, remain to be realized in South Asia.

Men and women both struggle with not being able to choose their marriage partners. Determining one's own spouse transgresses the control that families seek to exert over these decisions, yet the challenge to heterosexuality *per se* both in India and Nepal is also transgressive – to heterosex in totality.

Contesting the shape of heterosexuality

The working of classical patriarchy (Kandiyoti, 1988) in South Asia involves structures of male control, bolstered by hierarchies between women such that they have an investment in mechanisms which exert control over younger and lower status women. In terms of sex, the normative framework that defines appropriate heterosexual behaviour is upheld by men with the support of (senior) women. Family and community reputation and acceptability are significantly framed by appropriate behaviour of the girls and women of that group, especially their sexual behaviour. Unmarried parenthood and pre-marital pregnancy are both rare and unaccepted. Policing of girls, segregation, controlled entry into marriage, sexual relations being contained within marriage and female sexual fidelity are the basic elements of that framework. This is not a denial of the sexuality of women but a definition of legitimate consumption of that sexuality: women's sexuality is available to some men (husbands) but not to others and women themselves are not in control of these decisions.

There are of course 'right' and 'wrong' husbands. The usual considerations may apply such as employment prospects, shared cultural background – but in India social stratification and religious affiliation also matter. Not any man can be the right husband: class, caste and sub-caste, village and other background are taken into account and the calculation as to suitability is made by a family group in which the prospective spouses may have little or no say. The central problem facing the girl's family lies in ensuring that she preserves her virginity for her husband, that she reserves any sexual desire and exploration until marriage and that she accepts fully the determination of spouse by her elders and seniors. The role of the girl in this is to accept and conform: to marry as and when told, to wed the man chosen for her, accept intimacy with a stranger and be sexually at his demand for the entirety of her married life, including bearing him (preferably male) children. Indeed, the law recognizes sexual access as a right (conjugal rights as recognized in the Hindu Marriage Act) and failure to have sex as grounds for divorce.

Women's sexuality is a social headache, needing to be appropriated, controlled and channelled according to strict rules. Dress codes, separation of the sexes, veils, walls, *purdah* – are all ways of keeping men and women apart and therefore controlled: mixing with the opposite sex is potentially dangerous and romantic love is *ultra vires*. The family, primarily the older men of the family, shape, authorize or reject relationships within a framework of heterosexual marriage. Collective honour prevails over individual well-being and non-conformity is a transgression that must be managed and corrected. This version of normative heterosexuality supports the condemnation of sexually-active women, the ideology of male as protector and defender of female sexuality, of presumed male sexual rights of access to women's bodies and of women's status as fallen (i.e. sexually available) if beyond the ownership of one man.

A spike in reported 'honour' killings suggests that the management of non-compliance with marriage norms has become increasingly violent and transgressions by women seem to be particularly unacceptable. Control of women's sexuality and of the marital process remains in the hands of the collective; investment in its successful reproduction pays off for that group and the costs of non-conformity are also borne by the collective. Honour or shame can be won or lost in this domain as individual behaviour upholds or punctures honour and the collective gains or loses from (non-) conformity. There can be a strong incentive to correct or reclaim the loss of honour, and redress the shame, brought by non-conformity, which can lead to acts that involve force, violence or even death. It is a question of honour.

Honour

Recent international concern and horror regarding crimes committed in the name of honour have focused on Islamic contexts with scant attention paid to other environments. No doubt this has been influenced by the focus emerging at a time when the USA-led 'war on terror' and the aftermath of the Clash of Civilizations thesis has problematized Islam and the Muslim world. Yet there is no doubt that similar cultural patterns exist elsewhere and include frameworks of honour, collective efforts to control women's sexuality with the active participation of women and the ability to reclaim lost honour, that characterize 'honour' crimes (Sen, 2005); India being one.

The UN has noted honour killings in Egypt, Jordan, Lebanon, Morocco, Pakistan, Syria, Turkey, Yemen, the Mediterranean and Gulf countries and within migrant communities in France, Germany and the United Kingdom (Coomaraswamy, 2002). Western concerns about the treatment of women in Islamic contexts have been keen, yet men are not exempt from 'honour' crimes: those who stray outside the bounds of accepted or required behaviours can be made to pay a high price, including their lives. *Karo kari* killings in Pakistan are the oft-quoted example where men are killed along with errant women, to preserve collective honour.

Honour is pivotal in the maintenance of social credibility in India. Marriage rules exist across the country and in some parts of the country failure to abide by such rules offends collective honour (Chakravorty, 2005). Women are assumed to be unable or unfit to exercise choice in marriage (Chakravorty, 2005) and courts have supported parents who claim that their daughters have been kidnapped where a 'love marriage' is suspected.

Honour killings find little if any formal support from the State and the Indian judiciary has not invoked notions of honour in their decisions on such cases. Instead, they are accused of using technical arguments such as those concerning capacity to make decisions, to make judgements in order to define consent as meaning or at least including the consent of the parents of the girl (Chakravorty, 2005, pp. 326–7). Through such practices there is alleged to be widespread collusion by agents of the State (the police and the judiciary) with the denial of an individual's right to choice in matters of marriage and for the upholding of caste hierarchies and religious separation for the sake of collective honour.

There are some indications that it is predominantly the families of women that instigate or carry out the killings, though further data on this would be helpful. It appears to be women's transgressive behaviour that causes most offence: where a couple has transgressed it is often the woman's family that leads the efforts to correct the transgression. As the guardian of their female's sexuality, it is her family that has failed in its duty; the woman's family honour is thus stained. And after all, it is women who tempt men – women who must be covered, veiled, kept at home so as to ensure that men do not lose control.

More systematic research is needed to reach conclusions yet this pattern of control and the dispensability of women's lives is in line with other knowledge and evidence we have about gender in India, such as dowry deaths, acid throwing, widow burning, female infanticide, and sex-selective abortions. The latest census data (2011) show the persistence of worrying adverse sex ratios even though they have improved in a few states. If families cannot control 'their' women's sexual availability and confine its consumption to a man chosen by them, it seems that, in northern India at least, the uncontrolled woman can be eliminated; this option is for some preferable to supporting her choice or autonomy.

'Honour' killings in India: cases and context

Estimates of the scale of honour-related killings in India vary widely. A study commissioned by the National Commission for Women found 326 cases in one year, with 72 per cent involving inter-caste marriages and 90 per cent of perpetrators being from the girl's family (*Times of India*, 11 July 2010). Media reported an honour killing every four days in north India, based on a total of nineteen killings between 9 April and 30 June (*Times of India*, 1 July 2010), with three killings in the capital in a fortnight in 2010. Figures compiled by the India Democratic Women's Association record that, over one year, Haryana, Punjab and Uttar Pradesh account for about 900 honour killings and the rest of the country host another 100–300 (*Times of India*, 4 July 2010). Another estimate (Malhotra, 2010) has suggested over 1000 killings in a year in India among Muslims, Hindus and Sikhs, with Haryana, Punjab and western Uttar Pradesh accounting for 900 and marriage featuring as a dominant area of dispute.

The government of India earlier rejected reports of honour killings in the country saying these were inadequately researched or cognizant of the Indian situation (*Indian Express*, 12 October 2002). However, government responses have changed more recently, perhaps in light of the rash of media reports of 'honour' killings in 2009–10, which include the following:

- Haryana: A 22-year-old pregnant Brahmin journalist who had reportedly become engaged to a lower caste journalist was killed (death by asphyxiation/smothering); she was allegedly murdered by her family members, including her mother, for reasons of family pride (Times Online, 4 May 2010).

- Bihar: A low caste 15-year-old boy who had allegedly written love letters to a higher caste girl was beaten, had his hair shaved, was paraded through the street and then thrown under a train; fifteen members of a girl's family were arrested on suspicion of killing eight members of a boy's family, whose beheaded bodies were found floating in the river – the couple had married against prevailing marriage rules (Times Online, 11 February 2009).

- Delhi, June 2010: A couple who married against the wishes of their family was killed, allegedly by the woman's brother[2] (*Indian Express*, 18 January 2011).

- Punjab: A non-resident Indian was accused of bringing his step-daughter to India from Belgium, poisoning and hastily cremating her after she formed an attraction to a lower-caste young man in Belgium (*Times of India*, 30 June 2010).

- Bihar 2011: A Hindu-Muslim marriage disapproved of by parents resulted in the girl's father, brother and local council member allegedly forcing the husband to consume pesticide, eventually causing his death (*Times of India*, 17 Jan 2011).

- Delhi: A cross-caste relationship that parents feared would lead to elopement resulted in the couple, both aged 19, being killed, allegedly by being beaten by the girl's family with iron rods and then electrocuted by being 'forced to sit on iron trunks to which live wires were attached' (BBC, June 2010).

With up to seven honour killings reported each month in Haryana (Times Online, August 2009) and police reporting 'hundreds' of cases brought to them of couples being attacked by their relatives for marrying outside accepted social boundaries, the state has been labelled the 'honour killing capital' of India. The state announced the commencement of a pilot project intended to offer protection to couples considered to be at risk by offering a safe house, supported by outreach work with village councils intended to stem such violence (Times Online, August 2009).

Haryana has also witnessed a remarkable increase in the educational participation of girls, including at tertiary level: between 1980 and 1981 and 2006 and 2007 there was a fourfold increase in the number of girls attending college and a fivefold increase in girls studying to class 12 (compared to a less than twofold increase to that level for boys) (*Outlook India*, 12 July 2010). Are educated girls appearing to be growing in confidence and asserting their right to make choices, including in marriage? It has been argued that this might translate into assertion over inheritance of family property, a fear that may lie behind the search for the maintenance of family control over marriage partners (*Outlook India*, 12 July 2010). Inter-generational conflict may well be one factor behind 'honour' killings, with younger people wanting new ways of behaving and their parents seeking to uphold old norms (Ravi Kant in Sify News, 21 Jan 2011).

Panic over control of women spreads beyond Haryana. Local village councils have acted to restrict increasing choice exercised by women and girls, for example by banning the wearing of jeans (*Times of India*, 17 Jan 2011) and have even ordered honour based killings (*Outlook India*, 12 July 2010; BBC March 2010). Yet, justifications and excuses for honour killings can portray the killer as a victim, who has no choice but to act to protect (usually) his honour against a wayward child (often a girl): a Delhi *panchayat* member complained '[i]t is a social compulsion that a father is under, because his daughter has short-changed him by marrying against his will' (see for example *Times of India*, 1 July 2010). In 2010, comments by Haryana's Chief Minister expressing reservations about sub-caste marriages was considered by some to offer support to village councils that were complicit in or that explicitly ordered honour crimes (*Outlook India*, June 2010). Caste loyalties matter in Indian politics such that the cost of betraying or undermining caste structures can result in the loss of votes (*Times of India*, 1 July 2010). Yet the political pressure for formal political and judicial structures not to support such killings has prompted local councils in Punjab, considered to be among the worst affected of states, to condemn 'honour' killings (*Times of India*, 31 March 2011).

A Public Interest Litigation filed before the Supreme Court on killings related to the exercise of choice in marriage resulted in the Centre and eight governments being directed to report on steps taken to prevent such cases (Sify News, 2011). It calls for government to review the Indian Penal Code to introduce a definition of the crime. The Home Minister proposed all-women police stations as a solution but stated that he was not in favour of a special legal provision, preferring instead that such killings be treated as murder (Times Online, May 2009). A year later the Home Minister announced that he would introduce a Bill on honour killings that would propose a definition of crimes of honour (including stripping women and parading them in public as well as killings) and set out the punishment for these offences (Times of India, Aug 2010; Times of India, Jan 2011). In May 2011 the Supreme Court acknowledged what it saw as an increase in 'honour' killings and called for the death penalty to be applied in such cases (India Today, 10 May 2011).

The co-existence of progress for women and of attempts to exert increasing patriarchal control do not necessarily surprise but they do clash, with tragic consequences, on the issue of 'love marriages' in northern India. The impacts are felt by both women and men, with many lives lost. Forced marriage, controls on mobility, curtailment of education or employment and other means of enforcing compliance have long been known in India yet it seems now that 'honour' killings may be becoming an increasingly popular tool in the Hindu heartland.

The gradual opening of choice and love or romance in India may bring a host of new issues into social dynamics (e.g. household formation, divorce) yet the momentum is already underway. The extended family household is changing, there is increasing participation in education by girls; many pressures are bringing social change. Yet old structures and power holders do not easily relinquish their grip. Caste relationships, boundaries and arranged marriages, fundamental elements of Indian social structure that constrain accessibility to women's sexuality to acceptable men, seem to be increasingly challenged by a younger generation and violently defended by an older one. This has become a vicious battleground for a valuable prize: rightful ownership and control of women's sexual and reproductive lives.

Challenging heteronormativity

In the same period that northern India has seen violent responses to transgressive heterosexual relationships there has been progress towards the acceptance of homosexuality both legally and socially.

The mass of literature on gender issues in South Asia has as dominant themes: women's status, education, labour force participation and income generation, health and equality. Homosexuality has had relatively little attention (Thadani, 1996). If women seeking to choose their heterosexual partners is challenging to social conservatives then women choosing sexual intimacy that excludes men is no doubt especially troubling. The moral panic and social outrage that erupted over Deepa Mehta's film *Fire*, that explored unsatisfactory marriage and intimate, including sexual, relationships between women, illustrates the profoundness of the challenge posed by acknowledgement of lesbianism. It also showed the threat felt among social and religious conservatives by public discourse on women's sexual choices.

For men, the existence of the colonial law that outlaws homosexual activities ('against the order of nature', see Box 5.1) has been an outrage that has denied privacy and choice in intimate relationships. Indian nationalism somehow was not offended by this particular legacy of colonialism. Though the law had not actively been used in many years for prosecutions, it meant that gay men could not enjoy police protection and were liable to harassment or blackmail without redress. The law also compromised HIV work and realization of the right to health.

Yet, Indian history and social organization has long accommodated gender identity beyond a male/female binary, with the existence and importance of the

---

Box 5.1: Indian Penal Code, Section 377 (b)

Unnatural offences: Whoever voluntarily has carnal intercourse against the order of nature with any man, woman or animal, shall be punished with imprisonment for life, or with imprisonment of either description for term which may extend to ten years, and shall also be liable to fine.

Explanation: Penetration is sufficient to constitute the carnal intercourse necessary to the offense described in this section.

---

hijra[3] who have specific roles at key social occasions. And sexually segregated social life means that same-sex friendships and spaces enjoy greater approval than cross-sex friendships and mixed gender spaces (Vanita and Kidwai, 2001). The possibilities for same sex relationships are thus created and indeed preferred.

Literature and debates on homosexuality and transgender have grown over the last two decades in India (e.g. Jaising, 1992; Joseph, 1996; Thadani, 1996; Campaign for Lesbian Rights, 1999; Srivastava, 2004) and the idea that homophobia has a long history in the country has been challenged (Vanita and Kidwai, 2001). The health/HIV discourse has ushered into development concerns a (still limited) willingness to consider life beyond heterosexuality and marriage.

Section 377 of the Penal Code prohibits sexual acts 'against the order of nature' and captures any sexual behaviour other than penile-vaginal penetration. It has meant that anyone who is gay cannot turn to the State for protection against harassment or abuse and it has enabled blackmail. Criminalization of homosexual acts has had a detrimental impact on HIV work and the right to health, with health initiatives being compromised by the inability of men to acknowledge their behaviour to others.

The legal challenge to Section 377 came largely from organizations and activists in the HIV and health sectors. The criminalization of same sex sexual activity meant that those who the law made criminals were severely compromised and at risk when seeking health care in relation to HIV. A collection of groups led by the Naz Foundation and women's and human rights groups in the 'Voices against 377' coalition challenged this provision through a Public Interest Litigation in 2001. Eight years later, it resulted in the Delhi High Court bench of Justices Shah and Muralidhar declaring in July 2009 that Section 377 was at odds with provisions in the Indian constitution that guarantee equality before the law and the principles of non-discrimination and inclusiveness. The judgement showed a willingness to reconsider criminalisation.

Though sometimes misrepresented as India de-criminalising homosexuality (it has yet to come to the Supreme Court, where a determination will be made for the country as a whole) the decision is of huge significance and meaning. The case laid open fissures in government, with the Ministry of Health seeking decriminalization in order that health initiatives could proceed and the Home Ministry opposing decriminalization. Additional Solicitor General Malhotra in 2008 argued in the High Court that homosexuality is a social vice, a danger to peace and a cause of moral degradation (*Times of India*, September 2008) but in 2009 the new Law Minister, Moily, suggested it was time to repeal the provision. The government has signalled that it will not oppose the case when it comes before the Supreme Court, though many other parties will be doing so, including major religious groupings (Shah, 2010 and 2011; Muralidhar 2011).

The Delhi High Court decision should not be read in isolation to conclude that all is well for gay life in India. It remains difficult to be 'out' in India (PUCL, 2001) and experiences of harassment or acceptance vary, including by class (Merchant, 2010). Pressures to conform to heteronormativity have meant that in India, as in other countries, those who are gay have often had to mask their own preferences and behaviours through devices such as marriage. In the wake of the Section 377 decision, women who were brides of convenience began to file for divorce where their marriages had not been consummated or where they had knowledge of their husband's gay relationship (Sinlung, 2010).

Attempts to hold gay marriages, however informal, are strongly contested with one in Manipur in 2010 being broken up by the police at the behest of the families, two days after the ceremony (Sinlung, 2010). Yet, beyond the Delhi High Court decision there have been several developments that signal a loosening of the heterosexual stranglehold on Indian social life. Cultural discourse on homosexuality and gender identity has developed. The film *Fire* has already been mentioned – it was made and had a limited showing, even if opposed. Books such as that by Merchant (2010) illustrate the range of literature that addresses gay life, gay pride events take place in India, there are gay bookshops and film festivals (see Table 5.1). Lesbian organizations have been formed, such as LABIA, Symphony in Pink (both in Mumbai), Campaign for Lesbian Rights, Sanghini and Humrahi in Delhi, Olava in Pune and Prerana in Bangalore.

These legal and social changes suggest a direction of travel towards acknowledgement and even acceptance of homosexuality in India as existed in pre-colonial India. Homosexuality has not yet found acceptability across India but male homosexual behaviour has been reclaimed from its colonial illegality. The Section 377 decision was widely celebrated across LGBT communities and by many others yet much more remains to be done, especially for women who are seen to be rejecting men: the ideology of normative heterosexuality is

Table 5.1 Selection of developments on LGBT rights in India and Nepal

	India	Nepal
2005	• Category E (for eunuch) introduced in categorization of sex, on online passport application forms	
2007		• Recognition of third gender in the definition of citizenship • Decriminalization of homosexuality
2008		• Supreme Court gives consent to same sex marriage and instruction to the government to formulate a law; confirms rights to own property and right to employment
2009	• Election Commission – O (other) category on voting forms for eunuchs • S377 Delhi high court judgement	
2010	• Delhi Municipal Corporation makes pensions available to eunuchs • India's first mainstream gay film festival: the 'Kashish' Mumbai international queer film festival • First online gay bookstore opened • First gay condom • First gay pride event in Delhi since Section 377 decision, 2000 people attended (estimate)	• First gay pride parade • Pink Mountain travel agency launched to enable gay weddings • First gay wedding
2011		• Pink Mountain Travel Agency has bookings for weddings, most from women

especially powerfully policed for women. Sexually active women continue to suffer condemnation, the ideology of male as protector and defender of female sexuality remains in place, presumed male sexual rights of access to women's bodies prevail and the labelling continues of women as fallen or sexually available if beyond the ownership of one man.

Nepal

Developments in neighbouring Nepal over the past few years suggest a potential re-casting of sexual constraints and options. The journey appears to be smoother than in India and with less contestation, despite Nepal's reputation as a socially conservative nation.

Gender norms in Nepal share a great deal with the rest of South Asia, especially northern India, where premarital sex is strongly taboo, gender discrimination is deep and heterosexuality is the norm. Nepal is a major source country for the trafficking of girls across the region, fed in large part by the interaction of gender inequality and poverty. Nepal suffered a decade of armed Maoist struggle that eventually toppled the monarchy and saw the establishment of a constituent assembly in 2008. In the period immediately following the 'people's revolution' a remarkable series of events saw the increasing acceptance of homosexuality in law and politics with fundamental changes to the legal and social framework. Changes in the legal and social status of homosexuality and gender identity in Nepal owe a large debt to Sunil Pant MP and the Blue Diamond Society (BDS).

Unable to establish a gay rights NGO in 2001, Pant instead started a general human rights and health NGO, the Blue Diamond Society. Between 2001 and 2006 Pant's local support came primarily from women's NGOs in Nepal, INGOs and Western activists at a time when the country was suffering political violence and insecurity due to the armed insurgency. Pant became involved in the defence of transgender and gay people who were arrested, raped or harassed (Pant, 2011).

The Blue Diamond Society undertook HIV training, prevention work, condom distribution and extensive documentation of harassment faced by LGBT individuals. Pant also advocated changed behaviour among the police and military, lobbied for gay rights among the political parties and Maoists. Benefits seem to have been realized in the latter part of the decade.

As political space opened up at the end of the insurgency the BDS pressed for political commitment for action on LGBT rights and Pant took a case to court for equal rights. The Supreme Court gave broad and progressive decisions including the recognition of homosexuals and third gender people as natural persons with equal rights. The Court required the government to make citizenship identity available to those of a third gender, to end discriminatory legislation and policies, form a same-sex marriage committee and recognize homosexual and transgender rights in the new constitution. The court does not seem to have been hindered by the prevailing social conservatism in Hindu Nepal. With the end of the armed conflict and the move to electoral politics in 2008, Pant capitalized on the need among political parties to maximize their votes, asking them all to include lesbian and gay rights in their manifestos. The BDS was asked by the Communist Party of Nepal (Unified) (CPN(U)) to field a candidate in the elections; this is when Pant launched a successful electoral campaign and became Nepal's first openly gay MP. He accounts for his success by referring to the votes of closet gays and lesbians, especially among women in the security forces (Pant, 2011).

It was to take another set of discussions before membership was opened in 2010 to those whose votes were previously courted through manifesto changes; the Unified Marxist-Leninists (UML), Maoists and Nepali Congress all accepted LBGT members.

The draft constitution is strong on the language of equality, non-discrimination and social justice and names many groups who should enjoy rights, protections and special provisions (from Centre of Constitutional Dialogue website). This includes for example commitment on the preferential right to employment for single women, to ensure lives of dignity. There are repeated references through the text to equal treatment, special provisions and protections for specific groups including sexual minorities:

- The State shall not discriminate against any citizen in the application of general laws on grounds of religion, colour, caste, tribe, *gender, sexual orientation,* biological condition, disability, health condition, pregnancy, economic condition, origin, language or region, ideological conviction or other similar grounds.

- Special provisions can be made for 'the protection, empowerment or advancement of women, *dalits,* indigenous ethnic tribes (*adiwasis janjatis*), Madhesis or farmers, workers, oppressed regions, Muslims, backward class, minority, marginalized and endangered communities or destitute people, youths, children, senior citizens, *gender or sexual minorities,* the disabled or those who are physically or mentally incapacitated and helpless people, who are economically, socially or culturally backward.

- The State shall not discriminate among citizens on grounds of religion, colour, race, caste, tribe, *gender, sexual orientation,* biological condition, disability, health condition, marital condition, pregnancy, economic condition, origin, language or region, ideological conviction or other similar grounds.

There are repeated references to the rights of women and gender/sexual minorities and need for inclusiveness in the treatment of all. Two lawmakers out of 601 expressed concerns about the provisions yet their position may since have changed in the course of party debates (Pant, 2011). Difficulties in resolving debates on the new Constitution have lead to the deadline being repeatedly extended through 2011.

Conclusion

Patriarchy and heteronormativity dominate and infuse social structures and dynamics in South Asia and lie at the core of honour codes. Heterosexuality and collective (predominantly male) choice of spouse need to be enforced for honour codes to be upheld. These norms are being contested, reinforced and broken in South Asia. This chapter briefly considers two areas of contestation: the exercising of choice in selection of sexual/marital partners within heterosexual relationships and the establishment of homosexuality as legitimate and legal.

Rigid sexual norms remain constraints on men and women in South Asia. Caste boundaries for acceptable marriages remain strong, family control over selection of spouses continues and asserts its presence in the face of contestation, homosexuality remains criminalized in all but one state (Nepal) and one capital city (Delhi).

Nepal decriminalized homosexuality at the birth of a new epoch, along with the overthrow of the monarchy and during the period of drafting a new constitution. The dawning of a new era provided a similar impetus elsewhere – Soviet Russia, the new South Africa and Kosovo, for example. Nepal decriminalized a year before the Delhi High Court and remains the only state in the South Asia region to have done so on a national scale. Yet the change is not yet secure – the new constitution is yet to be adopted and decisions can change (Russia decriminalized in 1922 and re-criminalized in 1934).

India is undergoing rapid economic transformation and social developments that see increasing education among girls, with higher numbers of young women entering the labour force. Heterosexual marriage norms are being both challenged and asserted where women dare to transgress long-held marriage rules, with the loss of community (male) honour being re-established often through killings. The wider world thus opening up to women has a massive impact on the aspirations and confidence of young women, some of whom are beginning to contest the myriad forms of control over them that have traditionally been exercised by men and senior women. It is also the case that some young men are accompanying women on the journey towards increased individual choice, and both are paying with their lives for contesting heterosexual norms.

Transgressive heterosexuality appears to be being met with increasing violence in northern India yet the steps forward in terms of transgressive homosexuality appear to be being met with less venom, both in India and Nepal.

It might be expected that homosexuality, transgressions against heterosexuality, would be more unacceptable than resistance within the frame of heterosexuality. While this paper cannot give a comprehensive analysis, and abuse of LGBT communities certainly continues, a reading of recent events presented here suggests that transgressive heterosexuality *may* be costing more lives; transgressive heterosexuality may be the more disruptive to the social control of sexual relations.

How these dynamics will play out, whether there is increasing or decreasing tolerance, remains to be seen. It does not minimize the disrespect, rejection or abuse known by LGBT people to note that there is a qualitative difference in responses to the two strands of transgression discussed here.

Control of women's sexuality still remains at the heart of what it means to be a good family and an honourable community. Male sexuality does not carry the same import or meaning. In the public imagination it seems to me that homosexuality is more commonly understood to be about men and sodomy, and this is captured in the Section 377 debates. Lesbianism remains cloaked in lack of recognition if not silence. Do hot-blooded heterosexual men consider it inconceivable that women might have sexual lives and satisfaction without them? It may be so and if so, lesbian lives will not pose a threat until they are acknowledged to be real. And it is likely that until and unless it is perceived as a threat, women's choice of sexual lives without men will perhaps not be worth taking seriously. In Nepal, the Pink Mountain Travel agency capitalizes on Nepal's tourism industry and status as the first *South Asian* country to decriminalize homosexuality, to offer gay weddings to tourists. It currently has more bookings from women for weddings than from men (Pant, 2011). While these will be foreign women it may be part of larger picture in which women's sexual lives as free from men becomes increasingly recognized. It is not clear how this dynamic will move forward in India.

The State in both India and Nepal appears to be moving towards acceptance of the legitimacy, or at least tolerance, of homosexuality. At a time of political upheaval the creation of a new State dynamic and direction has enabled a positive space for the promotion of equality and non-discrimination in Nepal. Yet, the fact that Nepal is the only state in South Asia that has fully decriminalized homosexuality and has sought to enshrine this in a new Constitution offers a great beacon of hope in the region. It is as yet early days and this space remains to be watched, in both countries.

Similarly, State action on the policing of rigid social relations played out through control of male sexual access to women has also to take clearer shape. These will tell us a great deal about the future of sexual choice and autonomy in India and Nepal and how the battle for control of women's sexuality is played out.

Notes

1 Men who have sex with men.
2 The male victim's brother was later allegedly threatened by a policeman against testifying in court.
3 This is not to say that all are equally treated or respected, simply that their existence is an established part of social life.

References

BBC News, March 2010. Death penalty in India 'honour killings' case. *BBC News*, March. Available at: http://news.bbc.co.uk/1/hi/8595168.stm [accessed 30 May 2011].

BBC News, April 2010. India Caste councils back men over 'honour killings' *BBC News*, April. Available at http://news.bbc.co.uk/1/hi/8617576.stm [accessed 30 May 2011].

BBC News, June 2010. Delhi police make arrests after 'honour killing'. *BBC News*, June.

Campaign for Lesbian Rights, 1999. Lesbian emergence: a citizen's report. Campaign for Lesbian Rights: New Delhi.

Centre for Constitutional Dialogue (CCD), n.d. Committee on Fundamental Rights and Directive Principles, A resource centre to support the constitution making process in Nepal. Available at: http://www.ccd.org.np/new/index.php?cipid=22 [accessed 27 April 2011].

Chakravorty, U., 2005. From fathers to husbands: of love, death and marriage. In: Welchman and Hossain, eds. '*Honour*': *crimes, paradigms and violence against women*. London: Zed Books.

Coomaraswamy, R., 2002. Cultural practices in the family that are violent towards women. *Report of the Special Rapporteur on violence against women, its causes and consequences*, Ms. Radhika Coomaraswamy, submitted in accordance with Commission on Human Rights resolution 2001/49, 31 January 2002.

Hindustan Times, 2010. Honour killing: girl hacked to death by mother. *Hindustan Times*, 29 June. Available at: http://www.hindustantimes.com/Honour-killing-Girl-hacked-to-death-by-mother/Article1-564980.aspx [accessed 27 April 2011].

Indian Express, 2011. Cop held for threatening kin of honour killing victim. *Indian Express*, January. Available at: http://www.indianexpress.com/news/cop-held-for-threatening-kin-of-honour-killing-victim/738864/ [accessed 27 April 2011].

India Gazette, 2010. Manipur gets its first gay married couple. *India Gazette*, 25 March. Available at: http://story.indiagazette.com/index.php/ct/9/cid/701ee96610c884a6/id/616122/cs/1/ [accessed 27 April 2011].

India Today, Honour Killings: Supreme Court says those who kill for 'honour' deserve death sentence http://indiatoday.intoday.in/site/story/honour-killings-sc-for-death-sentence/1/137621.html [accessed 30 May 2011].

Jaising, I., 1988. Gay rights. *The Lawyer*, Feb-Mar.

Joseph, S., 1996. Gay and lesbian movement in India. *Economic and Political Weekly*, 17 August.

Kakar, S., 1990. *Intimate relations: exploring intimate sexuality*. India: Penguin.

Kandiyoti, D., 1988. Bargaining with patriarchy. *Gender and Society*, 2(3).

Malhotra, R., 2010. Socio-legal perspective of forced marriages. Conference on *International Child Abduction, Forced Marriage and Relocation*. London Metropolitan University, London UK, 2 July, 2010.

Merchant, H. ed., 2010. *Yaraana: gay writing from South Asia*. India: Penguin. (Expanded edition.)

Muralidhar, J.S., 2011. (Personal communication.)

Outlook India, June 2010. Congress for stern handling of honour killing cases. *Outlook India*, 23 June. Available at: http://news.outlookindia.com/item. aspx?685761 [accessed 27 April 2011].

Outlook India, July 2010. Dreams girl. *Outlook India*, 12 July. Available at: www.outlookindia.com/article.aspx?266071.

Pant, S., 2011. (Personal communication, January 2011).

People's Union for Civil Liberties, 2001. Human rights violations against sexuality minorities in India. Available at: http://www.pucl.org/Topics/Gender/2003/sexual-minorities.pdf [accessed 30 May 2011].

Ramnath, Nandini, n.d. The personal isn't always political in Mumbai. *Time Out Mumbai*. Available at: http://www.timeoutmumbai.net/client_coverstory/client_coverstory_details.asp?code=755 [accessed 27 April 2011].

Sen, Purna, 1998. A basket of resources: women's resistance to domestic violence in Calcutta. [PhD Thesis]. University of Bristol, UK.

Sen, Purna, 2005. Crimes of honour: value and meaning. In: Welchman and Hossain, eds. '*Honour': crimes, paradigms and violence against women*. London: Zed Books.

Shah, Justice A.P. 2010. (Personal communications with the author, December, 2010 and January, 2011.)

Sify News, 2011. Honour killings: conflict between tradition and modernity. *Sify News*, 21 January 2011. Available at: http://www.sify.com/news/honour-killings-conflict-between-rigid-tradition-modernity-news-national-kg1l4eibeaa.html [accessed 27 April 2011].

Singh, K., 1992. Sex in India. In: *Sex, scotch and scholarship*. Delhi: UBS Publishers.

Sinlung, 2010. More women in India divorcing gay men. *Sinlung*, 26 October 2010. Available at: http://www.sinlung.com/2010/10/more-women-in-india-divorcing-gay. html#ixzz1Cc2udDNi [accessed 27 April 2011].

Srivastava, S., ed., 2004. *Sexual sites, seminal attitudes: sexualities, masculinities and culture in South Asia*. India: Sage.

Telegraph, 2005. Divorce soars in India's middle class. *Telegraph*, 1 October 2005. Available at: http://www.telegraph.co.uk/news/worldnews/asia/india/1499679/ Divorce-soars-in-Indias-middle-class.html [accessed 27 April 2011].

Thadani, G.,1996. *Sakhiyani: lesbian desire in ancient and modern India*. London: Cassell.

Times of India, 2008. Centre: Homosexuality is a reflection of a perverse mind *Times of India*, 27 September 2008. http://timesofindia.indiatimes.com//india/Centre-Homosexuality-is-a-reflection-of-a-perverse-mind/articleshow/3530854.cms [accessed 30 May 2011].

Times of India, 2010. Honour killing: SC notice to Centre, Haryana and 6 other states. *Times of India*, 21 June, 2010. Available at: http://timesofindia.indiatimes. com/india/Honour-killing-SC-notice-to-Centre-Haryana-and-6-other-states/ articleshow/6073756.cms [accessed 27 April 2011].

Times of India, 2010. NRI held for suspected honour killing in Punjab. *Times of India*, 30 June 2010. Video story available at: http://timesofindia.indiatimes.com/ videos/news/NRI-held-for-suspected-honour-killing-in-Punjab/videoshow/6113739. cms [accessed 30 May 2011].

Times of India, 2010. Honour killing: North India wages a vicious war against love. *Times of India*, 1 July 2010. Available at: http://articles.timesofindia.indiatimes. com/2010-07-01/india/28294403_1_honour-killings-khap-nirupama-pathak [accessed 30 May 2011].

Times of India, 2010. More than 1000 honour killings in India every year: Experts. *Times of India*, 4 July 2010. Available at: http://timesofindia.indiatimes.com/india/ More-than-1000-honour-killings-in-India-every-year-Experts/articleshow/6127338. cms#ixzz1BYzPu34R [accessed 27 April 2011].

Times of India, 2010. Honour killing: its a global phenomenon. *Times of India*, 11 July 2010. Available at: http://articles.timesofindia.indiatimes.com/2010-07-11/ india/28318807_1_honour-killings-family-honour-reports-by-human-rights [accessed 30 May 2011].

Times of India, 2010. Bill on honour killings this session. *Times of India*, 6 August, 2010. Available at: http://articles.timesofindia.indiatimes.com/2010-08-06/ india/28320415_1_honour-killings-stringent-punishment-current-parliament-session [accessed 30 May 2011].

Times of India, 2011. Honour killing in Nawada. *Times of India*, 17 January 2011. Available at: http://timesofindia.indiatimes.com/city/patna/Honour-killing-in-Nawada/articleshow/7300100.cms [accessed 27 April 2011].

Times of India, March 2011, Panchayats adopt resolutions against honour killing, 31 March 2011, available at: http://timesofindia.indiatimes.com/india/Panchayats-adopt-resolutions-against-honour-killing/articleshow/7830912.cms [accessed 30 May 2011].

Times Online, February 2009. Times Online, February 2009. India: eight slaughtered over forbidden marriage. Available at: http://www.timesonline.co.uk/tol/news/ world/asia/article5711463.ece [accessed 27 April 2011].

Times Online, August 2009. Safe houses in India to protect newlyweds against 'honour killings'. *Times Online*, 14 August, 2009. Available at: http://www .timesonline.co.uk/tol/news/world/asia/article6795356.ece [accessed 27 April 2011].

Times Online, May 2010. Mother arrested over 'honour killing' of Indian journalist. *Times Online*, 4 May 2010. Available at: http://www.timesonline.co.uk/tol/news/ world/asia/article7115736.ece [accessed 27 April 2011].

United Nations, 1964. Convention on consent to marriage, minimum age for marriage and registration of marriages. (Entry into force, open to sig 1962). UN GA Res 1763 A (XVII) of 7 November, 1962.

Vanita, R. and Kidwai, S., 2001. *Same sex love in India*. London: St Martin's Press.

6

Agrarian Power and Agricultural Productivity in South Asia Revisited

John Harriss

Most Indian economists of Meghnad Desai's generation took some interest in agriculture – unsurprisingly so, since they grew up in a country in which agriculture remained the most important sector of the economy (it still accounted for 61 per cent of GDP in 1950–51, and for 76 per cent of employment). Meghnad was no exception to this general rule, and he worked on agriculture at Berkeley before he arrived at LSE. Then, his most significant contribution to work on agriculture in India came in the 1980s when, with the eminent political scientist Susanne Hoeber Rudolph from the University of Chicago and the feisty Bengali economist the late Ashok Rudra, he convened discussions for the Social Science Research Council of New York (SSRC), on the theme of 'Agrarian Power and Agricultural Productivity in South Asia'. A book of fine essays, with this title (hereafter *APAP*), based on these discussions, edited by Desai, Rudolph and Rudra, and with contributions by all three of them, together with Donald Attwood (an anthropologist), David Ludden and B.B. Chaudhuri (historians), Ronald Herring and Lloyd Rudolph (political scientists), and the economist the late Sukhamoy Chakravarti, was published in 1984. My purpose in this essay is to explain the context of the work contained in the book, and its significance, and then to reflect upon it in the light of the changed circumstances of the present, after almost thirty years in which India has generally experienced higher rates of economic growth than before, and in which agriculture now accounts for less than 20 per cent of GDP (though, significantly, still for around 50 per cent of all employment).

APAP was the most notable outcome of the initiative taken in the later 1970s by the South Asia Committee of the SSRC to launch work on the political economy of South Asia. As Susanne Rudolph explained in her introduction to *APAP* the working groups on South Asia that were established at that time differed significantly from those that the SSRC had set up before, in the 1960s, to study problems of development. Those earlier groups had been dominated by American political scientists working broadly within the frame of modernization theory and with structural-functional or behavioural perspectives. The South Asia groups, on the other hand, included numbers of scholars from South Asia, and from the United Kingdom and Canada as well as the United States, and from different disciplines. They also 'questioned the extent to which the historical sequences, value premises and social forms that dominated development in the West [the processes of 'modernization' as it was then understood] were relevant or desirable for Third World countries'; and, unlike those who preceded them, they were expressly concerned with 'how economic power and exploitation affected development' (both quotes Rudolph, 1984, p. 1 – the category 'Third World' was still current, and defensible, at the time). Rudolph also noted that the South Asia scholars 'focused on the need to delineate an approach from "within" to South Asian political economy'. They thought that '[t]he conceptual assumptions of neoclassical economics, in particular have been exceptionally immune to evidence of social and temporal variation', and so their idea was to create a research alliance across the social science disciplines, in an effort 'to approximate a more contextual understanding of economic processes'. They also sought to 'find scholars who recognized that political economy was known and practiced by John Stuart Mill and Karl Marx as well as Adam Smith' (all quotes Rudolph, 1984, p. 2). Given the catholicity of Meghnad's mind and interests, and his immersion in Marxian theory, we may imagine him as a young scholar ready to engage very enthusiastically with the work of the group (it was labeled 'SAPE 1' – South Asia Political Economy Project 1) concerned with agrarian power and agricultural productivity – though perhaps to the discomfiture of some of his colleagues in the Department of Economics at LSE who were less inclined to acknowledge the contributions of Marx, or indeed of Mill, to their discipline. His commitment to this interdisciplinary enterprise seems to have presaged Meghnad's taking over of the leadership, a decade later, of the LSE's venture of establishing the interdisciplinary Development Studies Institute (now the Department of International Development), which has remained committed to just the sort of approach exemplified by SAPE 1.

APAP in its time: the context

India's agricultural economy, outside some pockets of commercial farming, had stagnated throughout the latter part of the colonial period in the first half of the twentieth century, and productivity was much lower than elsewhere in Asia. The London *Economist*, in its issue of 16 August 1947, at the time of India's independence, expressed the hope that 'the energy of the new governments [of both India and Pakistan] will be concentrated without delay on the fundamental question of increasing agricultural production' (cited by Corbridge and Harriss, 2000, p. 10). As it turned out, however, relatively little attention was paid to agriculture by the planners of India's economic development until, twenty years after 1947, problems of food supply brought it to the forefront of their concerns. Some leading members of the Congress, the great political movement, now political party, that was the spearhead of India's struggle for freedom from colonial rule, had for long recognized the problem of agrarian class relations in India. At the heart of the problem, in their view, was landlordism – the concentration of economic power in the rural economy in the hands of a small number of very large landholders, usually absentees, who held sway over what was often a hierarchy of tenants with varying degrees of security of tenure – and the highly unequal distribution of landholdings, which meant that very many were uneconomic. The whole made for what Daniel Thorner, a fugitive in India from McCarthyism in his native United States, only a little later described as '[the] complex of legal, economic and social relations uniquely typical of the Indian countryside [that] served to produce an effect which I should like to call that of a built-in "depressor"' (Thorner, 1956, p. 16). With this term he referred to agrarian production relations that made it paying for landlords to live by appropriating rents, usurious interest and speculative trading profits from the impoverished mass of the peasantry – and thereby limited the possibilities of productivity-raising investment in technical change. The landlords had no incentive to invest; the impoverished peasant masses were left with no means of investment.

It was these conditions that the *Report of the Congress Agrarian Reforms Committee* of 1949 sought to change, through radical reform and the establishment of a pattern of village-based cooperative farming. Such ideas continued to be debated through the 1950s and they were put forward again in the 'Resolution on Agricultural Organisational Pattern' that was moved before the annual meeting of the Congress held in Nagpur in 1959. Meghnad Desai himself has argued that the defeat of this Resolution, thanks to the campaigning against it organized by Charan Singh, leader of rich peasants from Uttar Pradesh (and later, briefly, Prime Minister of India in 1979–80), finally marked the failure of the Nehruvian state to resolve India's 'agrarian question', and that this in turn substantially helps to account for the relative failure of planned economic development in the country. The final version of the India's First Five Year Plan (1951–6) did endorse the main recommendations of the Agrarian Reforms Committee, whilst stopping short of a generalized attack on private property, and legislation enacted in various major states between 1950 and 1954 did bring about a major change in the pattern of land ownership across large parts of the country, through the abolition of intermediary rights and tenures (that had been controlled by the tax-farming *zamindars*). But neither these reforms, nor subsequent legislation that was supposed to bring about redistributive land reform, brought about the end of 'landlordism'. In practice it was the larger occupancy tenants – a class of rich peasants – who benefited most from *zamindari* abolition and who increased their political power (already established within the Congress in the 1930s) and were able to undermine and frustrate further attempts at agrarian reform (as at Nagpur in 1959). Thorner's 'depressor' remained in place.

India's agriculture benefited from investments in irrigation development and the expansion of the cultivated area in the 1950s, and total agricultural production between 1952–3 and 1964–5 grew by 3.42 per cent per annum – though production of food grains grew only at 2.75 per cent, barely keeping pace with population growth. Under the most considered and significant of all India's economic plans, the Second Five Year Plan (1956–61, sometimes known as the Mahalanobis Plan, from the name of its principal designer) agriculture was treated as a kind of 'bargain basement', it being assumed that output could be increased primarily through institutional measures rather than requiring substantial outlays (Corbridge and Harriss, 2000, p. 60–5), and not long afterwards, in the mid-1960s, the country faced serious shortages of food. It was in this context that agriculture at last became a priority for planners and the government adopted what became known as the New Agricultural Strategy, intended to make agriculture more productive through technological investments and price incentives; and it was at this juncture that the new higher-yielding varieties of wheat and rice began to be introduced and the 'green revolution' took off, from the later 1960s.

Although the 'green revolution' had both a positive impact on the productivity of Indian food grains agriculture and ultimately a positive impact on poverty, through increased employment and a tightening of rural labour markets – reflected in increasing real wages in agriculture in the 1980s – and especially through lower food prices (Lipton with Longhurst, 1989), the principal beneficiaries were again the rich peasants who were in the best position to take advantage of the new technology. As was said at the time, though the technology of the green revolution was technically scale neutral, it was not 'resource neutral'. Thus it was that Indian scholars, stimulated at first by Ashok Rudra, began to debate the development of capitalist agriculture and the differentiation of the peasantry (along the lines laid out by Lenin with regard to Russia in *The Development of Capitalism in Russia* (Lenin, 1899), on which Meghnad commented in his collection of *Lenin's Economic Writings* (Desai, 1989)). At the same time, however, others – notably Amit Bhaduri – developed ideas about agrarian relations comparable with those of Daniel Thorner, into a more rigorous theory of 'semi-feudalism' (Bhaduri, 1973), providing a stronger theoretical basis for the idea that agrarian power relations blocked the transition to more productive capitalist agriculture. Meanwhile Krishna Bharadwaj in her work on production conditions in Indian agriculture (Bharadwaj, 1974) advanced ideas about what she referred to as the 'compulsive involvement in markets' (Meghnad has always argued with me that it should be 'compulsory involvement') of the mass of smallholding peasant producers in India. With this term she spoke of 'the category of the economically very weak sections of the peasantry ... all of whom have an extremely weak "bargaining" position in the markets. Yet they cannot avoid involving themselves in market operations ... The higher degree of monetization of inputs and outputs on very small farms [attested in farm management survey data] indicates this element of compulsive involvement in markets, reflecting conditions of distress' (Bharadwaj in Harriss, 1982, p. 272). Later Bharadwaj and Bhaduri both spoke of this in terms of the phenomenon of 'forced commercialization' (Bharadwaj, 1985). These latter arguments, in particular, about semi-feudalism and forced commercialization, justified the continued emphasis in the programmatic statements of left parties in India, on the need for redistributive land reform and fundamental changes in the organization of agricultural production (on lines, in fact, very much like those that had previously been advocated by the Congress party).

This, then, was the historical conjuncture and the intellectual context in which Desai and others of the SSRC's SAPE 1 began in the later 1970s to discuss agrarian power and agricultural productivity. As Susanne Rudolph says in her introduction to *APAP*, 'The central problematic ... was how local power structures impinge upon levels of and changes in agricultural production or productivity. The focus on local agrarian structures quickly expanded to suggest the relevance of translocal forces as well. But the question remained, do some [local] power relations obstruct productivity? Do others facilitate it?' (Rudolph, 1984, p. 12). The group was concerned with such questions as that of the persistence or not, in the context of the increasing commodification of Indian agriculture and the possible or actual development of agrarian capitalism, of the production relations described by Thorner as 'the depressor' and theorized by Bhaduri as 'semi-feudalism'. In other words, did the particular concentration of economic power in the South Asian countryside, reflected especially in inequalities in landholding, still constrain the development of agricultural productivity, or not? In the context of 'green revolution' did the historically often-observed inverse relationship between farm size and productivity – perhaps resulting in part at least from the 'compulsive involvement' in markets of small producers – still hold, or not? How did agrarian power structures vary across the region, with what consequences, and how were they changing?

APAP: arguments and their significance

APAP is an enormously rich book, its content ranging from Meghnad's own paper, concerned as he says, with the refinement of concepts, and which presents a model of an agrarian economy focusing on struggles for shares in the economic surplus, to B.B. Chaudhuri's overview of his own and others' historical research on 'Rural power structure and agrarian productivity in Eastern India, 1757–1947' and to Lloyd and Susanne Rudolph's first formulation of their idea of 'bullock capitalists' in their essay on 'Determinants and Varieties of Agrarian Mobilization'. For me, however, two themes, or sets of arguments, stand out. The first has to do with theory and methodology. The collection as a whole emphasizes the importance of locality (whilst not neglecting the importance of translocal influences), and in doing so it brings out the importance of specific histories. As Meghnad wrote 'given the uneven regional development of different parts of South Asia, a production of ecological and historical forces, it is incorrect to put a single label on the entire subcontinent' and 'when it comes to analyzing local situations, sufficient attention has to be paid to the historical background' (Desai, 1984, p. 176). This is an unexceptionable sort of statement, but should be read with reference to the context of the literature of that moment: many of the contributions to what was called at the time 'the mode of production debate', concerned with the development of capitalism, or not, in Indian agriculture, were marked by a formulaic, generalized history (Harriss, 1980). APAP as a whole, in contrast, shows the unevenness of the commercialization of agriculture across different regions of India, the acute difficulties of generalization and the bluntness of universalizing theory. Marxist theory was not spared, but the authors addressed, notably, the limitations of neo-classical economics. APAP demonstrates (especially in the papers by Rudra and Chakravarti) the persistent empirical divergence from neo-classical assumptions: 'the absence of a competitive labour market, the absence of free contractual labour, differential prices to big and small farmers, and fragmented credit markets' (Rudolph, 1984, p. 8). Of course, mainstream economists have done a great deal of work over the last twenty five years to take account of and to explain these 'divergences', but the recognition of the importance of history that the authors involved in APAP advocated has generally become much more established since the time they wrote. Two economists, Kenny and Williams have, for example, reviewed developments in economic growth theory, and in the empirical understanding of economic growth, and concluded that 'more energy should be directed toward understanding the complex and varied inner workings of actual economies rather than trying to assimilate them into abstract universal models' (Kenny and Williams, 2001, p. 16) – implying the value of substantive historical analysis (or, as they say 'historically-situated interpretations of the growth experience' (Kenny and Williams, 2001, p. 13)). More recently Woolcock, Szreter and Rao (the first and third of whom are from the World Bank) have argued forcefully for taking history seriously in regard to thinking about development policy. As they have said, the recognition of the importance of institutions in so much recent research in economics – though it was also exactly the subject of APAP – 'has led inexorably to the conclusion that "history matters", since institutions clearly form and evolve over time' (Woolcock, Szretzer and Rao, 2011, p. 70). So in significant ways APAP was ahead of its time. Contributors I think shared the view expressed by Susanne Rudolph that while the development of common frameworks was much to be desired, the impulse to generalize should be resisted (1984, p. 17). This is a mantra that has been taken seriously in the best work by institutional economists – by those who do take history seriously (Hodgson, 2001).

The second important set of arguments is that which provides substantive answers to the central problematic that *APAP* addresses. Against the powerful argument that '"semi-feudal" configurations [or "the depressor"] block the transition to a technically progressive capitalist agriculture' – an idea that was taken very seriously at the time by the Planning Commission's *Task Force on Agrarian Relations* – the central finding of *APAP* was that 'the relationship between power structures and productivity [is] highly variable' (Rudolph, 1984, p. 12–13). Chakravarti, Chaudhury and Herring (the latter in what is perhaps the most significant single contribution in the book) all advanced empirical evidence refuting the semi-feudal thesis. Herring summed up his own review of evidence and argument, saying that:

> Contrary to a great deal of received theory, there does not seem to be much evidence that traditional social organizations of production mandate agricultural stagnation. This does not mean that some structures of economic and political power locally are not immediate obstacles to productive investment ... but that at the farm level and the aggregate level the question of change over time is rooted in the size and disposition of the economic surplus in interaction with state policies toward agriculture and the resulting opportunity structure as perceived by those classes which command the lion's share of the surplus. *These questions are then empirical and cannot be settled at the theoretical level.* (Herring, 1984, p. 216, emphasis added)

A critical argument for Herring was that it is the deployment of the surplus that is crucial for agricultural productivity, and that the form of appropriation of surplus does not determine its deployment. He, and other contributors to *APAP* agreed that the concentration of scarce resources in the hands of powerful agriculturalists, often at the expense of the less powerful, commonly reduces the productive potential of small farms – but he pointed out that it could also encourage entrepreneurial risk-taking on the parts of some, at least, of the powerholders. In the context of a modernizing agricultural sector, the evidence – Herring believed – now showed that the classic inverse relationship between farm size and productivity, so often referred to as constituting an essential reason for advocating redistributive land reform, probably no longer held.

Generally, the argument of the book was that the association between power and productivity is shaped by variations in regional and ecological circumstances; and it was concluded (at least by Susanne Rudolph) that 'the case for altering the power structure has to rest mainly on political and equity grounds [not on grounds of its contribution to agricultural growth]' (Rudolph, 1984, p. 15). Herring argued, perhaps even more provocatively, that 'in a modernising agricultural sector, land control becomes less determinative of both political and economic power' (Herring, 1984, p. 203). These are arguments that I want to consider further in the context of what has been happening more recently in Indian agriculture.

APAP reconsidered

Amidst much controversy over the process and impacts of the great shift in economic policy in India that is commonly seen as having been initiated by the 'economic reforms' instituted by the Congress government in 1991, whilst the present prime minister Dr Manmohan Singh was Minister of Finance – though is now seen as having been initiated even earlier (see Kohli, 2006) – one set of facts is widely accepted: the agricultural economy has been largely neglected by the policy reformers, and agriculture has increasingly lagged behind the rest of the economy, which in turn is no longer affected nearly so much as it was in the past by variations in agricultural production.

It is extremely difficult, indeed, given the considerable variance in the performance of the agricultural economy from year to year – due to the highly uncertain climatic conditions characteristic of most of India – to draw clear-cut conclusions about growth trends, and much depends of course on which years or groups of years are taken for comparison over time. Still, there is no doubt about the fact that the growth of agriculture has lagged behind that of the rest of the economy. That this has been particularly marked in the period of high overall growth after 2003 was recognized both by the Prime Minister, Manmohan Singh, and by Montek Singh Ahluwalia, the Deputy Chairman of the Planning Commission, in speeches made in June 2010 (see *The Hindu*, 18 June and 20 June 2010). Both regretted that agriculture had been growing at a rate of only about 2 per cent per annum, as against the target of 4 per cent per annum set in the Eleventh Plan, and both spoke of the need to raise the growth rate. The estimates made by Bhalla and Singh (Bhalla and Singh, 2009) of the annual compound growth rate of value of agricultural output show this as having increased at the rate of 3.37 per cent per annum in 1990–3 over 1980–3, but at only 1.74 per cent in 2003–06 over 1990–3. Panagariya (Panagariya, 2008) has more bullish estimates but still shows the agricultural growth rate in 2000–2006 as having been lower than in the period 1951–65. The noted agricultural economist A. Vaidyanathan argues, however, that '[r]igorous statistical tests on official time series do not provide strong corroboration of a progressive deceleration of agricultural growth' (Vaidyanathan, 2006, p. 4011). But he points out as well that these data also show that the average of annual changes in total output, area and yields are lower, and much more volatile, over the fifteen years after 1989 than they were in the preceding period of twenty years. The problems of the agricultural economy over the recent past are strongly attested, quite apart from the evidence that is found in the apparently increased incidence of suicides amongst farmers (for a qualified view of which see Gruere and Sengupta, 2011).

What seems to have happened is that the productivity gains of the green revolution were pretty much exhausted before the end of the 1980s, with yield levels having reached a plateau, while the costs of cultivation continued to climb. This was, in part, because of the necessity for farmers to use increasing amounts of increasingly costly and increasingly ineffective plant protection chemicals, and fertilizers, while in major areas of agriculture dependent upon groundwater irrigation rapidly retreating water tables also increased the costs of cultivation (Harriss-White and Janakarajan, 2004). Public investment in agricultural infrastructure and research had declined (Ramachandran and Rawal, 2010), and alongside it, private investments as well (they have generally gone in tandem with public investments). Neither the earlier mode of state intervention in agriculture, however, nor the more recent liberalization policies, effectively addresses fundamental problems having to do with the inefficient and often wasteful use of agricultural resources – including the failure to use irrigation water efficiently, partly because of neglect of the maintenance of irrigation structures and limitations of their design; excessive use of chemical fertilizers; and degradation of soils. There is a long history of poor use of key agricultural resources in India, by comparison with China and elsewhere in East Asia. This was a theme developed years ago by Myrdal in his monumental *Asian Drama* (Myrdal, 1968). In the early 1950s, Myrdal showed, the overall productivity of agriculture (in relation to land) was roughly twice as high in China as in India – and it remains so still. In 1999–2000 yields of rice per hectare in China stood at 4.1 tonnes, while in India they were just under 2 tonnes (and still only 2.1 tonnes in 2009–10). The problems of agricultural productivity are connected with institutional weaknesses, as in irrigation management – which is also generally much more efficient in East Asia – and in credit and marketing organization, that are in turn compounded 'by government policies for [subsidized] pricing of water, electricity, fertilizers and credit which induce demand growth far in excess of available supplies ... and encourage inefficient use of scarce agricultural resources' (Vaidyanathan, 2006, p. 4013, see also Harriss-White and Janakarajan, 2004). And, it should be added, disproportionately benefit wealthier farmers in richer states such as Punjab, Haryana and Andhra Pradesh. Tackling such problems calls for more than just increasing public investment (see also Vaidyanathan, 2010, chapters 4 and 5).

How important, then, is agrarian power now, in accounting for the problems of agricultural productivity? How has the agrarian structure of India changed over the last quarter-century since the publication of *APAP*? A starting point in answering these questions is in the following three (interlocking) propositions (after Harriss, 2010, p. 144–7):

1 The differentiation and polarization of peasant classes has nearly frozen;

2 Land is no longer so important as the basis of status and power (exactly as Herring suggested in *APAP*) and neither does it serve to limit the livelihood possibilities of the poor;

3 The poor have loosened ties of dependence but exercise little leverage over the political space.

Some of those who contributed to the 'mode of production' debate of the 1970s thought that the differentiation of peasant classes – towards the establishment of an agrarian capitalist class and a substantial rural proletariat – was proceeding apace, but with the advantage of hindsight it is clear that Byres' argument that what was taking place was rather 'partial proletarianization', with small and marginal producers continuing to reproduce themselves, was substantially correct (Byres, 1981). The Indian agricultural economy is still characterized by extensive small-scale, household-based production. The distribution both of ownership and of operational holdings is distinctly pear-shaped, and what are described as 'marginal' operated holdings (of one hectare, or less, in extent) now account for 70 per cent of the total. Most such holdings are unlikely to be capable of 'providing enough work or income to be the main livelihood of the household' (Hazell, Poulton, Wiggins and Dorward, 2007, p. 1). The point is proven in findings of the Foundation for Agrarian Studies from village surveys in Andhra Pradesh, Uttar Pradesh and Maharashtra that it was virtually impossible in 2005–06 for households with operational holdings of two hectares of land or less (who account for all but a small share of all the cultivators in the country), to earn an income sufficient for family survival. The net annual incomes from crop production of very many households were actually negative (Ramachandran and Rawal, 2010). Household reproduction takes place now as a result of migration (both rural-urban and rural-rural, and short-term and long-term), of the remittances associated with it, and of increasing employment outside agriculture but still within the rural economy (though the levels of such employment have not grown very strongly in the recent past, and much of it probably is driven by distress). Some estimates suggest that there may be as many as 100 million migrant workers in the country, though a more reliable estimate from the National Commission on Enterprises in the Unorganised Sector is that the number of seasonal migrants is of the order of 30 million. As Bernstein has argued, more generally, the dominance of capital today is no longer expressed in 'classic' capital-labour relations. There are, he suggests, 'classes of labour' pursuing their reproduction 'through insecure and oppressive – and typically increasingly insecure – wage employment and/or a range of likewise precarious small-scale and insecure '"informal sector" ("survival") activity, including farming' (Bernstein 2008, cited by Lerche, 2010, p. 65).

The differentiation and polarization of peasant classes has, therefore, nearly frozen. Estimations made by Vikas Rawal (Rawal, 2008), using data from the 59th round of the National Sample Survey (NSS) for 2003–4 show that 31 per cent of rural households across the country as a whole own no land at all, and another 30 per cent own less than 0.4 hectare (or about one acre of land), while only a little over 5 per cent of households own more than three hectares (and just 0.52 per cent own more than ten). Still, the absolute numbers and the relative share in the rural population of households without land – which have for long been considerable – have been increasing, so differentiation has not quite frozen. The data from 2003–04 are not strictly comparable with those from an earlier round of the NSS, for 1992, but Rawal suggests that they show an increase of as much as six percentage points in landlessness, while inequality in land ownership also increased. Over most of the country, however, 'landlordism', as I defined it earlier, has unquestionably declined. The share of leased-in land in the total operated area, according to the NSS, declined from only 10.7 per cent in 1960-61 to just 6.5 per cent in the *kharif* (summer) season of 2002–03. Traces of classic landlordism remain, however. The dependence of very many in the rural economy upon borrowing money at usurious rates of interest has almost certainly increased again in recent years, as a result of financial liberalization (Ramachandran and Rawal, 2010), and those who are able to secure surplus product can still make speculative trading profits. Inequality in land ownership still gives considerable power locally – economic, social and political – to the relatively small numbers of larger landowners and the increasing numbers of capitalist farmers. How, then, can I argue that 'land is no longer so important as the basis of status and power'?

The proposition should certainly not be overestimated, but there is now a strong tendency for rural power-holders to invest outside agriculture, and in education, sometimes so as to secure employment in the public sector (see, for example Rutten, 1995 on the former, and Jeffrey, Jeffery and Jeffery 2008, on the latter). In other cases, as the profitability of agriculture has declined, or as a result of the ways in which members of landowning higher castes have sought to secure their continuing status distinction, there has been a tendency for them to move out of agriculture (Mayer, 1996 and Harriss, 2006 on the former and Gidwani, 2000 on the latter). Alongside these developments has come about the emergence of a new and very different generation of local leaders, as Krishna (Krishna, 2003) has explained with regard to rural Rajasthan, from amongst the educated but often unemployed younger men, including some from a *dalit* background. The class power of rich farmers coming mainly from upper-middle castes appears to have declined significantly since the Rudolphs wrote about it (using their terminology of 'bullock capitalists') in *APAP*. 'Farmers movements' that strongly represented the interests of the most intensively commercialized producers became a major factor in Indian politics in the 1980s (Brass, ed., 1995), but have declined substantially since the early 1990s. The fact that they are so divided, notably over reactions to the globalization of the Indian economy – supported by the Shetkari Sanghatana, one of the biggest farmers' organizations, and vehemently opposed by others, especially by the Karnataka Rajya Raitha Sangha (KRRS), which has been a darling of the anti-globalization movement internationally – does not help their case.

Jonathan Pattenden, from a village study of the KRRS, has shown that all the conditions that had been conducive to KRRS mobilizations in the 1980s started to break down by the middle of the 1990s. The intensification of commercial agriculture had created circumstances that provided for cross-class mobilization, and the burying of caste and class differences, for the time-being, by conflict between the peasantry generally, and the local state and merchants. At the same time the profitability of agriculture made available resources – notably of time, for richer peasants – for engaging in mobilization activity. The decline in the profitability of agriculture changed all of this. Non-agricultural activities and incomes became much more important and those more influential people who had been the local leaders of the KRRS became interested rather in 'gatekeeping activities' – roles in which they mediate between other people and the state, and are able to use these roles to secure resources for themselves (for example, from the allocation of ration cards). The significance of such roles – and the opportunities opened up by them – have been enhanced by political decentralization through *panchayati raj* and increasing political competition. In sum: '[t]he sense of togetherness that had accompanied the KRRS's rise had been replaced by a growing social fragmentation with people "looking after themselves"' (Pattenden, 2005, p. 1982). I would add that this account of changes that have taken place in rural Karnataka substantiates my point that land in itself is no longer so much the basis of power and status.

The collective class power of the rich peasantry/big farmers of India has diminished over the last two decades, therefore, while the ties of dependence upon them of poorer people, usually from lower castes, have unquestionably been weakened. Empirical examples of this come from village studies in the very diverse settings of Tamil Nadu, where *Dalit* labourers are no longer dependent in the way they were thirty years ago on the dominant landowners, and real wages for agricultural labour have at last broken through long-running stasis (Harriss *et al.*, 2010), and Bihar. In the latter case Singh concludes from his village study that: '[t]he importance of land as a factor of livelihood and dominance is decreasing and other factors of production are becoming more important ... more and more people are losing interest in village affairs. The urge to dominate over the lower castes always had a political-economic angle, and once the locus of the economy has partially shifted away from the village, the tendency to dominate is beginning to wither away' (Singh, 2005, p. 3173). Reports of the local impact of what is now called the Mahatma Gandhi

National Rural Employment Guarantee Scheme, that gives rural people the right to up to 100 days of employment in public works, further underline these points. Even if a significant share of the public resources devoted to the scheme are diverted through corruption, the fact of the right to and of the availability of such employment contributes significantly to the countervailing power of labour, and can push up rural wages (e.g., Harriss, Jeyaranjan and Nagaraj, 2010). In some cases this may have a negative impact, of course, on agricultural production and productivity because it can lead farmers to take land out of cultivation. Still, it is quite clear that local agrarian power is not what it was at the time when Meghnad and his colleagues of SAPE 1 met to discuss and to write about agrarian power and agricultural productivity.

But there is still a link between agrarian power, much modified though it now is, as a result of the changes that have taken place in India's economy, polity and society, and agricultural productivity. The fundamental problems, across the country as a whole, of the wasteful and inefficient use of agricultural resources, that I referred to earlier, do substantially reflect the continuing political weight of the 'farm lobby', diminished though it may be. Successive governments, nationally and at state level, have continued to find it extremely difficult to reduce the burden of subsidies that, as Vaidyanathan put (Vaidyanathan, 2006), 'encourage inefficient use of scarce agricultural resources'. Those who are locally powerful continue to manipulate, for example, the use of irrigation water, and the management of irrigation structures in ways that are wasteful and inefficient. The paradox (as it seems) that agrarian power undermines agricultural productivity remains, in this way, as powerful as ever it was.

Is there, then, still a case for redistributive land reform? The major left parties, the most important of them being the Communist Party of India (Marxist) (CPI(M)), and the (now banned) Communist Party of India (Maoist) (CPI(Maoist)), all continue to advocate the case for such 'land to the tiller' reforms. The CPI(M) argues in its current programme that the first task of a People's Democratic government in regard to agriculture remains to '[a]bolish landlordism by implementing radical land reforms and give land free of cost to the agricultural labourers and poor peasants'. The CPI(Maoist) – hostile to the CPI(M) though it is – argues in its *Party Programme* that the 'principal contradiction' in India remains that 'between feudalism and the broad masses of the people'. The central class contradiction in India, that must be resolved in order to bring about progressive social change, beneficial to the majority, is that between landlords and the mass of the peasantry. In support of this argument the *Programme* advances the following:

Despite the hoax of all land reforms, 30% of the total land is concentrated in the hands of landlords, who constitute only 5% of the population, while middle peasantry constitute about 20% of the rural population, whereas rich peasantry constitutes 10%. 65% of the total peasantry are landless and poor peasants, who own either no land at all or meager land. Extreme forms of semi-feudal exploitation are still prevalent in the countryside. The major prevailing forms of such exploitation are extortion of their produce through share-cropping, which is robbing them of their produce up to 50%, bonded labour, usurious and merchant capital and other forms of extra-economic coercion.

Consequently one of the primary tasks of the new people's democratic state, to be established by revolution, will be to 'confiscate all land belonging to the landlords and religious institutions and [to] redistribute it among the landless poor peasants and agricultural labourers on the slogan of "land to the tillers"'.

Vikas Rawal, from his study of household level data from the 48th and 59th rounds (Rawal, 1992 and 2003–04) of the National Sample Survey, on landholdings – and whose calculations, cited above, on the distribution of ownership holdings, lend support to some of the figures given by the CPI(Maoist) – provides a careful argument to show that there is still a potential for redistribution, even after decades in which there has been an enormous amount of subdivision of holdings (as Geof Wood has described from Bihar, personal communication). Rawal provides 'ballpark estimates', on the basis of the admittedly crude assumption of a uniform ceiling on ownership holdings of twenty acres, to show that 'there is about 15 million acres of ceiling surplus land in India'. As he goes on to say 'this is more than three times the total amount of land that has ever been redistributed under land reform programmes in all states' (Rawal, 2008, p. 47). This is not to say that there is a large potential for redistribution, given the fact that only a very small proportion of agricultural land in India has been redistributed hitherto, but still, it goes to lend weight to Michael Lipton's conclusion in his recent comprehensive restatement of the case for land reform, that '[i]n South Asia, still containing half the world's poor, 10 ha is in most countries a large owned farm [and] *there is scope for some further land reform*, but land shortage and growing [though still, surely, seriously inadequate – JH] non-farm work opportunities may largely limit it to creating tiny "home-gardens" for increasingly part-time rural farmers' (Lipton, 2009, p. 9, emphasis added).

Case there may be, for continuing to press for redistributive land reform, but there is little sign of political mobilization to make claims for it, even on the part of the CPI(M) which has been responsible for such success as there has been in India in bringing about reform, in its two bastions of Kerala and West Bengal. And now the CPI(Maoist), whilst it continues to hold to the programmatic statements cited earlier, appears in practice to have shifted its focus to struggles over the dispossession of especially tribal people in Central India, to make way for infrastructural, industrial and mining projects (Harriss, 2011). Susanne Rudolph's conclusion in *APAP* that 'the case for altering the power structure [presumably, through land reform, JH] has to rest mainly on political and equity grounds' might actually be amended, because land reform would contribute to weakening the influence of the 'farm lobby' that is partly responsible for the persistence of conditions in India that undermine agricultural productivity. There is no indication, however, that the case has any real political traction. Agrarian power will finally be reduced rather by the development of the non-agricultural economy, by the opening up of more employment opportunities outside agriculture (the lack of which is the great limitation of India's remarkable economic growth of recent years), and by the deepening of substantive democracy as decentralized democratic institutions become more powerful.

Times have changed since *APAP* was written, on the cusp of major transformations in the Indian economy, which it did not – of course, and understandably – anticipate. But still, its assessments of the trends in the agricultural economy at the time it was written, and of changes in agrarian relations, were in many ways remarkably prescient.

References

Bhaduri, A., 1973. Agricultural backwardness under semi-feudalism. *The Economic Journal*, LXXXIII.

Bhalla, G.S. and Singh, G., 2009. Economic liberalisation and Indian agriculture: a statewise analysis. *Economic and Political Weekly*, 44(52), pp. 34–44.

Bharadwaj, K., 1974. *Production conditions in Indian agriculture*. Cambridge: Cambridge University Press.

Bharadwaj, K., 1985. A view on commercialisation in Indian agriculture and the development of capitalism. *Journal of Peasant Studies*, 12(1), pp. 7–25.

Brass, T., ed., 1995. *New farmers' movements in India*. London: Frank Cass.

Byres, T.J., 1981. The new technology, class formation and class action in the Indian countryside. *Journal of Peasant Studies*, 8(4), pp. 405–54.

Corbridge, S. and Harriss, J., 2000. *Reinventing India: liberalization, Hindu nationalism and popular democracy*. Cambridge: Polity Press.

Desai, M., 1984. 'Power and Agrarian Relations Some Concepts and Measurements', in M. Desai et al (eds.) *Agrarian Power and Agricultural Productivity in South Asia*. Delhi: Oxford University Press.

Desai, M., 1989. *Lenin's economic writings*, London: Lawrence & Wishart.

Desai, M., Rudolph, S.H., and Rudra, A., eds., 1984. *Agrarian power and agricultural productivity in South Asia*. Delhi: Oxford University Press.

Gidwani, V., 2000. Laboured landscapes: agroecological change in central Gujarat, India. In: A. Agarwal and K. Sivaramakrishnan, eds. *Agrarian environments: resources, representations and rule in India*. Durham: Duke University Press, pp. 216–47.

Gruère, G. and Sengupta, D., 2011. Bt cotton and farmers' suicides in India. *Journal of Development Studies*, 47(2), pp. 316–37.

Harriss, J., 1980. Contemporary Marxist analysis of the agrarian question in India. Madras Institute of Development Studies, Working Paper 14. Madras: MIDS.

Harriss, J., ed., 1982. *Rural development: theories of peasant economy and agrarian change*. London: Hutchinson.

Harriss, J., 2006. Postscript: North Arcot papers. In: J. Harriss, ed. *Power matters: essays on politics, institutions and society in India*. Delhi: Oxford University Press.

Harriss, J., 2010. Class and politics. In: N.G. Jayal and P.B. Mehta, eds. *The Oxford Companion to Politics in India*. Delhi: Oxford University Press.

Harriss, J., Jeyaranjan, J., and Nagaraj, K., 2010. Land, labour and caste politics in rural Tamil Nadu in the twentieth century, Iruvelpattu 1916–2008. *Economic and Political Weekly*, 45(31), pp. 47–61.

Harriss, J., 2011. 'What is going on in India's "red corridor"? Questions about India's Maoist insurgency', *Pacific Affairs*, Vol.84, No.2, pp. 307–325.

Harriss-White, B. and Janakarajan, S., eds., 2004. *Rural India faces the 21st century*. London: Anthem Press.

Hazell, P., Poulton, C., Wiggins, S., and Dorward, A., 2007. *The future of small farms for poverty reduction and growth*. Washington: International Food Policy Research Institute.

Herring, R., 1984. Economic consequences of local power configurations in rural South Asia. In: M. Desai, Rudolph, S. and Rudra, A eds. *Agrarian power and agricultural productivity in South Asia*. Berkeley: University of California Press.

Hodgson, G., 2001. *How economics forgot history: the problem of historical specificity in social science*. London: Routledge.

Jeffrey, C., Jeffery, R., and Jeffery, P., 2008. *Degrees without freedom: education, masculinities and unemployment in North India*. Stanford: Stanford California Press.

Kenny, C. and Williams, D., 2001. What do we know about economic growth? Or, why don't we know very much? *World Development*, 29(1), pp. 1–22.

Kohli, A., 2006. Politics of economic growth, 1980–2005. *Economic and Political Weekly* 41(13) and (14), pp. 1251–59, and 1361–70.

Krishna, A., 2003. What is happening to caste? A view from some North Indian villages. *Journal of Asian Studies*, 62(4), pp. 1171–94.

Lenin, V.I., 1899. *The development of capitalism in Russia*. In: *Collected works*, Vol.3. London: Lawrence & Wishart (1960).

Lerche, J., 2010. From "rural labour" to "classes of labour": class fragmentation, caste and class struggle at the bottom of the Indian labour hierarchy. In: B. Harriss-White and J. Heyer, eds. *The comparative political economy of development*. London and New York: Routledge.

Lipton, M., with Longhurst, R., 1989. *New seeds and poor people*. Baltimore, MD: Johns Hopkins University Press.

Lipton, M., 2009. *Land reform in developing countries: property rights and property wrongs*. London and New York: Routledge.

Mayer, A., 1996. Caste in an Indian village: change and continuity, 1954–1992. In: C. Fuller, ed. *Caste Today*. Delhi: Oxford University Press, pp. 32–64.

Myrdal, G., 1968. *Asian drama: an inquiry into the poverty of nations*. New York: Twentieth Century Fund.

Panagariya, A., 2008. *India: the emerging giant*. New York: Oxford University Press.

Pattenden, J., 2005. Trickle-down solidarity, globalisation and dynamics of social transformation in a South Indian village. *Economic and Political Weekly*, 40(19), pp. 1975–85.

Ramachandran, V.K. and Rawal, V., 2010. The impact of liberalisation and globalisation on India's agrarian economy. *Global Labour Journal*, 1(1), pp. 56–91. Available at: www.digitalcommons.mcmaster.ca [accessed 30 June 2011].

Rawal, V., 2008. Ownership holdings of land in rural India: putting the record straight. *Economic and Political Weekly*, March 8, 2008, pp. 43–47.

Rudolph, S., 1984. Introduction. In M. Desai *et al.* (eds.) *Agrarian Power and Agricultural Productivity in South Asia*. Delhi: Oxford University Press.

Rutten, M., 1995. *Farms and factories: social profile of large farmers and rural industrialists in Western India*. Delhi: Oxford University Press.

Singh, S.B., 2005. Limits to power: Naxalism and caste relations in a South Bihar village. *Economic and Political Weekly*, XL(29), pp. 3167–75.

Thorner, D., 1956. *The agrarian prospect in India*. Delhi School of Economics: University Press.

Vaidyanathan, A., 2006. Farmers' suicides and the agrarian crisis. *Economic and Political Weekly*, September 23, 2006, pp. 4009–13.

Vaidyanathan, A., 2010. *Agricultural growth in India: role of technology, incentives and institutions*. Delhi: Oxford University Press.

Woolcock, M., Szreter, S., and Rao, V., 2011. How and why does history matter for development policy. *Journal of Development Studies*, 47(1), pp. 70–96.

7

Disability and Human Development[*]

Mozaffar Qizilbash

Introduction

The notion of human development has significantly altered and influenced the landscape of contemporary development thought. With its roots in the philosophical writings of Aristotle, Marx and Kant (amongst others), the idea has led to a significant conceptual shift away from a focus on material progress in development thinking towards one on human beings, seen as ends in themselves and not merely as means (Qizilbash, 2006c). In the history of development economics, the human development approach emerged from a range of different strands – including the work of the basic needs school (Streeten with Burqi, Haq, Hicks, Stewart, 1981) and Amartya Sen's writings on development conceived as 'capability expansion' (Sen, 1984, 1988 and 1999). Importantly, it was championed by Mahbub ul Haq at the United Nations Development Programme (UNDP) who led work on the *Human Development Reports* in the early 1990s. With contributions from Meghnad Desai and others – notably Sen – these reports introduced a series of measures of development. Desai's classic 1991 paper 'Human Development: Concept and Measurement' presents the initial formulation of the human development index (HDI) which has proven to be very influential. Over time these reports accommodated a wide range of issues, such as gender and sustainability, to show the relevance of the idea of human development to a variety of issues, underlining the point that the idea of human development involves a *paradigm* shift in development work. Desai has also made further important (if perhaps less well-known) contributions to this work (see, for example, Desai, 1995a and 1995b).

Recent work on disability and development has emerged somewhat independently of the contributions of the human development school. Writers in this literature have noted that there are clear links between research on

[*]A very early version of this paper was presented at the International Conference of the Human Development and Capability Association (HDCA), Groningen, 29 August-1 September 2006. My work on it began when I was visiting the Department of Philosophy at Harvard University in the Spring of that year. I am grateful to Sabina Alkire, Amartya Sen and Shelley Weiner for making that visit possible and for their help and support while I was at Harvard. I also thank Amartya Sen and participants at the HDCA conference for comments relating to the subject of this paper. I also thank Polly Vizard for her help and guidance. Any error is mine.

human development and disability while at the same time observing that the human development literature has not gone far in championing the cause of the disabled in the way that it has championed gender justice (Harriss-White, 1996 and Baylies, 2002). This is in spite of the fact that some of those working in the field of human development – including Sen and Martha Nussbaum – have engaged seriously with disability issues, especially in the fast-growing literature on the capability approach (see Comim, Qizilbash and Alkire, 2008). The chief purpose of this contribution is to make and explore a series of inter-connected claims. These claims are that: the human development approach provides a strong conceptual foundation for work on disability; recent works on capability and disability show that amongst the family of views which endorse the human development approach, the capability approach has significant strengths in addressing disability issues; work on human development can thus make a significant contribution to advancing justice for the disabled, and in particular there is scope for further advocacy in the *Human Development Reports*, which might include the publication of more extensive data, and the development of new measures which might to some degree capture the situation of the disabled in various countries.

This chapter is organized as follows: section 1 focuses on the relationship between disability and development; Sen's and Nussbaum's works on capability and disability are discussed in section 2; further conceptual issues about the relationship between capability and disability (notably the location of the capability approach in relation to the so-called 'individual' and 'social' models of disability) are discussed in section 3; some implications relating to data and various approaches to measurement are discussed in section 4; and section 5 concludes.

Development and disability

Both 'development' and 'disability' can be defined in a variety of ways. While conceptual issues relating to 'disability' and 'impairment' are discussed later in this paper, I start out with the following rough definitions: disability is a loss of ability or opportunity of some form which results from impairment. Impairment in turn involves some form of failure of bodily or mental function. Definitions of 'development' have multiplied over the years, but in this chapter I shall focus on 'human development'. The idea of human development emerged from a concern that development economics had grown so concerned with the expansion of per capita income that they had forgotten the human beings whom such an expansion should benefit. Its emergence in modern times has its roots in the work of the basic needs school which argued for the priority of meeting basic human needs in developing countries and Sen's writings which defined development as an expansion of 'capability' (Sen, 1988, 1990 and 1999). 'Capability' refers to what a person can be or do, the combinations of valued 'beings' and 'doings' or 'functionings' open to her and from which she can choose. Again the focus is on *people*. Indeed it is this focus, and an acceptance that people are the ends of development and not just the means to higher levels of per capita income which is the hallmark of the human development paradigm (Desai, 1991, Haq, 1995 and Sen, 2006a).

Since the human development paradigm is endorsed by a wide range of thinkers – including those who advocate the priority of basic needs and others who favour the capability approach – it is clear that there is no one unified 'human development view' but rather a family of views. Amongst this family of views two strands can be distinguished. One focuses narrowly on giving priority to meeting basic needs, and for that reason is not necessarily concerned with equality as a goal (Streeten et al, 1981). The other sees development in terms of improvement of the quality of human lives which is equitable or just (Qizilbash, 1996a, 1996b and 2006c). I refer to these two views as the 'narrow' and 'broad' versions of the human development paradigm. In this paper, I shall take the second of these views to be the approach which most closely approximates the notion of human development advanced in the UNDP's *Human Development Reports*, though the narrow version still no doubt has its adherents.

Even on this rather limited description of some of the views which endorse the human development paradigm, it is clear that these views are attractive for anyone concerned with incorporating disability issues within a development framework. First and foremost, the human development paradigm does not see human beings as merely the means of expanding production. It would not thus merely value them in terms of their productive capacity. Nor would it value the social loss to society from impairments and disabilities exclusively in terms of the loss of income or output measured in monetary terms. Even though there are significant losses from impairment and disability which can be measured in terms of the value of losses of output, so that – as Barbara Harriss-White notes – even traditional cost-benefit analysis supports community-based rehabilitation schemes (Harriss-White, 1996, p. 26), a framework which focuses on monetary gains and losses alone seems to be inadequate. Because the human development approach treats people as ends in themselves, it can provide a basis for a concern for, and action to ameliorate, the well-being of people with impairments even in the absence of any monetary gain from rehabilitation.

The link between the human development approach and disability here is not accidental but goes to the very heart of how we think about development. Indeed, in her path-breaking paper on the political economy of disability in India, Harriss-White (1996) also struggles with how to *define* development. Having noted that 'disability is a relative term because cultures define differently their norms of being and doing', she goes on to say that '[d]evelopment can be seen as a liberation from such social disabilities and from the systems of technology, reason and value producing them' (Harriss-White, 1996, p. 3). It is hard here to fail to see that if development is seen as an expansion of capability, a liberation from disability can be seen to *constitute* development irrespective of any further effect on output and indeed any cost-benefit calculation. Thus, it is natural to use some version of the capability approach to address disability. However, Harriss-White's attempt to conceptualise development in the context of disability also provides a case for the human development approach more broadly. Harriss-White sees standard assumptions made in economic evaluation to be part of a 'technocratized policy discourse [which] is actually the product of a set of values expressing a polity where economic productivity, measurable or imputable in monetary terms, is positioned in first place as a criterion for allocation' (Harriss-White, 1996, p. 14). One must conclude that – on Harriss-White's account – standard approaches to economic evaluation form part of the 'systems of technology, reason and value' which produce 'social disabilities'. The human development paradigm may – as I have suggested – in fact better address issues relating to impairment and disability because the notion of human development does not position economic productivity in 'first place as a criterion for allocation'. Beginning from an account of human development thus appears to have a great deal to offer.

While the arguments just made suggest that the human development paradigm has a great deal to offer, and suggest in particular that the capability approach may prove to be insightful in the context of disability, the distinction between narrow and broad views within the human development paradigm has not been used thus far in making central claims in its favour. If one takes a broad view of human development which incorporates a concern for justice, clearly the human development paradigm has more to offer as regards some standard concerns relating to disability. Indeed, both rights and participation have been central to advocacy relating to disability, and the human development literature has extensively engaged with each of these (UNDP, 1993 and 2000; and Nussbaum, 2000 *inter alia*). Ironically, it is precisely because some previous *Human Development Reports* do engage with these ideas that Carolyn Baylies (Baylies, 2002, p. 731–2) articulates a certain disappointment that the issue of disability has not received more attention in previous *Reports* – for example in the 2000 *Human Development Report* which is centrally concerned with rights.[1] Baylies also articulates a concern about one specific version of the capability approach – Martha Nussbaum's – which involves a specific list of capabilities. Baylies writes that: '[i]f it is, indeed, the case, as she seems to suggest, that each of the items on her list of functionings and capabilities is deemed essential to the living of a human life or a good human life, this framework could be read as leaving people with impairments as not human at all' (Baylies, 2002, p. 733). The fear then is that if some human functions are seen as necessary for human life – or a good human life – on the capability approach, this approach will exacerbate what Baylies sees as an already dangerous tendency which involves seeing disabled people as not entirely human. This version of the capability approach would then potentially marginalize the disabled. To consider this issue, I now discuss the capability approach in more detail.

Capability and disability I: Sen and Nussbaum

There are now a number of versions of the capability approach and I begin with Amartya Sen's formulation of it. As we have seen, the approach conceives of development as capability expansion. It also sees poverty as 'basic capability failure' – that is, a failure to achieve certain crucially important functionings up to certain minimally adequate levels (Sen, 1993, pp. 40–1). Finally, egalitarian justice is conceived in terms of 'equality of capability' (Sen, 1992). Sen's arguments for the relevance of capability as a 'space' for evaluating individual advantage and justice have often invoked examples involving the disabled from his earliest writings on capability, going back to his lecture on 'Equality of What?' (reprinted in Sen, 1982). In that lecture and in his subsequent writings Sen has argued that certain influential positions in moral philosophy – including utilitarianism and John Rawls' theory of justice – do not adequately take account of human diversity. In the case of utilitarianism, the goal is, typically, to maximize the sum or average of 'utility' (whether this is understood in terms of desire satisfaction, pleasure or happiness). Sen argues that focusing on utility alone can be misleading. His original discussion of this issue in 'Equality of What?' is concerned with egalitarian justice where, on Sen's reading, utilitarianism implies equality of *marginal* utility (i.e. the extra utility from an additional unit of some commodity or of income). He convincingly argues that in the case of a 'cripple' who is not as good at converting income into utility (at the margin) as a 'pleasure wizard', utilitarianism would give more income to the pleasure wizard. Furthermore, it may also be the case that the cripple has no disadvantage in relation to the able-bodied in terms of his level of *total* utility. Sen writes that the cripple may be quite well-off in terms of utility because:

> he has a jolly disposition. Or because he has a low aspiration level and his heart leaps whenever he sees a rainbow in the sky. Or because he is religious and believes that he will be rewarded in the after-life, or cheerfully accepts what he takes to be just penalty for misdeeds in a past incarnation. (Sen, 1982, p. 367)

This argument encapsulates one of Sen's fundamental worries about utilitarianism because it potentially undermines the very idea that utility is invariably a sensible basis for evaluating a person's well-being or quality of life (see also Sen, 1992, pp. 28–9). Sen's discussion also addresses Rawls' account of justice. In that account (Rawls, 1971, p. 93) egalitarian claims are judged in terms of an index of (social) 'primary goods', where these were originally conceived of as 'all purpose means' – goods one would desire whatever one's life plan. In later versions of his theory, Rawls (1993) conceives of these goods in terms of the needs of equal citizens, where citizens are equal in having two moral powers – which are the capacities to form and pursue a conception of the good and to have a conception of justice.[2] He also provides a list of primary goods, which includes: income and wealth; the social bases of self-respect; powers and prerogatives of offices and positions of responsibility in the political and economic institutions of the basic structure of society; freedom of movement and free choice of occupation against a background of diverse opportunities; and basic rights and liberties (also given by a list) (Rawls, 1993, p. 181). Sen's most basic claim in relation to this view is that a primary goods index will be insensitive to the differential rates at which people convert such goods into the objects they ultimately value. A disabled person may, for example, need more in terms of some primary goods than an able-bodied person to be able to do certain basic things (such as move around). Primary goods are explicitly conceived of as means in Rawls' theory, not as ends, and if it is what one is actually able to do with these goods which is fundamental, then evaluating individual advantage in terms of primary goods is likely to be inadequate when it comes to judging egalitarian claims. Sen argues that Rawls' account is for this reason no better than utilitarian accounts when it comes to evaluating the claims of the disabled (see for example, Sen, 1982, pp. 366–7; and 1992, pp. 28–9 and 79–84; 2009, pp. 258–262; and Brighouse and Robeyns, 2010). It is the failure of these various accounts to address the case of the disabled and, more generally to allow for human diversity, which led Sen to advance the notion 'basic capabilities equality' in 'Equality of What?' and subsequently to espouse 'capability equality'. So the motivation for pursuing the idea of capability relates to concerns about disability from the very outset. In the subsequent literature (e.g. Cohen, 1993, p. 63) this is taken to be a significant strength of the capability approach over rival views of justice.

It is worth noting, nonetheless, that Sen's example of the 'cripple' who might have a high level of utility may not be especially attractive to the disabled themselves. David Wasserman makes this point. He suggests that the challenge that disability poses for theories of justice has recently been framed in a way that is congenial to disability scholars and activists in part *because* it no longer invokes 'the fictional "happy cripple," Tiny Tim, resolutely euphoric in his impairment, illness and poverty' (Wasserman, 2005, p. 215). Inevitably Wasserman goes on to note that one of the reasons why the capability approach might not be congenial to people with disabilities is that 'Sen invokes Tiny Tim's euphoria in arguing that subjective welfare provides an inappropriate metric for equality and an inadequate conception of well-being, thereby treating the contentment of a crippled child as presumptively suspect' (Wasserman, 2005,

p. 220). Sen's argument about the ability of the disabled to find contentment in the face of disadvantage is, nonetheless, part of a broader strategy which raises worries about 'utility' based views. The suggestion is that if people adapt to unfavourable circumstances and learn to be happy or restrict their desires in these circumstances, then the 'utility' calculus may underestimate their disadvantage. He has now made this argument in a range of contexts including long term unemployment and gender injustice (Sen, 2006b, Qizilbash, 2006a and 2006b *inter alia*). Furthermore, the argument seems to be supported by psychological studies about adaptation, which suggest that the disabled often do adjust to their misfortunes (see Frederick and Lowenstein, 1996, p. 312). So even if Sen's discussion of the 'happy cripple' is not attractively formulated, its significance cannot be underestimated.

Given the central importance of disability in Sen's case in favour of capability as a space of evaluation, it is remarkable that the issue of disability has not been more salient in the human development literature. However, Sen's argument has been explored in various ways in both philosophy and economics. In economics, a number of studies have pursued his claims regarding the difficulties that the disabled may encounter when it comes to converting income into functionings. As Sen (Sen, 2004, p. 3 and 1999, p. 88) has himself noted, the disabled are handicapped vis-à-vis the able-bodied in terms of earnings – what he calls the 'earnings handicap' – but also in terms of the ability to convert 'money into good living' which he refers to as the 'conversion handicap'. Some empirical studies (notably by Burchardt and Zaidi, 2005 and Kuklys, 2005) have focussed on the 'conversion handicap' and shown that a failure to allow for it seriously underestimates the extent of poverty amongst households with disabled members when poverty is measured in income terms. These studies are examples of – what Sen (1999, p. 83) terms – the 'indirect approach' to applying the capability approach, in as much as they focus on income rather than capability itself, but adjust income measures to reflect the different rates at which people convert income into functionings. There are few if any studies which 'directly' apply the capability approach to disability at the empirical level by looking at capability and functionings rather than income. The UNDP's measures of human development, poverty and gender empowerment have used a more direct approach which does not merely look at income but also at direct measures of the quality of life. In this spirit some *Human Development Reports* provide data on the 'proportion of the population with disabilities' (see UNDP, 1997, pp. 176–7). There is, nonetheless, certainly a case for future *Human Development Reports* to provide more comprehensive information on disabilities and impairments and also for further data collection. I pursue this point in section 4.

The philosophical literature has explored issues relating to capability and disability in greater depth than the economics literature. Martha Nussbaum's work on justice, which develops her own version of the capability approach, has taken Sen's arguments further in various ways. However, it is Nussbaum's earlier work which has been most controversial and led to the worry that the capability approach – or at least her version of it – the 'capabilities approach' – may not treat the disabled as altogether human. Nussbaum's earlier writings on capability were informed by, and in some ways constituted, a reading of Aristotle's writings on justice, flourishing and human nature, and are, in that sense, 'neo-Aristotelian' (see especially Nussbaum, 1988 and 1995). On her reading of Aristotle's account of human nature, the exercise of certain functions is characteristic of humanity. The relevant functions are clearly related to Aristotle's view of human beings as rational, political animals. The upshot of this view is that if, for example, an impairment sufficiently compromises someone's mental functioning, the relevant being would no longer be classed as a human being. The argument is not supposed to exclude mere irrationality, but 'people who live without planning and organizing their lives' (Nussbaum, 1995, p. 117). Individuals whose form of life would be so far from the norm as no longer to classify as human might include 'the survivor of a frontal lobotomy' and 'people who suffer from some severe form of mental retardation' (Nussbaum, 1995, p. 117).[3]

This view is echoed in Nussbaum's writings on her capabilities approach – at least up to *Women and Human Development*. In many of these writings Nussbaum has articulated a detailed list of capabilities, grouped under ten headings: life; bodily health; bodily integrity; senses, imagination and thought; emotions; practical reason; affiliation; other species; play; and control over one's environment (political and material). She suggests that there are two thresholds relevant to the realization of the relevant capabilities. In relation to the lower of these thresholds she writes that 'we may judge that the absence of capability for a central function is so acute that the person is not really a human being at all, or any longer – as in the case of certain very extreme forms of mental disability, or senile dementia' (Nussbaum, 2000, p. 73). It is unsurprising that this view has caused some, like Baylies, to worry that the capabilities approach – and indeed work on human development – may not be a fruitful approach to disability. Certainly people with some serious mental disabilities would not be treated as human at all.

In her more recent discussion of disability in *Frontiers of Justice*, Nussbaum (2006) revises and develops her view. A great deal of her discussion of disability in this book is focused on contrasting social contract theories – exemplified by John Ralws' theory of justice – with her capabilities approach. Nussbaum generalizes and develops Sen's critique of Rawls. In doing so she focuses on difficulties in Rawls' treatment of the issue of disability. In Rawls' account: the principles of justice are agreed behind a veil of ignorance; the principles apply to the 'basic structure of society' (i.e. its major institutions etc.); and they cover the distribution of the benefits of cooperation amongst citizens, who have the two 'moral powers'. The difficulty arises with regard to those people who fall short of these powers. The principles of justice are not selected by (or for) such people and relevant issues about disabilities are put off to a later 'legislative stage'. To this degree, the issue of disability is marginalized in Rawls' theory. Nussbaum's major complaint is that this would mean that many disabled people would not qualify as citizens and their concerns would not be addressed in principles of justice which govern major social institutions. Nussbaum focuses on the lives of three disabled individuals: Sesha Kittay, who suffers from congenital cerebral palsy and severe mental retardation; her own nephew Arthur, who suffers from Asperger's syndrome and Tourette's syndrome; and Jamie Beroubé who was born with Down's syndrome. In a marked break from her earlier writings, Nussbaum sees all three as citizens whom any principles of justice must address. Echoing the central concerns of the literature on human development, Nussbaum finds fault with the idea – which she thinks underlies social contract views – that only *productive* members of society can be genuine citizens to whom the principles of justice apply (Nussbaum, 2006, p. 128). Sesha, Arthur and Jamie would certainly not – she thinks – be included as citizens on the basis that they are productive in augmenting social well-being. She notes (Nussbaum, 2006, p. 113) nonetheless that people with impairments are often unproductive, only because of the way in which society is organized. Here her writings echo the so-called 'social model of disability' which I turn to in the next section. Her capabilities approach sees people as ends in themselves. The notion of *dignity* is central to Nussbaum's approach. She claims that 'we do not have to win the respect of others by being productive. We have a claim to support in the dignity of our human need itself' (Nussbaum, 2006, p. 160).

This more recent version of the capabilities approach is informed by the experiences of disabled people and differs from Nussbaum's earlier writings at a number of levels. However, Nussbaum still classifies some people with sufficiently severe impairments as non-human. The chief difference between her earlier and later views relates to how serious the impairment has to be for a person to qualify as non-human. So she writes that:

> We can say of some conditions of being, say a permanent vegetative state of a (former) human being, that this just is not a human life, in any meaningful way, because possibilities of thought, perception, attachment, and so on are irrevocably cut off. (Notice that we do not say this if just one or more of a group of modalities is cut off: we say this only if the entirety of a group of them is cut off. Thus there is a close relation between this threshold and the medical definition of death. And we would not say this if any random one of the capabilities is cut off: it would have to be a group of them, sufficiently significant to constitute the death of anything like a characteristic human life. The person in a persistent vegetative condition and the anencephalic child would be examples.) (Nussbaum, 2006, p. 181)

Nussbaum (2006, p. 432) concedes that this constitutes a significant modification of her earlier view which, she says, 'might have been read to suggest that if any one of the capabilities is totally cut off, the life is no longer a human life'.

This reading of Nussbaum's work shows that her most recent version of the capabilities approach is not as controversial as her earlier writings. It does not suggest that the human development paradigm – which is strongly echoed in her more recent writings with the focus on human beings as ends in themselves and not worthy of respect only on grounds of productivity – must dehumanise people with impairments, even very serious impairments. However, more importantly, it is clear that Sen's and Nussbaum's discussions of this topic operate at different levels of ambition. Nussbaum's goal is to develop the capability approach as a (partial) theory of justice which might provide an alternative to social contract views. Sen's work on *capability* falls well short of attempting to develop such a theory. Even when he extends his own work so that it can be seen as an approach or 'theory' of, or general approach to, justice in *The Idea of Justice* (Sen, 2009, ix) which differs from Rawls' approach on a range of issues (Sen, 2009, especially pp. 52–74) he stresses the fact that the capability approach makes its key contribution by changing the *informational focus* of evaluation and he wishes to distinguish this contribution of the approach from that of other applications of the approach which (might) advance some 'design' for how society should be organized (Sen, 2009, pp. 232). His conceptual framework is nonetheless motivated by concerns relating to the quality of life of the disabled and arguably addresses issues relating to disability more adequately than utilitarian and Rawlsian views. In fact, most of the claims made in favour of the capability approach in the context of disability relevant to this paper are advanced in Sen's version of the approach and do not involve endorsing any view about what it is to be human.

Capability and disability II: individual and social models

While Sen's and Nussbaum's writings on disability have made a significant contribution to the literature on social justice and the evaluation of the quality of life, their work has not seriously engaged with *definitions* of impairment and capability. Recent work by Tania Burchardt and Lorella Terzi has attempted to locate the capability approach in relation to the most influential conceptual models of disability – the so-called 'individual' and 'social' models. One might guess that the underlying concepts advanced in the capability approach – functioning and capability – can indeed be used to mark the distinction between impairment and disability, with the first relating primarily to limitations in functioning and the latter relating to a failure of capability. This hunch is borne out by the recent literature, though – as we shall see – there are significant differences in the ways in which Burchardt and Terzi locate the capability approach in relation to 'individual' and 'social' models.

The 'individual model' sees impairment as the chief cause of disability, and the disadvantage which arises from disability is, for this reason, seen as a matter for the individual rather than society. Because limitations in functioning and participation are seen as part of a medical condition, the emphasis tends to be on rehabilitation. This model informs standard definitions of disability. For example, the International Classification of Impairment, Disability and Handicaps proposed by the World Health Organization (WHO) uses the following distinction between the concepts of impairment, disability and handicap: an impairment is 'an abnormality in the structure of the functioning of the body whether through disease or trauma; disability as referred to the restriction in the ability to perform tasks..., and handicap as referred to the social disadvantage that could be associated with impairment and/or disability' (Terzi, 2004, p. 142). It is worth noting that Nussbaum (2006, pp. 423–4) defines terms along roughly these lines in *Frontiers of Justice*, though she qualifies her delineation of these terms by noting that 'the line between impairment and disability is difficult to draw, particularly when the social context is not held fixed and is up for debate.' So her discussion uses terms which are influenced by the individual model.

The alternative to the individual model – initially outlined by Michael Oliver – is the 'social model' which sees disability as exclusively caused by social constraints. According to this model, impairment involves 'lacking a limb, or having a defective limb, organ or mechanism of the body' and disability is 'the disadvantage or restriction of activity caused by a contemporary social organization which takes no or little account of people who have physical impairments and hence excludes them from participation in the mainstream of social activities' (Terzi, 2004, p. 143). While as we have seen, Nussbaum defines her terms along lines influenced by the individual model, Tania Burchardt's chief goal in her paper on this subject is to suggest that there is significant common ground between the capability approach and the social model. On both, she suggests, a focus on income is inadequate, and will lead to an underestimation of the needs of the disabled (Burchardt, 2004, p. 740). Importantly, furthermore, just as the social model recognizes the importance of social barriers, the capability approach notes the important role of social factors in influencing the transformation of resources or income into a good life. Burchardt also argues that the focus on freedom in the capability approach is a distinctive feature of the approach which is shared by the social model. In particular, the social model rejects the notion of 'normal' functioning, and does not see liberation from disability in terms of 'living a life in conformity to some pre-defined notion of normality' (Burchardt, 2004, p. 742). Finally, as regards the question of identifying which abilities are important, the social model suggests that this is a matter for the disabled, rather than medical experts, to decide (Burchardt, 2004, p. 743). This, of course, might run contrary to Nussbaum's capabilities approach which proposes a list of capabilities in the context of justice for the disabled without any obvious involvement of the impaired. It may be more compatible with Sen's recent writings which suggest that the articulation of such a list is a matter for public debate (Sen, 2005), though I expect that he would be uncomfortable with the idea of excluding the able-bodied from such debate. Nussbaum has also explicitly argued against the idea that there should be a separate list specifically for the disabled (Nussbaum, 2006, pp. 186–190). In short, this is not an issue on which different versions of the capability approach take an unified view. One might add, nonetheless, that – as Burchardt (2004, p. 744) notes – standard issues about adaptation are relevant to this point. If public debate is influenced by an unjust status quo, because people have adapted to their living conditions – then the list which results from such debate might reflect that status quo. This would nonetheless be the case *even if* the debate were restricted to disabled people. Finally, Burchardt (2004, p. 746) sees disability as a form of capability failure, and to this degree sees the capability approach as useful in *defining* disability.

While Burchardt makes a strong case for an overlap between the central concerns of the capability approach and the social model of disability, Lorella Terzi has taken a rather different view criticizing the polarized opposition between the individual and social models in the disability literature while also suggesting that the capability approach offers a way of avoiding this opposition. Terzi's work on this subject begins with a critique of the social model (Terzi, 2004). The social model can certainly be criticised on the grounds that according to it all relevant limitations in one's ability to participate in society are caused by social organization. This view does not recognise any disability which might not be removed by some appropriate change in social arrangements. It offers a very strong contrast to the individual model which entirely locates the causes of disability in individual impairments. The correct approach must lie in between these extremes.

The capability approach has a number of advantages in this context. Firstly, it recognizes the importance of social factors in converting resources into a good life, but at the same time – in Sen's hands – emphasizes the importance of human diversity. Furthermore, while differences in personal characteristics are central to Sen's version of the approach, he does not use the notion of 'normal' functioning – and so does not emphasize the notion of 'abnormality' which is rejected by the social model in discussing disability (Terzi, 2005a, p. 452). Obviously, the fact that the capability approach uses the distinction between functioning and capability also helps to define the distinction between disability and impairment. On Terzi's account – which is influenced by the works of Allen Buchanan and John Perry – impairment relates to the loss of some aspect of functioning, while disability is an inability to perform some significant class of functionings that individuals in some reference group are on average and ordinarily able to do under favourable conditions (Terzi, 2005b, p. 214). On this account, impairment does not imply disability. Disability arises from the interplay between impairment and social conditions. Terzi makes a strong case for the view that a key strength of the capability approach is that it defines a middle ground between the individual and social models. This case is broadly faithful to both Sen's and Nussbaum's writings which show an awareness of both social influences and individual characteristics. For example, Nussbaum stresses the influence of social arrangements on the productivity of the impaired (as we have seen) while also recognizing the importance of individualized treatments and programs (Nussbaum, 2006, pp. 190). This and other strengths of the capability approach which are identified in the recent literature can inform work on human development, including the development of measures which might be used to highlight disability issues.[4]

Some implications for measurement and data collection

Data on disability in developing countries is limited and not necessarily comparable across countries. What data there is suggests that it is a very significant problem which needs to be much more seriously addressed than it has been in development research and policy. It suggests that around three quarters of the impaired live in developing countries (Baylies, 2002, p. 726). It also suggests that the disabled form a significant percentage of the world's (income) poor (Harriss-White and Sridhar, 2006, p. 126). Yet use of one measure of the quality of life which incorporates disability – the so-called Disability Adjusted Life Year – which is sometimes used by the World Bank can discriminate against the disabled by implying that if one had the choice between saving the life of a disabled or an able-bodied person one should save the able-bodied person (Sen, 1997, pp. 216–7).

What contribution can work on human development make to data collection and measurement issues relating to disability? As we have already seen, most existing applications of the capability approach to the issue of disability – at least within economics – focus on income, and adjust income poverty analysis to allow for the differential rates at which income is converted into the ability to lead a good life. There is certainly scope for expanding the range of such studies to developing countries. If such adjusted-measures of income poverty were used, clearly the proportion of poor households that contain a disabled member would rise. But, more importantly, corrections to headcount indices of income poverty at national level would help governments to target poverty better. They would also make poverty reduction policies less 'blind' to disability. This sort of intervention can be made at the level of national *Human Development Reports*.

At the international level, obviously, there is also a strong case for gathering more data – or at least advocating that such data needs to be collected. Such data would be suitable for inclusion and presentation in *Human Development Reports* and would form part of what Mahbub ul Haq (Haq, 1995) referred to as the 'human balance sheet'. Data collection exercises would obviously need to keep the distinction between impairment and disability clearly in mind. As we have already seen, this distinction mirrors the distinction between functioning and capability. Since many impairments are preventable, and since impairment need not imply disability, information is needed on both. A central role of the capability approach would be in helping to *identify* (respectively) the impaired and the disabled. As noted earlier, some previous *Human Development Reports* have reported on the proportion of the population who are disabled. The definition used in these reports (e.g. UNDP, 1997, p. 235) is the WHO definition which respects the distinction between impairment and disability. Nonetheless, worries have been expressed along the lines that relevant data may not clearly distinguish between disability and impairment. As Baylies (Baylies, 2002, p. 726) hints, this might be one reason why sometimes richer countries appear to have a higher proportion of disabled people than poorer nations. Of course, higher rates of age-related impairment in richer countries may be driven by higher life expectancy. However, in these countries it is also less likely that impairments will necessarily translate into disabilities (Baylies, 2002, p. 727).

Much of the impact of recent work on human development, whether in the UNDP reports or in the wider literature, has been made by innovative multi-dimensional measures such as the human development index, as well as various other less well-known measures of poverty and gender-related indices which these reports have introduced. That is the level at which Meghnad Desai has made his most important contributions to this literature. The question naturally arises: if appropriate and comparable international data emerges, is there a case for developing new measures relating to disability? There is a case for developing non-income measures relating to disability and potentially incorporating them in summary statistics presented in *Human Development Reports*. The main success of measures which have emerged from work on human development is that they pick up the misleading nature of income measures. Adjusting such measures is obviously a move in the right direction, but development of more direct measures would be desirable if it were feasible.

There are at least four more 'direct' approaches to developing a measure in the human development tradition which might highlight the issue of disability and at the same time help to monitor progress in relation to disability issues over time across countries. The first of these begins by conceiving of disability as a form of capability failure. The natural implication of this approach is that one would attempt to quantify the 'shortfall' relative to some maximum level which is attainable in various dimensions of capability for a range of different impairments. Shortfalls may be measured relative to a 'below-par' maximal level, reflecting the potential of the impaired as Sen (Sen, 1992, pp. 90–1) suggests may be very tempting. But there are potential dangers with defining a lower maximal level for the impaired. These difficulties lead Nussbaum (Nussbaum, 2006, pp. 188–190) to adopt the same threshold for all irrespective of impairment in her capabilities approach. These suggest that a measure of the 'attainment' of the impaired may sometimes be the better approach even when it is clear that the impaired cannot attain the same level as the able bodied so that an ideal of 'attainment equality' is out of reach (Sen, 1992, 90–91).[5]

A shortfall measure would be – at least in conceptual terms – similar to the UNDP's capability poverty measure (UNDP, 1996), its human poverty index (UNDP, 1997), related indices of capability poverty (Majumdar and Subramanian, 2001 *inter alia*) and more recent measures of multi-dimensional poverty (Alkire and Foster, forthcoming). Because a genuine capability measure would attempt to capture the extent that impairments are disabling and affect what people can do and be, it should be sensitive to changes in the society which lessen the disabling effect of social institutions and environmental factors that can make it easier for those with specific impairments to lead good lives. It would not simply be a measure of impairments or of limitations in functionings which result from the relevant impairment. It would be a measure of the limitations in opportunity or capability to function (in various ways) as a result of an impairment. Such a measure would be demanding as regards information since it would pick up the difference between capability and functioning failure.

While this seems – at least conceptually – the most obvious approach for those who attempt to apply the capability approach, there is nonetheless still a value in developing measures which focus on impairments. If social change (at least as regards disability) is not likely to be rapid and, as seems undisputable, many impairments are preventable, then measures which pick up the incidence and severity of impairments would also be informative and less informationally demanding than a measure of capability failure. They would operate at the level of functionings rather than capability. Of course, going further, a functionings based analysis may also look at the range of functionings which the impaired are deprived of – capturing problems not only with rather basic functionings but also potentially others such as social and political participation. At the international level, measurement for the purposes of international comparisons would no doubt be focused on impairments about which there is international consensus and limited controversy.

A related approach to measurement would look at the *access* that people with impairments have, including their access to buildings, public spaces, paid employment and so on. This more indirect approach would naturally focus selectively on access involving specific functionings (such as being able to move around, participate in social and political life and employment). It may in practice be less demanding at the level of information than some approaches which look at capability or functioning failure. But it may nonetheless be necessary to gather data and advocate the necessity for this at an international level. Finally, a version of this approach more akin to that involved in the UNDP's gender empowerment measure (UNDP, 1995) would look at the extent to which people with impairments are able to participate in society at various levels. It would naturally include participation in the labour market, as well as other areas of social and political life. This 'empowerment' approach again may be easier to implement on informational grounds. Issues relating to the selection of functionings and the weights given to the selected functionings in such measures may arise in all the approaches just outlined as they do in most capability or functioning based measures relating to human development and the participation of people with impairments in relevant selection exercises would obviously be important.

Finally, Burchardt has suggested one possibility which may prove attractive from the point of view of advocacy. The suggestion is inspired by Sen's well-known measure of 'missing women' which dramatises the issue of gender injustice. The analogue measure would attempt to capture the number of 'missing impaired' in various contexts. For example, one might – as Burchardt (Burchardt, 2004, p. 746) suggests – consider the difference between the employment rates of those who are and are not impaired and infer the number of 'missing people with impairments'. As she notes, any such measure would be based on fairly strong assumptions – such as an assumption about the preferences of various people who are and are not impaired as regards paid employment. It would nonetheless provide a potentially dramatic measure of the disadvantages or exclusion that the impaired face. Such a measure need not be restricted to participation in the labour market and might be used in diverse contexts where the impaired are noticeable by their absence.

Conclusions

The human development approach has a lot to offer to the analysis and understanding of disability because it treats people as ends in themselves and does not see people as valuable only to the degree that they are productive (given the relevant social context). In the light of this, and the significance of the issue of disability and development, the relative reticence of *Human Development Reports* on disability issues is surprising. Recent work on capability and disability – by Sen, Nussbaum and others – suggests that amongst the different approaches which adopt the human development paradigm, the capability approach is particularly suitable in the context of disability. Aside from having advantages in relation to accounts of justice and the quality of life, the approach avoids the limitations of both the individual and social models of disability. Finally, an examination of definition and measurement issues in the light of this discussion opens up various possible approaches to measurement and data collection. Numerous approaches can be used operating at the levels of capability and functionings, as well as access, empowerment and exclusion. Some of these are more demanding at the level of information than others. Collecting and presenting data on disability while clearly recognizing the distinction between impairment and disability and the related distinction between capability and functioning failures is a key challenge if these approaches were implemented. This preliminary discussion mapping the landscape where the human development paradigm might be brought to bear on disability issues suggests that its application would considerably and fruitfully extend the reach of the human development paradigm.

Notes

1 It is worth noting that a more general disappointment has also been expressed with the lack of attention given to disability issues in development studies more broadly. On this see Harriss-White (1996) and Yeo and Moore (2003).

2 Rawls' conception of primary goods was revised in the 1975 edition of his *A Theory of Justice* which was produced for German translation. See Rawls (1999, p. xiii).

3 Similar judgements are, she tells us, involved in 'Aristotle's treatment of "monstrous births" and in his policies concerning abortion and the exposure of severely handicapped children' (Nussbaum, 1995, p. 118).

4 While explaining the strengths of the capability approach in relation to issues relating to disability, I have not argued that the approach is superior to some alternatives – such as the basic needs approach. It might be argued that a strength of Sen's capability approach is that it treats people as agents not merely as recipients of aid or help (Sen, 1999, p. 19). This may be seen as an advantage of the capability approach over needs approaches. However, needs approaches do typically also emphasize participation and autonomy (Streeten, with Burqi, Haq, Hicks, and Stewart, 1981 and Doyal and Gough, 1991). Furthermore, some (like Gasper and van Staveren, 2003) have argued that Sen's capability approach does not sufficiently take account of human interdependence and care. This would clearly count as a weakness of his version of the approach. This criticism cannot be levelled at Nussbaum's writings (particularly, Nussbaum, 1996) which give considerable attention to care in relation to disability. However, evaluating the relative merits of the capability and needs views in relation to disability is beyond the scope of this paper. I merely note that there is considerable common ground between versions of the two approaches (see Qizilbash, 2001).

5 It is notable here that in discussing these issues Sen acknowledges the importance of Rawls' contribution in highlighting the priority to be given to the least well-off group – within which the severely disabled may be included – which is compatible with Sen's own concerns. In this respect, in spite of various other differences, there is (potentially) complementarity (and sometimes less difference than one would

expect) between Sen's work – and indeed work in the capability tradition – and work in the Rawlsian tradition. On this see also Richardson (2006) and Robeyns (2008). There is not space here, however, to consider defences of the Rawlsian primary goods index. Rawls' own defences can be found in Rawls (1993 and 1999).

References

Alkire, S. and Foster, J. (forthcoming). Counting and multi-dimensional poverty measurement. *Journal of Public Economics.*

Baylies, C., 2002. Disability and the notion of human development: questions of rights and capabilities. *Disability and Society* 17(7), pp. 725–739.

Brighouse, H. and Robeyns, I., 2010. *Measuring justice: primary goods and capabilities* Cambridge: Cambridge University Press.

Burchardt, T., 2004. Capabilities and disability: the capabilities framework and the social model of disability, *Disability and Society* 19(7), pp. 735–751.

Burchardt, T. and Zaidi, A., 2005. Comparing incomes when needs differ: equivalization for the extra costs of disability in the UK, *Review of Income and Wealth* 51(1), pp. 89–114.

Cohen, G.A., 1993. Equality of what? On welfare, goods and capabilities, in Nussbaum, M.C. and Sen, A. eds. *The quality of life.* Oxford: Clarendon Press.

Comim, F., Qizilbash, M. and Alkire, S., 2008. *The capability approach: concepts, measures and applications.* Cambridge: Cambridge University Press.

Desai, M., 1991. Human development: concept and measurement. *European Economic Review* 35, pp. 350–357.

Desai, M., 1995a. Greening the HDI? In: McGillivray, A. ed. *Accounting for change* London: New Economics Foundation.

Desai, M., 1995b. Measuring political freedom in Barker, E. ed. *On Freedom: A Centenary Anthology.* London: LSE Books.

Doyal, L. and Gough, I., 1991. *A theory of human need.* Basingstoke: Macmillan.

Frederick, S. and Lowenstein, F., 1996. Hedonic adaptation, in Kahneman, D., Diener, E. and Schwartz, N. eds., *Well-being: the foundations of hedonic psychology.* New York: Russell Sage Foundation.

Gasper, D. and van Staveren, I., 2003. Development as freedom – and what else? *Feminist Economics* 9(2–3), pp. 137–161.

Haq, M., 1995. *Reflections on human development.* Oxford and New York: Oxford University Press.

Harriss-White, B., 1996. The political economy of disability and development with special reference to India, UNRISD DP 73.

Harriss-White, B. and Sridhar, P., 2006. Disability and development. In: Clark, D.A. ed. *The Elgar companion to development studies* Cheltenham: Edward Elgar.

Kuklys, W., 2005. *Amartya Sen's capability approach: theoretical and empirical applications.* Berlin: Springer.

Majumdar, M. and Subramanian, S., 2001. Capability failure and group disparities: some evidence from India for the 1980s. *Journal of Development Studies* 37, pp. 104–140.

Nussbaum, M., 1988. Nature, function and capability: Aristotle on political distribution. *Oxford studies in ancient philosophy* 6 (Suppl. Vol.), pp. 145–184.

Nussbaum, M., 1995. Aristotle on human nature and the foundations of ethics. In: Altham, J.E.J. and Harrison, R., eds. *World, mind, and ethics. Essays on the ethical philosophy of Bernard Williams*. Cambridge: Cambridge University Press.

Nussbaum, M., 2000. *Women and human development: the capabilities approach*. Cambridge: Cambridge University Press.

Nussbaum, M., 2006. *Frontiers of justice: disability, nationality, species-membership*. Cambridge Mass.: Belknap Press.

Qizilbash, M., 1996a. Capabilities, well-being and human development: a survey, *Journal of Development Studies* 33, pp. 143–162.

Qizilbash, M., 1996b. Ethical development, *World Development* 24(7), pp. 1209–1221.

Qizilbash, M., 2001. Development, common foes and shared values. *Review of Political Economy* 14(4), pp. 463–480.

Qizilbash, M., 2006a. Capability, happiness and adaptation in Sen and J.S. Mill, *Utilitas* 18(1), pp. 20–32.

Qizilbash, M., 2006b. Well-being, adaptation and human limitations. *Philosophy* (Supplementary Volume), pp. 83–109.

Qizilbash, M., 2006c. Human development in D. Clark. In: *The Elgar companion to development studies* Cheltenham: Edward Elgar.

Rawls, J., 1971. *A theory of justice*. Oxford: Oxford University Press.

Rawls, J., 1993. *Political liberalism* New York: Columbia University Press.

Rawls, J., 1999. *A Theory of Justice. Revised Edition*. Oxford: Oxford University Press.

Richardson, H., 2006. Rawlsian social-contract theory and the severely disabled. *Journal of Ethics* 10, pp. 419-462.

Robeyns, I., 2008. Justice as fairness and the capability approach. In: Basu, K. and Kanbur, R. eds. *Arguments for a better world: essays in honor of Amartya Sen, Volume 1 Ethics, welfare and measurement*. Oxford University Press.

Sen, A.,1982. *Choice, welfare and measurement*. Oxford: Blackwell.

Sen, A., 1984. *Resources, values and development*. Oxford Blackwell.

Sen, A., 1988. The concept of development. In: Chenery, H. and Srinivasan T. eds. *Handbook of development economics Vol 1*. Amsterdam: North Holland.

Sen, A., 1990. Development as capability expansion. In: Griffin, K. and Knight J. eds. *Human development and the international development strategy for the 1990s*. New York: Macmillan.

Sen, A., 1992. *Inequality re-examined*. Oxford: Oxford University Press.

Sen, A., 1997. *On economic inequality*. Expanded Edition with a Substantial Annexe by Foster, J.E. and Sen, A. Oxford: Clarendon Press.

Sen, A., 1999. *Development as freedom*. Oxford: Oxford University Press.

Sen, A., 1993. Capability and well-Being. In: Nussbaum, M. and Sen, A. ed. *The Quality of life*. Oxford: Oxford University Press.

Sen, A., 2004. Disability and justice. Keynote speech, Second International Disability Conference, World Bank.

Sen, A., 2005. Human rights and capabilities. *Journal of human development* 6(2), pp. 151–166.

Sen, A., 2006a. The human development index. In Clark, D. *The Elgar companion to development studies* Cheltenham: Edward Elgar.

Sen, A., 2006b. Reason, freedom and well-being, *Utilitas* 18(1), pp. 80–96.

Sen, A., 2009. *The idea of justice*. London: Allen Lane.

Streeten, P. (with Burki, S.J., Haq, M., Hicks, N. and Stewart, F.) 1981. *First things first: Meeting basic human needs in the developing countries*. London: Oxford University Press.

Terzi, L., 2004. The social model of disability: a philosophical critique. *Journal of Applied Philosophy* 21(2), pp. 141–157.

Terzi, L., 2005a. Beyond the dilemma of difference: the capability approach to disability and special education needs, *Journal of Philosophy of Education* 39(3), pp. 443–459.

Terzi, L., 2005b. A capability perspective on impairment, disability and special needs: towards social justice in education, *Theory and Research in Education*, 3(2), pp. 197–223.

UNDP, 1993. *Human development report 1993*. Oxford and New York: Oxford University Press.

UNDP, 1995. *Human development report 1995*. Oxford and New York: Oxford University Press.

UNDP, 1996. *Human development report 1996*. Oxford and New York: Oxford University Press.

UNDP, 1997. *Human development report 1997*. Oxford and New York: Oxford University Press.

UNDP, 2000. *Human development report 2000*. Oxford and New York: Oxford University Press.

Wasserman, D., 2005. Disability, capability, and thresholds for distributive justice in Kaufman, A., ed. *Capabilities equality: basic issues and problems*. London and New York: Routledge.

Yeo, R. and Moore, K., 2003. Including disabled people in poverty reduction work: 'Nothing About Us, Without Us'. *World Development* 31(3), pp. 571–590.

8

The G20

A New Experiment in Global Governance

Montek S. Ahluwalia*

It is a pleasure to contribute to this Festschrift for my good friend Meghnad Desai. I have known Meghnad for many years in a staggering variety of avatars: as a one-time Marxist economist, a mainstream economist/econometrician at LSE, a Labour Party activist, a Labour Member of the House of Lords (I was his guest in the gallery when he spoke in support of Tony Blair's decision to send British troops into Iraq), a keen and surprisingly good cook, an insightful observer of the Indian political scene, a regular columnist in one of India's leading newspapers, a biographer of one of the best-loved Bollywood icons of yesteryear, most recently a late-blossoming novelist, and above all a wonderful raconteur and bon vivant!

Meghnad's multifaceted personality allows the widest possible latitude in choosing a subject for an essay in his honour. As he is quintessentially a global citizen, I thought it would be both appropriate and topical to write on the G20 and its role in global governance. Section I presents an assessment of the performance of the G20 in the first two years when it was dominantly concerned with managing the global crisis. Section II presents an assessment of the challenges facing the G20 in undertaking a more holistic reform of the international monetary system. Section III comments briefly on other tasks before the G20 and Section IV comments on the issue of the legitimacy of the G20 as a mechanism for improving global governance.

The first two years: managing the crisis

The decision to convene the first meeting of what later became the G20 at the summit level[1], was taken shortly after the collapse of Lehman Brothers

*The author is currently the Deputy Chairman of the Planning Commission, Government of India and also the Sherpa for India for the G20 Summits. The views expressed in this paper are personal and do not necessarily reflect the official position of the Government of India. Thanks are due to Parthasarathi Shome, Kaushik Basu and Manmohan Kumar for helpful comments.

transformed what, until then, had been viewed as a serious but limited problem affecting the housing loan market in the United States into a full-blown financial crisis.

Both Prime Minister Brown of the United Kingdom and President Sarkozy of France called for a second Bretton Woods-type Conference to examine the functioning of the system as a whole. The severity and breadth of the crisis dictated that consultations would have to go beyond the G8 and involve a larger group of emerging market economies, which now accounted for a substantial share of global output and trade, and an even larger share in global growth. President George Bush therefore invited the leaders of the Group of 20 to meet in Washington DC in November 2008, to discuss measures to deal with the crisis. The leaders met again on two occasions in 2009, first in London and then in Pittsburgh, and twice again in 2010, first in Toronto and then in Seoul. To examine whether these meetings were successful in handling the crisis, we first consider the end results, and then the nature of the specific actions taken.

The position as far as end results is concerned is summarized in Table 8.1, which shows the outcomes in terms of growth rates of GDP for the world and also for the advanced countries and emerging market and developing countries separately. Projections made for 2009 and 2010 by the International Monetary Fund (IMF) in its successive World Economic Outlook (WEO) updates are shown, along with the actual outcomes.

After growing at 5.4 per cent in 2007, world output growth slowed down to 2.9 per cent in 2008. The advanced economies were initially projected to contract by 0.3 per cent in 2009, while the developing countries were projected

Table 8.1 Growth Rates of GDP Projected and Actual (percentage growth over previous year)

	2007	2008	2009			2010		2011
			WEO (Nov 08)	WEO (April 09)	Actual Outcome	WEO (April 09)	Actual Outcome	Projection
1) World Output	5.4	2.9	2.2	−1.4	−0.5	2.5	5.0	4.4
2) Advanced Countries	2.7	0.2	−.03	3.8	-3.4	0.6	3.0	2.4
3) Emerging Market & Developing Economies	8.8	6.1	5.1	1.5	2.7	4.7	7.3	6.5

to grow at 5.1 per cent but these projections were subsequently revised sharply downwards in the WEO update for April 2009, which showed the world contracting by 1.4 per cent and advanced countries contracting by 3.8 per cent, while the developing countries grew by only 1.5 per cent.

The rapid downgrading of growth prospects in 2009 led to a substantial policy response described later in this section. As it turned out, the world performed better in 2009 than was initially feared. The contraction in 2009 for the world as a whole was only around 0.5 per cent, instead of 1.4 per cent projected earlier. The advanced countries contracted by 3.4 per cent instead of 3.8 per cent projected earlier and the emerging economies did much better, expanding by 2.7 per cent instead of 1.5 per cent predicted earlier.

The recovery in 2010 was stronger than originally expected. The WEO for April 2009 initially estimated growth in world output in 2010 at 2.5 per cent but world output actually grew at 5.0 per cent in 2010. The advanced countries grew at 3.0 per cent and the developing countries at 7.3 per cent, instead of the 0.6 per cent and 4.7 per cent respectively, projected in April 2009.

Given the scale of the shock, which at one time seemed reminiscent of the Great Depression, the fact that the world economy recovered smartly after only one year of negative growth has been remarkable. The recovery has not been without problems: unemployment has remained stubbornly high in industrialized countries and inflationary pressures have surfaced in emerging market countries. The sustainability of the recovery is also clouded by the sharp increase in public sector deficits and debts in most of the advanced economies, including in particular, the United States, Japan and many of the European countries. The fragility of the Eurozone at the time of writing (mid 2011) added a new source of concern. These are worrying problems but they do not negate the fact that the worst-case outcome of a prolonged depression following the 2008 crisis was avoided. Whether this is because of the corrective policies followed as a result of the G20 consultations, or whether the earlier projections were simply over pessimistic, is difficult to establish with certainty. However, the benefit of doubt should surely go to the G20.

Understanding the nature of the crisis

Correct diagnosis is the first step in defining correct solutions and one of the stated objectives of the first meeting in Washington in November 2008 was to achieve a better understanding of what caused the crisis. The G20 consultations did well in this area because they helped move the public debate away from somewhat simplified perceptions of the causes of the crisis, towards a more nuanced understanding, which helped evolve a consensus on how to move forward.

Initially, there was a tendency to over simplify by tracing the crisis solely to the excessively large surpluses in some countries, notably China and the oil exporting countries, and the recycling of these surpluses back to the U.S.

in the form of large reserve holdings of US dollar securities. The build up of reserves was seen as reflecting a conscious decision not to allow the currency to appreciate, thus interfering with the mechanism for adjustment. The inflows resulting from reserve accumulation were seen as causing excess liquidity in the United States, which drove down long-term interest rates, promoting risky forms of financial innovation and reckless lending in search of higher yield, which in turn produced financial fragility.

On this view, much of the blame for the crisis lay with the relentless drive for exports as a source of growth, facilitated by an exchange rate that was deliberately undervalued. This in turn suggested that corrective steps should focus on the need to introduce 'discipline' on surplus countries, including pressure for appreciation of the currency. Not surprisingly, this view was strongly opposed by the surplus countries, who typically argued that the other side of large surpluses was large deficits, which reflected macro-economic imbalances that should have been tackled internally.

After much discussion among Finance Deputies and Ministers, the G20 Summit endorsed a more balanced assessment, recognizing the multiple causes of the crisis. Unsustainable global imbalances and the absence of self-correcting mechanisms had plagued the global economy for several years, and certainly represented one part of the problem. However, there were several other factors that were also responsible for the financial vulnerability that led to the crisis. These were: (i) the regulatory philosophy of financial regulators in some of the major industrialized countries, which placed too much faith in the efficiency of financial markets, (ii) the unwillingness to tighten money supply despite asset price bubbles created by excess liquidity, (iii) inadequate understanding of the risk associated with several of the new financial products created by financial innovation, (iv) toleration of excessive leverage in financial institutions, especially in the shadow banking sector, which contributed to system vulnerability, (v) inadequate capital buffers and a procyclical bias built into Basle II mark-to-market practices, (vi) unrealistically low assessment of risk for securitized assets based on poor credit rating practices and (vii) compensation practices in the financial sector which greatly encouraged excessive risk taking.

The relative role of all these factors was not spelt out precisely in the Washington communiqué, but they were sufficiently acknowledged to avoid placing blame on only some elements. This set the stage for evolving a common position on what might be an appropriate architecture for financial sector reform and also lay the basis for exploring mechanisms of macro-economic coordination to overcome global imbalances.

Policies to counter recession

Issues related to reforming the financial regulatory system occupied the headlines in the immediate aftermath of the crisis but these were essentially relevant over a longer time horizon. The financial sector was so shell-shocked in the short term that there was little danger of excessive risk-taking and the immediate problem was how to inject liquidity and overcome an irrational unwillingness on the part of banks to lend. The more urgent task was to counter the downturn in the real economy.

There was considerable resistance in many quarters to adopting expansionary Keynesian policies. Part of the problem was the initial tendency in Europe to see the crisis as a problem of the Anglo Saxon banking system, whereas the fact was that global financial interconnectivity had made large parts of the European banking also vulnerable, a weakness that would exert a contractionary effect on the real economy.

Despite differences in perception, the G20 consultation in London in June 2009 did produce a consensus in which most of the industrialized countries resorted to varying degrees of fiscal and monetary expansion compared to what was envisaged earlier. This was not the result of any formal agreement on the extent to which fiscal policy would be expansionary, or monetary policy eased, in particular countries. The most that can be said is that the consultation process helped to evolve a consensus that enabled G20 leaders to state that primacy must be given to economic recovery, leaving it to individual countries to choose the extent of fiscal or monetary expansion they would attempt. In other words, the countries acted in concert though they did not actually coordinate.

The commitment to pursue expansionary policies was reiterated at the Pittsburgh Summit in September 2009. The communiqué specifically referred to a determination to avoid any 'premature withdrawal of stimulus' although it was also noted that exit strategies would be prepared to withdraw support in a 'cooperative and coordinated way' when the time is right. The G20 had a difficult balancing act to perform. Both external and internal public sector imbalances in the industrialized countries pointed to the need for fiscal consolidation, but private sector balance sheets had been so damaged by the asset price collapse caused by the crisis that private demand could not be expected to take up the slack and indeed, was expected to have a contractionary effect.

By the time of the Toronto meeting in June 2010, perceptions had changed. A recovery was clearly underway, and although there were worries about a possible 'double dip' recession, concern about the consequences of fiscal imprudence had also increased. The Conservative-Liberal coalition which had come to power in the United Kingdom was committed to an earlier exit from fiscal stimulus and this re-inforced German views on this issue. The G20 communiqué from Toronto, therefore, signalled a stronger commitment for an earlier exit for countries with serious fiscal challenges. The concerns of those worried about the contractionary effect of an early exit were sought to be addressed by stating that fiscal deficits would be halved by 2013, thus indicating the goal at the end of three years without specifying the annual phasing. It was hoped that this approach would reassure markets about the longer term commitment to restoring fiscal sustainability, while avoiding immediate contraction in demand.

A missing element in the discussion on policies to counter recession was that there was no strong commitment on the part of surplus countries to expand domestic demand to counter demand contraction in deficit industrialized countries. In the absence of such a commitment, the stimulus would have to be continued in deficit countries if the level of economic activity was to be maintained, even if it worsened the public debt balance. This meant that demand was being sustained, but the underlying global imbalances were not being corrected. That correction could only occur if the G20 could achieve the more difficult task of coordinating macro-economic policy across countries, with surplus countries expanding demand while deficit countries contracted.

Co-ordinating macro-economic policy

The advantages of coordination of policy have been discussed extensively in the literature. When a single country has an imbalance, and the rest of the world is broadly in balance, it is reasonable to expect that corrective action has to be taken primarily by the country with the imbalance, and coordination with other countries is less important. However, when some countries have unsustainable deficits and others have excessive surpluses, as has been the case for several years, what is needed is symmetric adjustment in which both the deficit and the surplus countries undertake some adjustment. The willingness to accept demand deflation in a deficit country would be greater if there were assurance that demand elsewhere is being increased simultaneously, mitigating the negative effect on employment. Equally, the willingness to inflate demand in surplus countries should be higher, if fears of overheating are reduced, because of the knowledge that demand elsewhere is being reduced. Coordination can therefore lead to an optimal outcome in such a situation.

IMF surveillance conducted under Article 4, involves surveillance of the policies of each country individually, and is ill suited to achieving coordination of policies across countries. The IMF also undertakes broader assessments of the global economic situation through the World Economic Outlook, the Global Financial Stability Reports, and more recently through the Fiscal Monitor, but these do not involve discussion of individual country policies in the context of what other country policies might be.

The need for multilateral consultations to deal with global imbalances was recognized in the middle of the last decade when the United States current account deficit rose year after year, reaching 6 per cent of GDP in 2005. There was widespread concern that if these large imbalances, affecting the major reserve currency country, were not reduced through some form of soft landing, a much more disruptive hard landing would become inevitable. Departing from past practice, the IMF sought the cooperation of the five entities that account for the bulk of the surpluses and deficits – the United States, the eurozone, China, Japan and Saudi Arabia – to undertake a multilateral discussion of the actions each might be willing to take to address the problem.

This initiative was not particularly successful. Raghuram Rajan, then Chief Economist of the IMF, reports that to prepare for the international meetings, the Fund engaged in preliminary discussions with each of the five to see if some agreement could be evolved. The outcome, described in Rajan (2010), is sobering: 'The response from our interlocutors was pretty uniform. Countries agreed that the trade imbalances were a potential source of instability and economic reforms were needed to bring them down before markets took fright. But each country was then quick to point out why it was not responsible for the imbalances and why it would be so much easier for some other country to push the magic button to make them disappear... When the consultations eventually concluded in 2007, the Fund declared that they had been a success: there had been a free and frank exchange of views, which is bureaucratese for total disagreement.'

The G20 rightly chose not to be discouraged by this earlier failure and embarked on a bold new initiative to develop a mechanism for policy coordination among the G20 countries through a Mutual Assessment Process (MAP). Unlike the normal IMF surveillance process, in which the IMF is the principal interlocutor, the MAP process is expected to be led by the G20 countries themselves, with the IMF, along with other international organizations, only providing technical assistance.

A two-stage framework for this multilateral process was developed. In the first stage, seven statistical indicators were used to identify countries with large external and internal imbalances. The indicators include three, which relate to the external balance (balance of trade in goods and services, income and transfer balance, and net external balance) and four, which relate to internal balance (primary budget balance, public debt, private debt, and private savings). These indicators have been used by the IMF in different ways to identify imbalances which appear large. On this basis, seven systemically important G20 countries as having large imbalances, and the policies of these countries will be subjected to special scrutiny in the second stage.[2]

Each G20 country has also been asked to submit its projection of major macro-economic variables based on a common template over a five year horizon. These individual country projections will be analysed by the IMF as part of the MAP to assess what they imply for the global economy. Since the G20 account for about 78 per cent of global output, aggregation of the individual country projections does provide a reasonable basis for scaling up to global GDP, and comparing the aggregate of the country projections with the global projections made by the IMF. It also provides a basis for assessing whether individual country projections are based on assumptions about global outcomes which correspond to the actual global outcome that would result if individual countries proceed as projected. Inconsistency between the global growth assumed in individual country projections, and the global projections resulting from the aggregation of individual projections or from the IMFs global forecasts, can be resolved through interaction. This would give the IMF a basis for assessing what global growth and global imbalances would be if the countries policies proceed on the lines indicated.

In the case of the seven G20 countries selected for second stage scrutiny, the individual country projections will be analysed on the basis of indicative guidelines regarding policy action that might be appropriate to correct the imbalances, taking account of the specific circumstances of each country. From this process, it is expected that the IMF will be able to define an "upside scenario" for the global economy, assuming that the seven systemically important countries follow the policies which can lead to the upside scenario. This upside scenario can then be viewed as the goal which successful policy co-ordination can achieve.

The IMF assessment, along with reports by other international organizations, will be presented to the Framework Working Group (FWG) of G20 finance officials and the FWG will then present a single MAP report to the finance ministers. The FWG's MAP report is expected to reflect the collective view of G20 members, informed by reports produced by the IMF and other international organisations. The MAP report after being considered by the Finance Ministers will be presented to the Cannes Summit in November 2011.

It remains to be seen whether the proposed MAP process will be more successful than the IMF's last attempt at multilateral surveillance in 2007. A key difference is that instead of the IMF conducting the process, it is country driven, with the IMF only providing technical assistance. However, that by itself does not make it any easier. Participating countries are likely to defend their own positions strongly, but are less likely to take strong positions when differences arise between other countries. The absence of an external arbiter pronouncing on these issues has the advantage of avoiding what may otherwise appear as intrusive intervention by the IMF, but it will also make it difficult to resolve differences. The danger in such situations is that difficult issues will be obfuscated through creative drafting rather than meaningfully resolved.

The technical complexity of each step of the exercise should also not be underestimated. It is very difficult to determine objectively when an imbalance in a particular country is unsustainable, especially if the assessment is meant to be forward-looking rather than simply a statistical exercise identifying outliers based on past trends. It is even more difficult to determine what precise mix of policies is appropriate to address the imbalance in a particular country. Such assessments can only be made on the basis of some implicit assumption about the structure of the economy, which determines its response to policy intervention, and the time lags involved. There is enormous room for honest differences of opinion on each of these issues. The margin of error involved in estimating the extent of change needed in particular policy instruments to achieve a given outcome is so large that judgement rather than technical analysis has to play the dominant role. Besides, since the policies of one systemically important country will affect other countries, it will always be possible to argue – as countries did on the last occasion – that the correction of an imbalance in any one country depends more on changing the policies of other countries.

The IMF routinely makes projections about the world economy and also makes judgements about broad directions of policy based on various economic models of the world economy and its regional components. These projections can also be questioned on the same basis, but countries have much less incentive to question projections about the world economy, and even recommendations on broad policy directions for groups of countries or regions. They will subject country specific policy conclusions to much greater scrutiny.

Despite these difficulties, it can be argued that the value of the process is much more in the process itself, and the impact that it may have over time in developing a shared approach among participating countries, rather than in the ability to resolve current differences. Coordination of policy among sovereign countries is never easy, and is unlikely to be achieved through collective decision making based on some form of voting to resolve differences. It is more likely to occur because the policy of each country is influenced, gradually if not immediately, by the collective sense of the community of G20 members. In other words, multilateral surveillance has to be viewed as an exercise in persuasion.

The IMF has an important role in this process, even if it is not the arbiter of outcomes, by providing high quality technical inputs, and also indicating where the case for policy change is compelling and where it is more marginal. However the IMF's ability to ensure that technical issues are not lost sight of is limited by the structuring of the MAP exercise, in which the IMF's input is primarily at the FWG level, after which the FWG prepares the report that goes to the finance ministers and the summit. There is a case for the G20 establishing a technical advisory group of eminent experts who might be asked to comment on the technical work of the IMF, and also on the consensus emerging from the FWG. The views of these experts should be available in subsequent stages to ensure that difficult issues are suitably highlighted for the Summit rather than papered over. Such a mechanism is particularly necessary since there is no G20 secretariat.

Creating a new architecture for financial regulation

The need for reform of the financial system was recognized as a priority in the very first meeting in November 2008. Subsequently, there have been several expert reports on the subject, including assessments by regulators within individual countries. Much of what is involved is technical and not what one would expect leaders to pronounce upon. However, the G20 Summits can claim to have imparted a sense of urgency on the need to act, and also endorsed the broad direction of action.

At the first meeting in November 2008, the G20 endorsed the principle that financial markets must remain open, competitive and transparent, but they must be much better regulated to reduce risk-taking behaviour and avoid pro-cyclicality. It was also made clear that better regulation did not mean establishment of a supranational financial regulator which had been talked about. As the November 2008 communiqué put it, 'Regulation is first and foremost the responsibility of national regulators who constitute the first line of defence against market instability. However, our financial markets are global in scope, therefore, intensified international cooperation among regulators and strengthening of international standards, where necessary, and their consistent implementation is necessary to protect against adverse cross-border regional and global developments affecting international financial stability.' Those who favour stronger supra-national regulators may not be happy with this decision, but it was the only approach acceptable, including by emerging market countries.

The erstwhile Financial Stability Forum, which had been set up after the East Asian crisis, but which did not include emerging market countries, was broadened to include all G20 countries and renamed the Financial Stability Board (FSB). This was clearly an important act of democratization, increasing ownership by the emerging market countries of action taken by the FSB. The FSB was expected to work with the international standard-setting bodies and encourage them to develop a new architecture for financial regulation.

An important outcome of this effort is the set of new Basle III standards, issued by the Basle Committee on Banking Supervision. The new standards contain many significant improvements such as (i) improved quality and transparency of the capital base, (ii) provisions for capital buffers which can be built up in good times and drawn down in bad, thus reducing pro-cyclicality, (iii) leverage ratios that put a limit on total leverage, and (iv) various measures designed to limit risk, including the use of longer-term data horizons to estimate probabilities of default. The target for full implementation is December 31, 2019 which gives considerable room for national regulators to determine the pace of adherence in a manner that will be least disruptive. The G20 can legitimately claim that it is because of the commitment expressed at the highest level that Basle III took only two years to complete, whereas Basle II took ten years!

This is not to say that all aspects of financial architecture have been resolved. Some of the most difficult issues in dealing with financial stability have yet to be addressed. Basle III covers banks, but does not directly address potential vulnerability arising from the shadow banking system which is very large compared to the banks in industrialized economies. Problems associated with cross border resolution in banking crises, and also the problems of institutions that are too big to fail, also remain unresolved. The supervision of financial institutions operating in more than one jurisdiction, based on a college of supervisors approach, has also yet to be tested in practice.

These weaknesses notwithstanding, there is no doubt that a start has been made with considerable convergence of thinking among all the major countries. The task of creating a new financial architecture is bound to be an ongoing process and at this stage it is likely to make more progress if taken out of the limelight summits.

Strengthening the International Financial Institutions

One of the important achievements of the G20 in the first two years is the strengthening of the International Financial Institutions (IFIs) by providing additional financial resources and also improving the voice of developing countries within the institutions. The provision of additional resources was viewed as especially important as it would enable these institutions to help developing and transition countries to cope with a global downturn which was expected to reduce their exports and possibility also trigger a reversal of capital flows.

IMF quotas were doubled to about SDR 477 billion, a much bolder step than was earlier thought likely. This was accompanied by an interim increase in the size of the New Arrangements to Borrow, pending the quota increases becoming effective. A new issue of Special Drawing Rights (SDRs) amounting to SDR 270 billion was also agreed, providing unconditional liquidity to many countries in need. Two new IMF facilities were introduced which provided much greater flexibility to borrowers. One of these is the Flexible Credit Line, for countries with very strong fundamentals and a track record of implementation. The facility provides large resources upfront with no policy conditionality. The other new facility is the Precautionary Credit Line, which is also meant for countries with strong fundamentals, but which have some moderate vulnerabilities. This facility therefore entails some conditionality, aimed at addressing these vulnerabilities, and disbursement is trenched.

Long-standing demands for increased representation from the developing countries have also produced some response. Quota shares have been adjusted by shifting 6 per cent of the total share to the 'dynamic emerging markets and developing countries' and another 6 per cent shift from 'overrepresented' to 'underrepresented' countries. The net effect has been to reduce the quota share of the older European members and the United States though still leaving the United States with enough voting share to have an effective veto on major issues, which require an 85 per cent vote.

The multilateral international development banks are an important part of the international financial system from the perspective of developing countries. They are less important than they used to be for the emerging market group within the developing countries, but they remain very important for smaller developing countries that lack access to capital markets. The World Bank's capital was increased by 50 per cent the Asian Development Bank by 100 per cent and the Inter American Development Bank capital by 70 per cent. Quota shares of the developing countries in the World Bank have also been increased as a consequence of the increase in the IMF.

It can be argued that these decisions had been under consideration for some time and could have been taken in the normal course. However, anyone familiar with the resistance and inertia that prevented movement earlier, would agree that the direct engagement of the G20 leaders at the summit level, prompted no doubt by the crisis and the need to respond to developing country demands, helped resolve what otherwise might have taken much longer, and indeed may not have come to as satisfactory an outcome.

A moratorium on protectionism

Finally, the moratorium on additional protectionist measures, which was a part of the commitment of the G20 repeated in successive communiqués, deserves to be counted as an important achievement. It can be argued that these commitments were not strictly observed, since many G20 countries introduced some measures that could be described as increasing the level of domestic protection. However, all these actions were strictly monitored by the WTO, which reported back to G20 leaders at each summit. The gist of the WTO assessment thus far has been that while almost all countries introduced some measures, the overall impact of the measures was small.

The G20 did therefore live upto the promise of avoiding any serious risk of a relapse into protectionism which would have been devastating for the world economy. In this respect the world was spared the protectionist-type reaction witnessed at the time of the Great Depression, when the Smoot Hawley Act was passed in the United States.

Reforming of the International Monetary System

In addition to crisis management, a task which has once again moved to the front burner because of the Eurozone crisis, the G20 must also turn to the broader issue of whether the present International Monetary System (IMS) is capable of meeting the needs of the global economy or whether some basic structural redesign is needed. Some important steps have already been taken, but these amount to fixing the system where it was obviously broken. A holistic review of the system as a whole is needed and this is expected to be part of the agenda at the Cannes Summit in November 2011.

Weaknesses in the present system

A central issue that must be addressed at the outset is whether the present system of exchange rates between major currencies should continue or whether there is a change that is feasible and desirable. This paper proceeds on the assumption that no practical alternative exists to the present system of floating exchange rates between the currencies of major countries, (treating the Eurozone as one unit for this purpose) with other countries adopting a variety of exchange rate arrangements ranging from free floating to various types of managed floats, soft pegs, or even hard pegs if preferred. The main weaknesses of the system, which any restructuring of the IMS must address, are the following: (i) excessive volatility in exchange rates, combined with persistent misalignment reflecting the absence of automatic adjustment mechanisms (ii) excessive dependence on the US dollar as the reserve currency, which also reduces pressures on the United States to adjust, (iii) excessive volatility of capital flows reflecting high levels of capital mobility with not enough underlying stability in the world economy and (iv) insufficient assurance of availability of international liquidity, especially in crisis situations. These weaknesses obviously feed on each other. Persistent misalignment of exchange rates can lead to large reserve holdings in dollar assets and this in turn raises the threat of currency instability following a possible portfolio shift.

No grand design for reform has emerged thus far although considerable useful work has been done on this issue e.g. the Report of the Palais Royale Initiative (2011) and a report to the European Commission by Angeloni et al. (2011).

Reducing volatility and mismanagement

There can be no doubt that the global real economy would benefit from lower volatility of exchange rates and smoother adjustment when exchange rates are misaligned. In a world of floating exchange rates, this is best achieved by more effective policy coordination across countries to avoid the kind of imbalances which can otherwise create destabilizing exchange rate movements. The G20 MAP initiative is designed precisely to address this issue. If it does make some progress, the G20 can legitimately claim to have created one of the major building blocks for ensuring a well functioning global economy in today's world.

The problems of achieving coordination are formidable Deleveraging in the industrial world will mean weak private demand, while existing and projected public sector imbalances in these countries limit the scope for fiscal policy.

Monetary easing in the industrialized countries has also reached the limit of its possibilities, with low interest rates threatening another asset price bubble, and also potentially large spillover effects on emerging market countries through volatile capital flows. East Asia has depended heavily on exports and needs to shift rapidly to a domestic demand-led strategy with greater exchange rate flexibility.[3] However, perceptions vary on the pace at which the shift can occur. Germany too has relied heavily on export demand and presents similar problems. It is sometimes argued that the German surplus is offset by deficits in other Eurozone countries, and as long as the Eurozone as a currency area, is in balance, the German surplus should not matter. However, the deficits in some of the Eurozone countries are not sustainable unless there are assured fiscal transfers bailing them out. If this is not feasible, and demand in these countries has to be contained, then global rebalancing will require an increase in German domestic demand. It remains to be seen how effectively the MAP can resolve these problems.

Dominance of the dollar

The dominance of the US dollar, relative to the other reserve currencies has long been a source of asymmetry in the system, giving the United States the 'exorbitant privilege' of being able to finance its deficit by issuing claims denominated in its own currency. Since this dominance is not due to any international agreement or compulsion, but is solely the result of market choices, it can be argued that it is a legacy phenomenon. On this view, the importance of the US dollar will decline gradually. It will, of course, remain one of the major reserve currencies, and indeed the most important for quite some time, but a better balance with other currencies will emerge on its own.

However, the massive accumulation of US dollar assets in reserves increases the risks of exchange rate volatility if reserve holders seek to diversify their holdings. One way of solving this problem is to allow dollar reserves to be converted into SDR reserves, reducing the danger of portfolio switches away from the dollar. The mechanism envisaged is one in which holders of dollar reserves can convert their excess reserves into SDR denominated reserves held in a special account in the IMF. These SDR denominated assets could be used by holders to settle claims with other central banks, or converted into desired currencies by the IMF using the dollar assets originally deposited with it.

Countries could achieve the same objective by diversifying their reserve holdings to reflect the same proportion of different currencies as the weight of the component currencies in the SDR, but this process would involve a net offloading of dollars in currency markets with consequent exchange rate effects. Freezing the dollar holdings in a special account in the IMF forestalls such pressures in currency markets, but it entails an exchange risk for the special account if the dollar depreciates over time. The need for a substitution account of this type was discussed in the late 1970s, but it never took off because the issue of who would bear the exchange risk could not be resolved.[4]

Role of the SDR

The case for giving the SDR a larger role in the IMS has been a recurring theme in the literature on international monetary reform. It has been raised again recently by Zhou Xiaochuan, in a much quoted article 'Reform of the International Monetary System' which suggests that the SDR should progressively replace the dollar in global reserves and should also become a multilaterally controlled mechanism to increase global liquidity. There are several different issues that arise in this context that need to be addressed.

It is sometimes asserted that increased reliance on the SDR will help reduce volatility in exchange rates between the major currencies. Since the SDR is itself a basket of currencies, and not a separate currency, it is not immediately obvious how it can actually add to stability of other currencies except by preventing large dollar holdings from being offloaded in the market. Fluctuations in the exchange rates of currencies composing the basket result from the operation of currency markets, which in turn are driven by changes in the underlying economic fundamentals of the corresponding economies, or expectations about these fundamentals. Efforts to reduce exchange rate fluctuations must therefore focus on measures which will dampen sudden changes in those fundamentals, or manage the changes better. This takes us back to co-ordination mechanisms such as the MAP, which have to be used to generate more orderly adjustment processes. Conversion of dollars into SDRs in a special account would reduce the risk of volatility, but this is possible only if the exchange risk problem can be resolved.

The case for enlarging the role of the SDR is sometimes made in terms of the need for regular new allocations of SDRs. Regular allocations would add a steady dose of liquidity, based on multilaterally determined rules which could build in an element of counter-cyclicality. Since the SDR is not "outside money" but only a line of credit, it should not have significant inflationary impact. To the extent that the availability of unconditional liquidity reduces the need for building up owned reserves, it can be said to avoid behaviour that is otherwise contractionary. The quantitative impact of modest but regular new allocations on inflation will be small. Even after the recent increase in SDR allocations, the total outstanding stock of SDRs is only 4 per cent of total foreign currency reserves.

The fact that the resulting liquidity would be distributed to countries in proportion to their share in Fund quotas has been criticised as a departure from purely market-based criteria for providing credit, but this criticism is overdone. Extending some additional liquidity to weaker countries can be justified on equity grounds, especially since the poorer countries suffer so many other disadvantages.[5] What regular SDR allocations will do is increase the cushion of confidence that countries have, while also creating considerable potential liquidity which would be useful in abnormal times, when private capital markets freeze.

If we want to increase the role of the SDR in global reserve holdings, it makes sense to increase the usability of the SDR in non-official transactions. Several proposals for doing so have been advanced, and could be implemented in a gradual manner. These include the issue of SDR denominated bonds by the IMF and also the promotion of SDR denominated pricing of major commodities. Wider use of the SDR as a unit of account in invoicing of world trade will certainly dampen the effect of fluctuations among the major currencies on prices denominated in SDRs. However since the prices that affect the real economy are the domestic prices in individual countries, based on the currencies in use, a mere dampening of SDR denominated prices is only an averaging phenomenon.

Finally, if the SDR is to continue as an important part of the international monetary architecture, it makes sense to establish transparent rules whereby currencies of countries which meet certain criteria of economic size and currency convertibility can be included in the basket. The Renminbi is the obvious currency which could be added to the SDR basket, though it would be necessary for it to have much greater flexibility for use in capital transactions, which in turn implies much higher exchange rate flexibility. The issue of exchange rate flexibility is particularly relevant since otherwise adding the Renminbi into the SDR basket only amounts to increasing the weight of the US dollar. Logically, there should be periodic review of the composition of the SDR basket providing for both entry and exit of currencies. Looking further ahead, say over the next twenty years, the role of both the yen and sterling are likely to decline. A case can also be made for well-defined, rule-based surveillance, by the IMF, of the currency regime of countries whose currencies are in the SDR basket.

Managing capital flows

It is generally agreed that long term capital flows, including especially Foreign Direct Investment (FDI), can improve global allocation of resources and bring about faster growth of developing countries. However, the volatility of capital flows, 'with sudden stops' and surges, poses serious risks. This is the main factor explaining the 'fear of floating' which characterizes many developing countries, and explains their adoption of exchange rate regimes which allow for flexibility, but retain the option of intervening including by the introduction of capital controls. Developing countries therefore need a framework for regulation of capital flows, which enables them to reap the benefits of global financial integration, while limiting the risk involved.

A sound financial sector is clearly one element of such a framework. One of the lessons of the East Asian crisis of 1997 was that weak financial institutions intermediating foreign flows can expose countries to serious currency mismatch risks, which can generate extreme financial vulnerability, which in turn can provoke a crisis. Most Asian countries have already taken significant steps to deal with this problem and the ongoing global efforts to strengthen the financial system will help further in this respect. Building owned reserves is another mechanism to insulate the economy from volatile capital flows and many emerging economies have taken steps in this direction. The possibility of using capital controls is another mechanism for managing capital flows.

The use of capital controls was a contentious issue in the 1990s, when the conventional wisdom in industrialized countries held that developing countries should liberalize the capital account. There were influential voices arguing against this position – notably Bhagwati (1998) and Williamson (1991) – but the general thrust of opinion, especially in the United States, strongly favoured capital account liberalization. The Articles of Agreement of the IMF do not give it a mandate to oversee the capital account – a hangover from the days when the Fund was created, when the capital account was closed everywhere except the United States. In the second half of the 1990s, the IMF tried to get support for an Amendment of the Articles that would give it a mandate to cover capital account transactions. The effort was strongly resisted at the time by developing countries because it was feared that Fund conditionality would be used to coerce countries to liberalize the capital account.[6]

The intellectual climate today has changed dramatically with virtually universal acceptance that developing countries need to retain some instruments for control over capital flows. The question which arises is whether we should continue with the present arrangements, in which there is no restraint whatsoever on the controls a country may impose, or whether there should be some agreed international discipline on the action that governments might take to control capital flows, and the surveillance to which this should be subjected. The case for having some discipline is simply that if interconnections on account of trade are regulated by international agreements, then interconnection by way of financial flows should also be subject to some agreed discipline. Of course, trade is different from finance and exact parallels are potentially misleading. However, this should not lead to an automatic rejection of the idea, especially if it is made clear from the outset that the discipline proposed for controls over capital flows should not be designed to push developing countries to acceptance of greater openness.

The issue that needs to be considered is whether we should move to a system where Governments have the choice of deciding the levels of openness to capital flows they choose, but having done so, agree to a discipline on what controls can be introduced beyond that level, and in what circumstances, and also for what period. The objective is only to introduce predictability about what measures can be introduced purely at the discretion of the Government, and what will require some form of international surveillance. A proposal along these lines was outlined in Ahluwalia (2000).

Access to multilateral financing

The recent crisis has clearly demonstrated that the global system needs the IMF as a credible lender of last resort and not just for the developing economies, and transition economies as was once thought. The crises in Greece, Ireland, and Portugal have demonstrated that the IMF may have to be brought into play even for weaker industrialized countries. Some important steps have been taken to strengthen the IMF, but it can be argued that what has been done is an ad hoc response, and not a systemic redesign of the architecture enabling the IMF to play the role it may have to play in future crises. The unprecedented monetary easing resorted to by the US Federal Reserve shows how, in extreme situations, it may become necessary to create additional liquidity on a massive scale.

This raises the issue of whether the IMF should be empowered, based on suitably weighted voting, to create SDRs which it could allocate to itself to use in the event of a crisis. This would take us part of the way to Keynes' original suggestion of creating an International Clearing Union which could issue a new currency to be called Bancor. The SDRs so created could be extinguished when the emergency is over, so that the Fund does not continue to enjoy more liquidity when it is not needed. Suggestions along these lines have been made on several occasions e.g. Ahluwalia (2000) but have not been accepted. There is no reason why the Fund should not be empowered in this way to create liquidity. If the IMF's governance structure is judged to be adequate, the creation of liquidity would be subject to appropriate oversight. If the governance structure is not adequate, it should be suitably modified. This would be a major structural reform, going beyond a mere 'fix what is broken' approach.

Increased voice of developing countries in the IMF

As part of the reform of the system, it is necessary to accelerate the process of giving greater voice to the emerging markets and developing countries in the IMF. The new quotas approved in 2010, which will become effective after ratification, have made some difference. As shown in Table 8.2, the combined voting share of the four European members of the G20 (i.e. Germany, United Kingdom, France and Italy) will decline marginally from 17.5 per cent to 16.37 per cent and the share of the eight emerging market countries will increase from 12.42 per cent to 15.91 per cent. Even so, the voting share of these countries will be much lower than their share of world GDP, which is 28.34 per cent on

Table 8.2 Distribution of GDP and Voting Share Among the G20

1. Industrialized Countries	GDP Share		Voting share	
	PPP	Market Exchange Rate	Present Position	After 2010 change
EU	20.43	25.88		
USA	19.74	23.30	16.727	16.479
Japan	5.80	8.68	6.225	6.138
Germany	3.96	5.27	5.803	5.308
Russia	2.99	2.33	2.386	2.587
UK	2.93	3.57	4.286	4.024
France	2.89	4.11	4.286	4.024
Italy	2.39	3.27	3.154	3.016
Korea	1.96	1.60	1.364	1.731
Canada	1.79	2.50	2.554	2.214
Australia	1.19	1.96	1.312	1.332
Sub-Total	**66.07**	**82.47**	**48.097**	**46.853**
2. Oil Exporter				
Saudi Arabia	0.84	0.71	2.799	2.010
3. Emerging Markets				
China	13.58	9.34	3.806	6.071
India	5.47	2.44	2.337	2.629
Brazil	2.92	3.32	1.714	2.218
Mexico	2.11	1.65	1.467	1.796
Indonesia	1.39	1.12	0.854	0.951
Turkey	1.29	1.18	0.607	0.953
Argentina	0.87	0.59	0.869	0.661
South Africa	0.71	0.57	0.770	0.634
Sub-Total	**28.34**	**20.21**	**12.424**	**15.913**

the basis of GDP in PPP (purchasing power parity) terms and 20.21 per cent on the basis of market exchange rates.

The next quota review is scheduled to begin in 2013 and be completed by 2014. With more rapid growth projected in the emerging market countries, we can expect a further shift in quota and voting share in their favour. There is a case for accelerating this process by abandoning the existing quota formula, which gives too much weight to foreign trade and reserves. These variables have no particular rationale either as indicators of the need to borrow, or of the ability to contribute. In a world of capital mobility, borrowing needs will be largely unrelated to the size of foreign trade or the current account deficit, and this has been recognized by effectively delinking borrowing limits for individual countries. We should move to a new formula that uses some combination of GDP at PPP and at market exchange rates, as the base for determining quota contribution and therefore voting rights. Countries that do not wish to contribute on this basis can be allowed to withhold contribution at the cost of lower voting rights, and perhaps also some limitations on access.

Other tasks before the G20

The mandate of the G20 covers not only international monetary and financial issues but also other international economic issues. Several of these are already on the agenda and some present especially difficult problems.

Completion of Doha Round

One of the most important issues which is on the agenda of the G20 is the need to ensure successful completion of the Doha Development Round. The G20 have recognised the importance of this item in the global economic agenda by consistently calling for an early conclusion of the Round. Unfortunately, there has been very little progress towards this objective. Trade Ministers have met frequently in Geneva, but the negotiations seem to have reached an impasse. Given the importance of open trade for the growth prospects of the developing countries, it can be argued that the G20 should take on the responsibility of breaking the deadlock to deliver on what has been promised to the developing countries.

The central problem is that some of the industrialized countries have decided that what had emerged thus far in the negotiations – and was in that sense 'on the table' – is simply not good enough and that 'greater ambition' is therefore needed. In practical terms, this means re-opening issues which most participants thought were settled earlier at Hong Kong. Since all such decisions are part of a negotiating process, many participants feel that whatever was agreed was part of a quid pro quo, and re-opening anything involves re-opening everything. This of course would be equivalent to declaring the Round dead, and starting afresh.

The Doha Development Round is the first round of multilateral trade negotiations to have been explicitly described as a development round. Failure to conclude the round will be viewed as a major set back for global governance especially as the Round was meant to deliver disproportionate benefits to the developing countries. In the circumstances, the G20, as the principal forum for discussing international economic issues, will be expected to give a political push to the stalled talks. In some ways, the very usefulness of establishing the G20 as the principal forum of the major industrialized and emerging market countries, to discuss international economic issues, stems from the assumption that it can take up issues that are otherwise blocked in the normal ministerial forum, and bring them for resolution at the highest political level. It remains to be seen whether, by the time of the Cannes Summit, the G20 can take some new initiative in this area.

Climate change negotiations

A similar test could arise for the G20 in terms of their ability to resolve what look like insuperable barriers to making significant progress on the Climate Change Negotiations. A detailed review of the state of the climate change negotiations is beyond the scope of this paper, but the issues are similar to those in the trade talks. There is an established international forum where this issue is being discussed, but the negotiations in that forum are making very little progress.

There have been some positive developments. The Copenhagen Accord appeared to produce a broad framework of agreement among many participants, which could be developed further. There is also growing agreement on the need to cooperate in some well-defined areas taken in isolation. These are welcome developments and there is merit in being realistic and encouraging progress wherever it is possible. But sooner or later, the world will have to face the fact that a credible deal on climate change will not be possible unless much faster progress is made on how to share the burden involved.

Arguably, the last two years have been the worst years to look for such agreement. Most countries have been pre-occupied with their own domestic problems which include fiscal stress. Hopefully, after the world has got back to economic normalcy, there will be greater willingness to re-engage substantively. Nevertheless, it will be a huge challenge to orchestrate cooperative action on the scale needed and to bear the costs involved. The G20 will certainly be judged by what it contributes to overcome obstacles in this area.

Other issues

There are several other items on the G20 agenda including unemployment and social security, agriculture and food security, energy security and energy subsidies, transparency in commodity markets, action against corruption etc. The Seoul Summit added development to this already extended agenda. These are important areas in which countries should engage in dialogue to develop commonality of views. But they do not pose any difficult issues for decision in the near future and are therefore not likely to be the basis for judging the usefulness of the G20.

The Legitimacy of the G20

Any assessment of the role of the G20 in global governance has to address the legitimacy issue: can a self selected group of countries ever have international legitimacy? The short answer is that it cannot. However, the real value of the G20 as an international forum is not because it is a legitimized forum for international negotiations, but rather as a more representative replacement for the G8, as the principal forum for discussion of international economic issues.

The need for a broader forum was long evident. The old arrangement, in which the industrialized countries operated as an exclusive club, effectively taking key decisions within the G7/8, and having them ratified later in the relevant international forum, was no longer workable. The steadily rising weight of emerging market economies required that these countries had to be included in consultations on international issues for any meaningful results to be obtained. The G8 Summit in Gleneagles in 2005 acknowledged this reality by inviting five emerging market countries – China, India, South Africa, Brazil and Mexico – to participate, albeit only as invitees for some sessions. This practice was continued in subsequent summits. However, the ambiguous status of the new invitees in this arrangement was a source of discomfort. Celso Amorin, Foreign Minister of Brazil gently satirized the arrangement as the developing countries 'being invited to join for coffee'!

Some expansion of the G7/8 was, therefore, inevitable. It could have occurred by adding some more countries to the G8 plus 5. In the event, it occurred because President George Bush decided to convene a summit of the countries which were already members of the G20 at the level of finance ministers. The creation of that group has an interesting history. The decision to set up a group of finance ministers to discuss international monetary and financial issues was taken at the Asia-Pacific Economic Cooperation (APEC) Summit meeting in Vancouver in 1997, immediately after the outbreak of the East Asian crisis, The United States then invited 22 Finance Ministers to meet in Washington in 1998 at the Willard Hotel (which led to the group being called the Willard Group of 22). The membership expanded to 33, at the next meeting of the group in 1999. However, recognizing the unwieldiness of meetings with 33 countries, the G8, at the Berlin Summit in 1999, decided to establish a permanent Group of 20 finance ministers and central bank governors that would meet regularly to discuss issues related to the international monetary and financial system.

The country composition of the Group of 20 established in 1999 determined the country composition of the G20 Summit. It included all the important industrialized countries, and also the major emerging market countries. Together, the group accounts for 78 per cent of global GDP. However, it leaves out some emerging market countries which have a larger weight than some that are included. Clearly, regional balance considerations played a role in the selection of countries in 1999. There was also no representation for small countries.

Recognizing the limitations of this grouping, the G20 leaders have attempted to broaden participation by a formula which involves five additional invitees. Spain which was not part of the G20 as originally constituted has been made a permanent invitee, in acknowledgement of the size of its GDP. In addition, the head of one of the two African regional organizations will be invited as also a representative of the Association of Southeast Asian Nations (ASEAN). The host of the G20 Summit will have the discretion to invite two other countries. The G20 are also actively pursuing policies of outreach to engage CSOs, business leaders, and other countries, on items on the summit agenda.

None of this can confer formal legitimacy to the group. But it does help to create an environment in which the activities of the G20 are more transparent, and open to comment by others who are not members. In the end, the effectiveness of the group will depend on the fact that the countries included in the group account for almost 80 per cent of global GDP. If consensus is reached in this group, it should be possible to translate it into a global consensus. The translation is easy in the case of international financial and monetary issues, since decisions in the relevant international fora are taken on the basis of weighted voting. It will be more difficult in other fora such as the WTO or the United Nations Framework Convention on Climate Change (UNFCCC), where the tradition is to operate through consensus. But it should not be impossible.

Conclusion

Has the G20 lived up to the expectations raised when it was established? The answer to this question can be unambiguously positive as far as the first two years are concerned, though its crisis management capacity will once again be tested by the Eurozone crisis.

The group can certainly claim to have succeeded in averting a prolonged global downturn through concerted, if not fully coordinated, policy action. It can also claim to have taken a number of initiatives to reform financial sector regulation and to strengthen the IFIs. It has also initiated an ambitious process for policy co-ordination across countries which is widely regarded as an essential element for effective management of an interconnected global economy.

It can be argued that some of these policy decisions were relatively easy. The fact that the world was teetering on a precipice in early 1999 imparted a sense of urgency that something had to be done. The specific actions taken to counter the recession – fiscal and monetary expansion – were also politically popular, as they appeared to be responding to the need to protect jobs. The only critics were the anti Keynesians, warning about inflationary consequences several months ahead. The action taken to tighten financial regulation was also politically popular, as it resonated well with public anger at "greed in Wall Street", which was seen as responsible for loss of jobs and the destruction of value in homes. The only dissenters were those who felt that excessive regulation might dampen flexibility and innovation, but they were willing to bide their time, and find ways to dilute the restrictive steps later.

The strengthening of the IFIs represented an agenda that had been on the table for some time, and while it had been resisted earlier, it is now seen as a relatively low cost way of helping developing countries, and also some of the new eurozone members, to obtain finance to tide them over the crisis. Given the extraordinary amounts being used for bail outs in the industrialized countries, it would have been odd to deny much more modest amounts to help other countries.

The new Multilateral Assessment Process (MAP) which has the ambitious objective of bringing about effective coordination of macro policy across countries, is potentially very important but is still a work in progress. Unlike the other initiatives taken in the first two years, this does not represent a case of fixing the system where it is visibly broken. It is potentially a game changer. However, to be successful, it must produce a process which persuades sovereign governments to rethink their domestic policy options in the light of their global spillover effects, and in the light of some assurance that other countries will act in a manner to achieve an 'upside scenario'. It would be unrealistic to expect any easy victories here. Something like the MAP is necessary if we want to ensure continued viability of a highly interconnected global economy but, it will, at best, be a long haul, and countries should prepare themselves for a possibly rough ride.

Will the G20 be able to ensure a continuing good record of performance in the years ahead? This is a much more difficult question to answer since the problems the G20 now face are much more difficult. The 2008 crisis is over but the ongoing Eurozone crisis is in some ways more difficult. The first discussion of the outcome of the MAP at the summit level in Cannes in November 2011 will give some indication of how far the G20 can engage in meaningful discussion of difficult issues, involving decisions made by sovereign governments which have to pass the test of domestic political acceptability. It will also be the occasion to judge whether there is real appetite for considering structural reforms in the IMS.

Saving the Doha Development Round, which at present seems to going nowhere, will require extraordinary political leadership. It could be argued that the G20 is not the right forum to discuss these issues, but on that consideration it shouldn't be addressing many of the other issues either. If the Doha Development Round is important, it should be the responsibility of the G20 to try and restore momentum by giving a political push to what at present seems a hopelessly mired activity.

If the Doha Round is difficult, the Climate Change Negotiations, which are the next major ongoing item on the international agenda, are even more difficult. However, there is clearly more time to build a broader consensus on these issues.

Notes

1 The G20 was originally established in 1999 as a forum of finance ministers and central bank governors of 19 important advanced and emerging market economies plus the EU to discuss issues related to the functioning of the international monetary and financial system. It has met annually since then. The first meeting of the Heads of Government of these 20 countries was held in November 2008 in Washington DC.

2 The G20 have not announced the list of countries but the list has been discussed publicly. Angeloni and Pisani-Ferry (2011) report that the list consists of the United States, United Kingdom, France, Germany, Japan, China and India.

3 There is recognition of the need for such a shift, and China's Twelfth Five Year Plan explicitly talks of a consumption-led strategy with a lower growth rate.

4 The extent of exchange loss would depend on the net effect of the change in exchange rates plus the differential between the interest earned on dollar securities and the interest paid on the SDR holdings.

5 It should be noted that the rule of proportionality to quotas ensure that the bulk of the additional liquidity provided goes to countries that will not use it. It is instructive that 90 per cent of the new SDR allocation made in the post crisis period remains unused.

6 The timing was particularly unfortunate since the proposal came up in the meeting of the Interim Committee in Hong Kong in 1997, just as the East Asian crisis was breaking out. The move failed, and the initiative was shelved.

References

Ahluwalia, M.S., 2000. Reforming the global financial architecture. Economics Page 41 Commonwealth Economic Paper Series.

Angeloni, I., Benassy-Quéré, A., Carton, B., Darvas, Z., Destais, C., Gauvin, L., Pisani-Ferry, J., Sapir, A. and Vallee, S., 2011. Reforming the International Monetary System – Options and Implication. Report submitted to the European Commission.

Angeloni, Ignacio and Jean Pisani-Ferry (2011) "The G20: Characters in Search of an Author" Paper prepared for the Bank of Korea Annual Conference May.

Bhagwati, J., 1998. The capital myth: the difference between trade in widgets and trade in dollars. *Foreign Affairs* 77.

Camdessus, M., Lamfalussy, A. and Padoa-Schioppa, T., 2011. Reform of the International Monetary System: A cooperative approach for the twenty first century. Palais Royal Initiative.

Rajan, R.G., 2010. *Fault lines; how hidden fractures still threaten the world economy.* NJ: Princeton University Press.

Williamson, J., 1991. On Liberalising the Capital Account. In: O'Brien, R. ed. Finance and the International Economy. Oxford: Oxford University Press.

Xiaochuan, Z., Reform in International Monetary System, *BIS Review* 41/2009.

9

The Hydra-headed Crisis

David Held, Mary Kaldor and Danny Quah

We are living at a time of successive crises – the Haiti earthquake, famine in East Africa, the Taliban attack on Kabul, the collapse of Lehman Brothers, the Boxing Day Tsunami, Hurricane Katrina... No sooner does one crisis disappear from the headlines, than another pops up in a different part of the world. Perhaps this is just because we are more aware of crises in faraway places than in the past. The explosion in information and communications technologies has allowed us to receive and indeed experience images and texts not only from the media but from friends and families and indeed anyone with a camera or a mobile and access to the internet, and, at the same time, to be able to blog, twitter and comment upon what appears to be instant reportage from whatever crisis zone dominates airwaves at that particular moment.

But there is more to successive crises than growing communication, important though that is. We argue that all these crises are interconnected. They are all, in different ways, the expression of something more fundamental – a transformation of our social, economic and political relations, of which growing communications are just one element – and the failure of our governing institutions to adapt to this transformation. In the twentieth century, the nation state and the bloc were the mechanisms for managing social, economic and political relations; trust in our institutions was in large part based on the fact that we believed that they had the will and the capacity to cope with crises and to manage risk. Now that crises (financial, economic, security, or ecological) transcend borders, we have lost confidence in those traditional mechanisms. Yet the kind of global arrangements that are required have still not been constructed. This is the central paradox of our time: the collective issues we must grapple with are increasingly of global scope and reach and yet the means for addressing them are national, weak and incomplete.

A crisis is an emergency – a moment of extreme peril when time seems to stop, a moment of suspense when no one can be sure what will happen or how the crisis will end. It is also an illumination, a moment of truth, when people are more receptive to alternative ways of seeing the world. Our goal is to investigate and give substance to those new ways of thinking through rigorous conceptual and empirical research and to put forward ideas and proposals that might enable us, at least for a while, to escape what appears to be an ever deepening spiral of crisis.

In developing our argument, we focus on three overlapping categories of crisis: economic and financial, security, and environmental. We will draw from our analyses of these crises some common threads that have to do with the failures of public provision, the lack of governance and the lack of trust in governance. And in the final section, we put forward some new directions for both policy and research.

Economic and financial crisis

The financial crisis of 2008 has been widely interpreted as a failure of regulation and the consequence of excessive faith in markets. We agree with this interpretation but, at the same time, we argue that there was more to the crisis. As Joseph Stiglitz puts it in a recent book, understanding the crisis is like peeling the layers of an onion. Each explanation raises new questions. Why did the neo-liberal ideology become the dominant ideology in the 1980s and 1990s? Why did it sweep the corridors of power both nationally and internationally? Were there alternatives?

Money and the management of money is an expression of underlying power relations. The dollar became the world's reserve currency in 1945, replacing sterling in a matter of five years. In fact the US economy had grown to be the largest in the world by 1872. But it took the Great Depression and two world wars to depose sterling. Since then it has been America's political and economic power that has underpinned the role of the dollar. That successful American economic model has enjoyed huge increases in productivity based on mass production and the intensive use of energy, especially oil. It was only, however, after the Second World War that the United States was able to boost aggregate demand through increased consumer and military spending, and the spread of the American model to many parts of the world. It was at this point that the United States emerged as a powerful political and military actor; it was able to shape the international monetary system through the Bretton Woods arrangements and to foster worldwide economic growth through the provision of economic and military assistance.

But that model began to run into difficulties by the early 1970s. As other countries caught up with the United States, the trade surplus began to decline; at the same time the American model of growth was coming up against diminishing returns as it became harder to sustain productivity growth. As the US trade balance plunged into deficit in 1971 from increased spending during the Vietnam War, that episode called into question America's military pre-eminence. The same year saw the end of the system of fixed exchange rates and, two years later, dramatic increases in the price of oil.

It is in this context that the new wave of neo-liberalism has to be understood. The protagonists of supply side economics argued that excessive state interference was the cause of the slowdown in productivity growth. Deregulation and privatization would release new creative energies. The so-called Washington Consensus (privatization, liberalization, and fiscal and monetary discipline) became the dominant set of recipes emanating from the Bretton Woods institutions. These recipes were imposed on indebted countries throughout the developing world and elsewhere. Paradoxically, as a result of the 2008 global financial crisis, the United States and the United Kingdom emerged as significantly indebted countries but, of course, they have not been made to follow the strict Washington Consensus discipline usually reserved for such behaviour. For nearly two decades, the United States enjoyed strong growth through massive expansion of credit. The consequences were ballooning trade deficits and dramatic increases in overall indebtedness. But because the dollar remained the reserve currency, underpinned by America's political as well as economic clout, the country was always able to borrow to cover the deficit. The United States was able to use what the former French President de Gaulle called its *'privilège exhorbitant'* to suck in capital from the rest of the world, allowing capital to flow uphill from poor countries to richer ones.

As this continued through the early years of the twenty-first century, the United States and its supporters saw no immediate difficulties with its economic performance. Instead, many observers blamed so-called Asian thrift for causing a global savings glut in this time that, had the United States not stood ready to absorb it through increased consumption, would have led even earlier to global recession.

The deregulation of the financial sector led to a series of financial innovations – particularly the growing use of plastic. It also facilitated the mobilization of capital for new sectors potentially capable of generating new productivity gains – the revolution in information and communications systems. But enthusiasm for the new technologies ran ahead of productive possibilities, which were constrained by the continued emphasis on energy intensive military and consumer products, as well as skewed income distribution. After the bursting of the dot.com bubble in 2000, the financial sector began to develop ever more creative ways of increasing return based on asset inflation, particularly housing, rather than organic improvements in productivity. The financial sector swelled as banks lent to other banks, dealing in increasingly exotic financial instruments. Unnoticed, this massive build-up replicated many times over the risks of the original outlays.

The immediate cause of the 2008 global financial crisis was defaults on excessively-securitized sub-prime mortgage loans. But, of course, US (and UK) indebtedness had also soared due to involvement in costly wars and because of the Bush tax cuts. Indeed, the US defence budget, even excluding the supplemental cost of wars, is roughly equivalent, at $700 billion, to the entire Obama stimulus package. Estimates of US costs of the conflicts in Afghanistan and Iraq vary but some calculate that it could be in excess of a trillion dollars. By 2008, household, banking and corporate debt had reached 350 per cent of US GDP and 300 per cent of UK GDP (Gamble, 2009).

Of course, the US deficits did stimulate growth in other parts of the world, particularly China and India since Americans could afford to buy goods made in the rest of the world. Even though the United States remains the largest single national economy, if we were to attempt to plot the world's economic centre of gravity, we would find that it has moved dramatically towards the East. In 1976, the world's economic centre of gravity could be located west of London, at a point in the Atlantic ocean somewhere between the United States and the United Kingdom. Over the last thirty years, the economic centre of gravity has drilled nearly 2000 km, one third of the planet's radius, eastwards and into the interior towards China and India. On the one hand, this is all to the good: the rise of India and China has lifted millions out of poverty, profoundly re-drawing the map of human welfare. On the other hand, it has been the poorest people in parts of Africa, among others, who have been unable to compete in global markets and have borne the brunt of the Washington Consensus. Global inequality has increased in the context of deregulation and the lack of global public redistribution. One sixth of the world's population, roughly a billion people, remain desperately poor.

The policy implications of this explanation for the financial crisis go well beyond improved financial regulation – important though that is. It suggests that what we need is a new global regulatory framework based on a genuine global medium of exchange and unit of account, rather than one based on a single national currency, which then confounds needed adjustments in the international financial and trading system. But above all, it shows that there is a need to transform the pattern of development from the energy, consumer and military intensive model, if there are to be new opportunities for sustainable growth in economic terms, that is to say, growth that yields increases in productivity to match income redistribution.

Security crisis

The worst security crisis imaginable is an inter-state war like the two world wars or the Cold War. Perhaps because of the horror of that experience, most national security capabilities are designed for that contingency. Yet in the twenty-first century, the risk of inter-state wars seems remote. Indeed, of the sixteen major armed conflicts that were active in fifteen locations around the world in 2008, not one was a major inter-state conflict.[1] Instead we are facing the spread of insecure spaces where people fear being killed, kidnapped, robbed, tortured, raped or expelled from their homes; where they may lack access to water, food, electricity, or healthcare; or where they are increasingly vulnerable to natural or manmade disasters. Such spaces range from parts of global cities to whole regions. Cité Soleil in Port au Prince in Haiti is one such example, characterized by a toxic mixture of crime and poverty where police and UN peacekeepers dared not enter even before the earthquake. But so is the Horn of Africa, Central Asia, especially Afghanistan and its neighbours, and the Caucasus. Into these spaces rush private actors such as warlords, criminal gangs, militias, jihadists, pirates, adventurists and mercenaries, creating a market in violence that transcends borders and reaches into the heart of the developed world through terror, drugs, illegal migration...

Insecure spaces are also described as ungoverned spaces. They are characterized by what are variously described as fragile, weak, failing, failed, collapsed, shadow or quasi-states. This phenomenon is often attributed to backwardness, the incomplete character of the state-building process. But actually it may well be the opposite, the unravelling of the state-building process under the impact of globalization. Typically, these spaces exist in areas that were formerly governed by authoritarian or totalitarian states. The rise of neo-liberalism in the West in the 1980s and 1990s was paralleled by a wave of political and economic liberalization in the rest of the world for a variety of reasons – disillusion with populist ideologies based on socialism or post-colonial nationalism; declining state revenues either because of the decline in foreign aid as the Cold War came to an end or due to the failures of planned economies and the consequent increase in indebtedness; and growing travel and communications, which opened up the possibilities of alternatives. Samuel Huntington dubbed the spread of democratization in Latin America, Africa and Eastern Europe the 'third wave of democratization'.

During the transition from authoritarianism to democracy the risks of instability are greatest. Political liberalization was accompanied by economic liberalization. Perversely this gave rise to a process that is the opposite of state-building. Many countries had already experienced an erosion of the tax revenue base because of declining legitimacy and growing incapacity to collect tax; growing corruption and clientelism under the last years of dictatorship; and declining investment (both public and private) and, consequently, production. Declining tax revenue leads to growing dependence on external and private sources through, for example, rent seeking or criminal activities. Reductions in public expenditure as a result of the shrinking fiscal base as well as pressures from external donors and lenders further erode legitimacy. A growing informal economy associated with increased inequalities, unemployment and rural-urban migration, combined with the loss of legitimacy, weakens the rule of law and may lead to the re-emergence of privatized forms of violence – organized crime and the substitution of 'protection' for taxation, vigilantes, private security guards protecting economic facilities, especially international companies, or paramilitary groups associated with particular political factions. In particular, reductions in security expenditure, often encouraged by external donors for the best of motives, may lead to breakaway groups of redundant soldiers and policemen seeking alternative employment.

Of course, the impact of globalization is positive as well as negative. External donors and outside powers have pressured governments to introduce political reform as a precondition of economic reform, to reduce corruption, increase respect for human rights, and introduce democratic institutions. Support from outside powers and international NGOs for civil society has helped to strengthen domestic pressures for democratization. It can be argued that where domestic pressures for reform are weak and civil society is least developed the opening up of the state both to the outside world and to increased participation through the democratization process is most dangerous. In a number of countries, the process of democratization is largely confined to elections. Many of the essential prerequisites of democratic procedures – rule of law, separation of powers, freedom of association and of expression – are not in place. And even where procedures are more or less in place, decades of authoritarianism may have left the political culture vulnerable to populist ideologies based on the appeal to various forms of exclusive prejudices. Much contemporary political violence can be explained as a form gerrymandering – expelling people in order to win elections.

These are the circumstances that underlie contemporary insecurity. It is the lack of state authority, the weakness of representation, the loss of confidence that the state is able or willing to respond to public concerns, and the inability and/ or unwillingness to regulate the processes of privatization and informalization that gives rise to a combination of political and criminal violence. Moreover, this unravelling process tends to be reinforced by the dynamics of the violence, which has the effect of further reordering political, economic and social relationships in a negative spiral of insecurity – an ongoing crisis of fear which is no longer bounded in either time or space.

It is this pattern of insecurity that is most likely to spread as a consequence of dramatic occurrences like flooding, storms and earthquakes, or shortages of resources such as water, in the context of climate change. Some argue that the conflict in Darfur is the first climate change conflict. The dependence of the global economy on oil and other resources has also been associated with what has come to be known as the 'resource curse', as competition for resource rents degenerates into instability and those rents finance further violence.

Yet our security capabilities still consist predominantly of national armed forces, based on the organizational principle of geopolitical state interests. Global military spending, fuelled by such preconceptions, has increased significantly in recent years: global military expenditure in 2008 is estimated to have totalled $1.464 trillion, representing an increase of 4 per cent in real terms compared to 2007, and an increase of 45 per cent over the period 1999–2008.[2]

To put this in perspective, that represents $217 for every person on the planet, thirteen times that spent on all types of development aid, 700 times the amount spent on global health programmes, and roughly the same as the combined GDP of every country in Africa. The effects of the global financial crisis – in particular, growing government budget deficits and the economic stimulus packages that are aimed at countering the crisis – seem to have had little effect on military spending, with most countries, including the United States and China, remaining committed to further increases in the years ahead.

The use of conventional military forces in insecure areas merely results in a worsening of insecurity as we have witnessed in Iraq, Afghanistan, Chechnya or Palestine. What is needed are global security forces, much like emergency forces within a well-governed state – combining medical, fire fighting and policing capacities. The aim would not so much be the security of borders but the safety of human beings wherever they live. Even though a learning process is underway among multilateral institutions like the United Nations and indeed among the military who have experienced contemporary insecurity firsthand, it remains utterly inadequate. At present, for example, total global spending on multilateral operations such as peacekeeping forces was just $8.2 billion, or 0.56 per cent of total global military expenditures (SIPRI Multilateral Peace Operations Database). The danger of this growing security gap is only beginning to be grasped.

Environmental crisis

Until the middle of the last century, most known forms of negative environmental impact were largely localized. Since then, the impact and scale of environmental change has dramatically intensified, with problems such as declining biodiversity, deforestation, and a plethora of water resource problems becoming effectively globalized. In particular, climate change is already with us. The Arctic ice cap has been shrinking at 3 per cent a year since 1978. Eleven of the hottest years since 1850 have occurred in the last twenty years, and the last decade is the hottest on record. Global climate change has recently been called a threat more serious than that of international terrorism, and the greatest market failure the world has ever seen (see King 2004; Stern and Tubiana 2008).

Climate change and other human-induced damage to the environment are, of course, associated with the spread of the energy-intensive model of development. But insecurity is also a cause of environmental degradation. Even though production and energy use often decline, insecure spaces are more prone to deforestation, declining biodiversity, and illegal trading in commodities like ivory, rare animals, or timber. Moreover it is the poorest and most insecure areas that are most vulnerable to natural shocks and have least resilience, as the crisis in Haiti has dramatically illustrated.

Archibishop Desmond Tutu has talked about the prospect of 'adaptation apartheid' (UNDP, 2007/8, pp. 73–207). The asymmetrical costs of climate change stand in great contrast to the massive global asymmetries in carbon footprints. As the UNDP has recently pointed out, a single standard air-conditioning unit in Florida emits in a year more carbon dioxide than the average person in Cambodia or Afghanistan does in a lifetime; the population of New York State has a higher carbon footprint than the 766 million people living in the 50 least developed countries of the world (UNDP, 2007/8, pp. 43–44). And while countries like China and India are increasing their per-capita carbon footprint at a dangerous rate (especially given their large populations and projected level of industrialization), the historical picture is sobering – with the mass of responsibility lying with already industrialized states such as the United States and Britain (UNDP 2007/8, p. 41; World Resources Institute).[3]

The challenges to reaching a coherent and effective global deal on climate change are formidable. While democracies by and large have a better record on dealing with environmental degradation than autocracies, they find it extremely difficult to overcome collective action problems which affect future generations. They are hamstrung by a number of structural weaknesses – the short-termism of the electoral cycle, interest group concentration, and a focus on swing voters – which handicap their ability to solve long-term environmental problems. Civil society pressure and enlightened leadership can make a clear difference, yet bringing the domestic policy preferences of diverse countries together is proving hugely difficult, as the UN climate change conference in Copenhagen in 2011 illustrated.

The governance problem

All these domains suffer from the same paradox. A global strategy is required and yet power is organized on a national basis whether we are talking about formal authority or informal politics.

Of course, global institutions exist that are supposed to deal with finance, economic development, security and the environment. But these institutions are fragmented and access to power is very unequal. In the economic domain, there is the International Monetary Fund, the World Bank, the World Trade Organization, and the International Labour Organization. There is also the United Nations Development Programme, the United Nations Conference on Trade and Development, a range of regional organizations like the European Union, the North American Free Trade Agreement, and the Association of Southeast Asian Nations, not to mention a host of ad hoc financial institutions like the Basel Committee on Banking Supervision (established in 1974 in direct reaction to the contagious effects of cross-border bank failures) or the Financial Stability Forum (established in 1999 after widespread concerns over the contagion of financial instability following the East Asian financial crises).

In the security field, the United Nations Security Council is the only organization that can legally authorize the use of force beyond borders but it is dependent on the voluntary provision of security capabilities from individual nations and a range of emerging regional institutions such as NATO, the European Union, the Commonwealth of Independent States, the Organization for Security and Co-operation in Europe, or the African Union and the Economic Community of West African States Monitoring Group. Of course nowadays, security capabilities also include humanitarian organizations like the United Nations High Commissioner for Refugees, UNICEF, as well as many international NGOs and private security companies. And the current global environmental governance regime features a diverse set of players whose roles are largely uncoordinated among each other: the UN Environment Programme, the Global Environment Facility, the Environment Management Group, the Organisation for Economic Co-operation and Development Environment Directorate, the Commission for Sustainable Development, the UN's Economic and Social Development Council, and the Environmental Chamber of the International Court of Justice, to name the most prominent (see Mabey, 2007; Keohane and Raustiala, 2008).

Compounding this institutional fragmentation is the problem that most of these institutions are intergovernmental and accountable to national governments rather than those in need, and they tend to be dominated by the most powerful countries, notably the United States. This is particularly salient in relation to financial governance. Despite the wide membership of the International Monetary Fund (IMF), its voting rules skew decision-making power toward the United States.[4] This has wider implications than is often assumed, especially given the fact that private interests within the United States have been shown to influence IMF policies through the lobbying of Congress (Broz, 2008). Other governance institutions, however, have operated on a different decision-making basis but still exclude the vast majority of the world's population from any representative hand in formal decision-making.

For example, the Basel Committee on Banking Supervision, the global institution effectively setting the regulatory standards worldwide, has maintained a highly exclusive approach to its membership. For decades, it did not expand its membership to include formal representation of developing countries, and until 2008 its membership reflected the status of international financial power in the 1970s rather than the 2000s. During this period nothing changed in the Committee's membership, while countries like Japan, France and Germany experienced a relative decline in the position of their largest banks, and countries like China and Brazil a relative increase (Held and Young, 2009).

This meant that up to and including the worst of the global financial crisis, many countries without any formal representation in the Basel Committee had a much more prominent role in banking than many of those within it.[5]

In the security field the problem is that the United States accounts for half of world military spending. Other big spenders are France, the United Kingdom, China and Russia. But the big spenders are the least adjusted to contemporary security needs and the least committed to multilateral security missions. Most military spending goes towards large sophisticated weapons systems designed for a future world war. Although France and the UK have played active and constructive roles in UN missions, they currently face hard choices between moving towards new types of security capabilities or continuing to buy big systems like aircraft carriers or nuclear weapons.

In the environmental domain where more states have a voice, as became clear in Copenhagen, the dominant players brought enough bargaining power to the table to ensure that no global deal went through that might damage their interests. The Copenhagen Accord is marked by the absence of long-term emission targets, the omission of watertight pledges on new funding, and no clear indications of how to turn the Accord into a legally binding treaty. The big emitters – the United States, China, India and the countries of the European Union – will continue to be able to act without a binding framework to enforce emission reductions and speed up the pace of a transition to a low-carbon economy.

But above all, the problem is the national basis of politics. National members of intergovernmental institutions, by and large, are preoccupied with short-term national considerations. Some smaller states recognize that their interests can only be pursued in a safer, greener, more just world, but the larger states still put what they see as the interests of their populations in the next election cycle above the global public interest. And even where national interests could be considered to coincide with global public interest, they are often constrained by entrenched institutional attitudes as well as special interests.

Politics does, of course, spill over borders. People committed to causes like peace, human rights, tackling poverty or the environment, often find their access blocked at national levels by traditional political parties of left and right, and so engage at local and global levels. And this is not only true of progressive causes – Islamists, fundamentalist Christians, and others – also organize on a cross-border and local basis. Transnational activism does have an influence on global discourses – climate change for example. And it also means that some of these global issues can be addressed at sub-national levels; global cities like London, Chicago, or Medellin have often been at the forefront of new approaches to reducing carbon emissions, community policing, or reducing inequality.

But the problem of overcoming institutional fragmentation and making global institutions effective and accountable to a global public, as opposed to national and sectoral interests, remains the central challenge of our time.

The way forward

The world system we now have is one where global institutions and rules reflect historical patterns in the distribution of economic, political, and cultural power. It is a system that has not been able to adapt rapidly enough to the eastwards shift in the global distribution of economic activity. It is a system that, because of asymmetric obligations between debtors and creditors, has been unable to adjust in the face of massive global imbalances arising, in turn, from that ongoing shift in economic activity.

Established modes of national governance have the power to tax, subsidize, and provide public goods in ways designed to improve the lot of their societies. Much needed modes of global governance, on the other hand, raise new challenges. What instruments and targets are the legitimate ones to consider in this new world? What authority and legitimacy can be accorded to such systems that they can successfully tackle the problems emerging in the modern global economy and polity?

Some such problems arise from differences in national behaviours: aggregate consumption and savings leading to trade imbalances that do not self-correct. Others arise from the inability of individual countries to internalize global externalities: climate change and environmental degradation or the inappropriateness of national military forces to tackling new global risks. What global consensus can be built on the tools and goals appropriate in each case?

The main point, of course, is that all these crises are connected. They can only be addressed through shifting development away from the energy intensive consumerist model. We can only solve the economic crisis if we can generate sustainable growth and this can only be done through matching potential productivity gains from new technologies with appropriate expenditure on a global low-carbon infrastructure, and the redistribution of resources to the most vulnerable. We can only solve the security crisis if we address the problems of poverty and disease, as well as the instability arising from excessive dependence on commodities like oil, and if we restructure military budgets towards new security needs. And we cannot address climate change without a different model of development and a different model of security. Just as in the 1930s, we need to increase aggregate demand in the context of huge productivity increases brought about by the new economy. But the increase in aggregate demand has to be global rather than national and it has to involve energy saving and other global goods.

This cannot be achieved without representative and effective global institutions that have the capacity to create credible regulatory frameworks and to invest directly in the provision of global public goods and the mitigation of global public evils. It was Max Weber who said that institutions are determined by their sources of revenue. In our judgement, effective global institutions should be funded by new streams of resources, including a financial market transaction tax and a carbon tax.

Whether there is the political will to make this happen is another matter. Can the 1945 multilateral order be reforged and rebuilt, to reflect the changing balance of power in the world and the voices of non-state actors that have emerged with such force and impact over the last few decades? The crucial tests ahead concern the creation of new, effective and just global deals on trade rules, financial market regulation, climate change, the renewal of a nuclear non-proliferation treaty, as well as global investment in a low-carbon future, and in the capabilities to cope with crises. These are tests for the here and now and not some remote future. We face a choice between an effective and accountable rule-based multilateral order, or the fragmentation of the global order into competing regional power blocs pursuing their own sectional interests. Or worse, the spread of ungovernable parts of the world accelerating a vicious downward spiral of global ills – an ongoing Hydra-headed crisis.

Notes

1 According to the SIPRI Yearbook, 2009, the most comprehensive open-source account of developments in global conflicts and security (2009, p. 60).

2 The United States accounts for the majority of the global increase – representing 58 per cent of the global increase over the last ten years, largely due to the wars in Iraq and Afghanistan. However, the United States is far from the only country to pursue such a determined course of militarization. China and Russia have both nearly tripled their military expenditure, while other regional powers – such as Algeria, Brazil, India, Iran, Israel, South Korea, and Saudi Arabia – have also made substantial contributions to the total increase. Of the five permanent members of the UN Security Council, only France has held its spending relatively steady, with a rise of just 3.55 per cent over the last decade.

3 For example, the cumulative estimate of per capita emissions for the United States and Britain's history has been estimated to be 1,100 tonnes of CO_2 per capita, but just 66 tonnes for China and 23 tonnes for India.

4 See Rapkin and Strand, 2006; on the impacts of United States domestic politics on the IMF, see Broz and Hawes, 2006.

5 On the relationship between participation and accountability in financial governance, see Germain, 2004.

References

Broz, J.L. and Hawes, M.B., 2006. Congressional politics of financing the International Monetary Fund. *International Organization*, 60(2), pp. 367–399.

Broz, J.L., 2008. Congressional voting on funding the international financial institutions. *Review of International Organizations*, 3, pp. 351–374.

Gamble, A., 2009. *The spectre at the feast: capitalist crisis and the politics of recession*. London: Palgrave Macmillan.

Germain, R., 2004. Globalising accountability within the International Organization of Credit: financial governance and the public sphere. *Global Society*, 18(3), pp. 217–242.

Held, D. and Young, K., 2009. Parallel worlds: the governance of global risk, finance, security and the environment. LSE Global Governance Working Paper.

Keohane, R. and Raustiala, K., 2008. Toward a post-Kyoto climate change architecture: a political analysis. Discussion Paper 2008-01. Cambridge: Harvard Project on International Climate Agreements, July.

King, D., 2004. Climate change science: adapt, mitigate, or ignore? *Science*, Vol. 303, January, p. 177.

Mabey, N., 2007. Sustainability and foreign policy. In: D. Held and D. Mepham, eds. *Progressive foreign policy: new directions for the UK*. Cambridge: Polity Press.

Rapkin, D. and Strand, J., 2006. Reforming the IMF's weighted voting system. *The World Economy*, 29(3), pp. 305–324.

SIPRI Yearbook, 2009. p. 69. Stockholm: SIPRI.

SIPRI Multilateral Peace Operations Database, n.d. Stockholm: SIPRI, [online]. Available at: http://www.sipri.org/databases/pko) [accessed 17 April 2011].

Stern, N. and Tubiana, L., 2008. A progressive global deal on climate change. Paper Presentation, 5 April. Available at: http://documents.scribd.com/docs/mo91frl3sskk5a2q7i9.pdf [accessed 17 April 2011].

Stiglitz, J.E., 2010. *Freefall: America, free markets, and the sinking of the world economy*. UK: Penguin Books Ltd.

UNDP, 2007/8. *Human development report 2007/2008*.

World Resources Institute, n.d. Climate analysis indicators tool (CAIT) [online]. Available at: http://www.wrl.org/climate/project/description2.cfm?pld=93.

Meghnad Desai: Selected Writings

Books

Desai, M., 1974. *Marxian economic theory*. London: Gray Mills (now Blackwell). Turkish Translation, 1977. Istanbul: Birikim, 1977; Spanish Translation, 1977. Mexico City: Siglo Ventiuno; Japanese Translation, 1978. Chapters 7–10. Tokyo: University of Tokyo Press.

Desai, M., 1976. *Applied econometrics*. UK: Philip Allen. Reprinted, 1977. USA: McGraw Hill.

Desai, M., 1979. *Marxian economics*. Oxford: Blackwell. Japanese Translation, 1981; Portuguese Translation, 1984. Rio de Janeiro: Zahar Editors.

Desai, M., 1981. *Testing monetarism*. London: Frances Pinter Publishers Ltd, 1981. Reprinted, 1982. USA: St Martin's Press. Translated in Spanish, 1989. Fonda de Cultura Economica/Economics Contemparaneo.

Desai, M., 1995. *Macroeconomics and monetary theory. The selected essays of Meghnad Desai, volume 1*. Cheltenham: Edward Elgar.

Desai, M., 1995. *Poverty, famine and economic development. The selected essays of Meghnad Desai, volume II*. Cheltenham: Edward Elgar.

Desai, M., 2002. *Marx's revenge: the resurgence of capitalism and the death of statist socialism*. London, New York: Verso. (Translated in Korean, Chinese, Spanish, Greek and Portuguese.)

Desai, M., 2004. *Development and nationhood: essays in the political economy of South Asia*. Delhi: Oxford University Press.

Desai, M., 2004. *Nehru's hero: Dilip Kumar in the life of India*. Delhi: Roli Books.

Desai, M. and Ahsan, A., 2005. *Divided by democracy: why is India a democracy and Pakistan is not a democracy*. D. Page, ed. Delhi: Roli Books.

Desai, M., 2006. *Rethinking Islamism*. London: I.B. Tauris.

Desai, M., 2006. *The route of all evil: the political economy of Ezra Pound*. London: Faber and Faber.

Desai, M., 2009. *Dead on time* (fiction). London: Beautiful Books; Delhi: Harper Collins.

Desai, M., 2009. *The rediscovery of India*. India: Penguin.

Books (edited)

Kumar, D. and Desai, M. eds., 1983. *The Cambridge economic history of India 1757–1970*. Cambridge: Cambridge University Press.

Desai, M., Rudolph, S. and Rudra, A. eds., 1984. *Agrarian power and agricultural productivity in South Asia*. Berkeley, California: University of California Press.

Desai, M. ed., 1988. *Lectures on advanced econometrics by Denis Sargan*. Oxford: Blackwell.

Desai, M. ed., 1989. Introduction. *Lenin's economics writings*. London: Lawrence & Wishart; New York: New Horizons.

Desai, M. and Redfern, P. eds., 1995. *Global governance: ethics and economics of the world order*. London: Pinter Publishers.

Desai, M. ed., 1995. Introduction. *LSE on equality*. London: LSE Books.

Desai, M., Arestis, P. and Dow, S. eds., 2002. *Methodology, microeconomics and Keynes: essays in honour of Victoria Chick, volume 2*. London: Routledge.

Desai, M., Arestis, P. and Dow, S. eds., 2002. *Money, microeconomics and Keynes: essays in honour of Victoria Chick, volume 1*. London and New York: Routledge.

Desai, M. and Said, Y. eds., 2003. *Financial crises and global governance*. London: Routledge.

Chapters in books

Desai, M., 1966. An econometric model of the world tin economy 1948–1961. *Econometrica*. Reprinted 1977. In: Dutton and Starbruck, eds. *Computer simulation of human behaviour*. New York: John Wiley.

Desai, M. and Henry, S.G.B., 1970. Fiscal policy simulation for the UK economy, 1955–1966. In: K. Hilton and D. Heathfield, eds. *Econometric study of the United Kingdom*. London: Macmillan.

Desai, M., 1974. The theory of capitalist development. In: M. Dobb, ed. Published in Italian in *Instituto Giangiacomo Feltrinellu: storia del Marxismo contemporaneo*. Feltrinelli.

Desai, M., 1975. Emerging contradictions of slow capitalist development in India. In: R. Blackburn, ed. *Explosion in a subcontinent*. London: Penguin.

Desai, M., 1976. Consumption and pollution. In: I.R.C. Hirst & W.D. Reeke, eds. *The consumer society*. University of Edinburgh, Scotland. 1 June 1973. London: Tavistock.

Desai, M., 1978. Asking questions and understanding the answers about how the Chinese economy works. In M. Jeffrey and N. Caldwell, eds. *Planning and urbanism in China: progress in planning, Vol. 8, Part 2*. Oxford: Pergamon Press.

Desai, M., 1980. Stabilisation of primary product prices: lessons of the international tin agreement. In: A. Sengupta, ed. *Commodities finance and trade: the north south negotiating process*. London: Frances Pinter.

Desai, M., 1981. Marxian political economy. In: T. Bottomore, ed. *Modern interpretations of Marx*. Oxford: Blackwell.

Desai, M., 1982. The tasks of monetary theory: the Hayek/Sraffa debate in a modern perspective. In: M. Baranzini, ed. *Contributions to economic analysis*. Oxford: Blackwell.

Desai, M., 1983. Economic alternative for Labour. In: J.A.G. Griffith, ed. *Socialism in a cold climate*. London: Allen and Unwin.

Desai, M., Harvey, A., McKenzie, C.R., and Blake, D., 1983. Irregular Data Revision. In: A. Zellner, ed. *NBER conference volume*.

Desai, M., 1983. Teoria y politica monetaria en la 'teoria general'. *Information commercial Espanola*. Enero (January). Keynes centenary volume.

Desai, M., Keil, M. and Wadwhani, S., 1984. Incomes policy in a political business cycle environment: a structural model for the UK, 1961–1980. In: A.J.H. Hallett, ed. *Applied decision analysis and economic behaviour*. Dordrecht: Martinus Nijhoff.

Desai, M., 1984. The share of wages in national income UK 1860–1970: an econometric model of the growth cycle. In: R. Goodwin, A. Vercelli and M. Kruger, eds. *Nonlinear models of fluctuating growth*. Berlin: Springer Verlag.

Desai, M., 1984. Wages, prices and unemployment a quarter century after the Phillips curve. In: D.F. Hendry and K.F. Wallis, eds. *Econometrics and quantitative economics*. Oxford: Blackwell.

Desai, M., 1986. Building a process of democratic planning: a comment. In: Z. Tzannatos, ed. *Socialism in Greece*. Aldershot: Gower.

Desai, M. and Low, W., 1987. Financial innovations: measuring the opportunity for product innovations. In: M. De Cecco, ed. *Changing money*. Oxford: Blackwell.

Desai, M., 1987. Power and agrarian relations: concepts and measurements. In: M. Desai, S. Rudolph and A. Rudra, eds. *Agrarian power and agricultural productivity in South Asia*. Berkeley, California: University of California Press.

Desai, M., 1987. The political economy of WOE (the world oil economy). In: J. Rees, ed. *The international oil industry*. London: Macmillan.

Desai, M., 1988. Drawing the line. In: P. Golding, ed. *Excluding the poor*. London: Child Poverty Action Group.

Desai, M., 1988. Economic aspects of famine. In: G.A. Harrison, ed. *Famine*. Oxford: Oxford University Press.

Desai, M., 1989. Is Thatcherism the cure for the British disease? In: F. Green, ed. *The restructuring of the UK economy*. London: Harvester.

Desai, M., 1989. Potential life time (PLT): a proposal for an index of social welfare (published in Spanish as Duracion potencial de Vida (DPV) planteamiento sobre un indice de bienestar social). In D. Bracho, ed. *Towards a new way to measure to development*. August.

Desai, M., 1989. The scourge of the monetarists: Kaldor on monetarism and money. *Cambridge Journal of Economics*. Reprinted 1988. In: Lawson, Palma and Sender, eds. *Kaldor's political economy*. London: Academic Press.

Desai, M., 1990. Birth and death of nation states: speculations about Germany and India. In: M. Mann, F. Halliday and J. Hobson, eds. *Rise and decline of the nation state*. Oxford: Blackwell.

Desai, M., 1990. Econometric modelling of early warning systems for famines. In: J. Dreze and A. Sen, eds. *The political economy of hunger, vol. II*. Oxford: Oxford University Press.

Desai, M., 1991. Kaldor between Hayek and Keynes: or did Nicky kill capital theory? In: E. Nell and W. Semmler, eds. *Nicholas Kaldor and mainstream economics*. New York: Macmillan.

Desai, M., 1991. Methodological problems in quantitative Marxism. In: P. Dunne, ed. *Quantitative Marxism*. Cambridge: Polity Press.

Desai, M., 1991. The transformation problem. In: G. Caravale, ed. *Marx and modern economic analysis*. Aldershot: Edward Elgar.

Desai, M., 1991. The transition from socialism to capitalism. (Paper read at the Conference on 'Structural Change in the West', Cambridge 1989.) In: M. Mann, F. Halliday and J. Hobson, eds. *Structural change in the West*. Oxford: Blackwell.

Desai, M., 1992. A Keynesian model for a post-monetarist open economy. In: H. Brink, ed. *Themes in modern macroeconomics*. Houndmills: Macmillan.

Desai, M., 1992. The underworld of economics: heresy and heterodoxy in economic thought. In: G.K. Shaw, ed. *Economics, culture and education*. Aldershot: Edward Elgar.

Desai, M., 1992. Well-being and lifetime deprivation: a proposal for an index of social progress. In: M. Desai, A. Sen and J. Boltvinik, eds. *Social progress index. A proposal, regional project to overcome poverty*. Bogota: UNDP, pp. 67–95.

Desai, M., 1993. A prophet denied: Ambedkar and the partition of India. *The Ambedkar centenary volume*.

Desai, M., 1993. Constructing nationality in a multinational democracy: the case of India. In: R. Michener, ed. *Nationality, patriotism and nationalism in liberal democratic societies*. St. Paul Minnesota: PWPA, pp. 225–241.

Desai, M., 1993. Income and alternative measures of well-being. In: D.G Westendorff and D. Ghai, eds. *Monitoring social progress in the 1990s* (UNRISD). Aldershot: Avebury, pp. 23–39.

Desai, M., 1994. Equilibrium, expectations and knowledge. In: J. Birner and R. van Zijp, eds. *Hayek, co-ordination and evolution: his legacy in philosophy, politics, economics and the history of ideas*. London & New York: Routledge, pp. 25–50.

Desai, M., 1995. Economic reform: stalled by politics? In: P. Oldenburg, ed. *India briefing*. New York and London: M.E. Sharpe, pp. 75–95.

Desai, M., 1995. Global governance. In: M. Desai and P. Redfern, eds. *Global governance: ethics and economics of the world order*. London: Pinter Publishers.

Desai, M., 1995. Global trends in industrial development 2000. *30 years of industrial development 1966 – 1996*. United Nations Development Organisation (UNIDO). International Systems & Communications Ltd (ISC), pp. 220–229.

Desai, M., 1995. Greening of the HDI? In A. MacGillivray, ed. *Accounting for change*. London: The New Economics Foundation, October, pp. 21–36.

Desai, M., 1995. Measuring political freedom. In: E. Barker, ed. *LSE on freedom*. London: LSE Books.

Desai, M., 1995. The natural rate of unemployment: a fundamentalist Keynesian view. In: R. Cross, ed. *The natural rate of unemployment*. Cambridge: Cambridge University Press, pp. 346–361.

Desai, M. and P. Redfern, 1995. Trade cycle as a frustrated traverse: an analytical reconstruction of Hayek's model. In: M. Colonna and H. Hagemann, eds. *Money and business cycles: The economics of F.A. Hayek, vol. 1*. Aldershot: Edward Elgar.

Desai, M., 1995. What is left of Keynes. In: R. Skidelsky, ed. *SMF occasional paper no.10*. London: Social Market Foundation.

Desai, M., 1996. Globalisation and sustainable development In: S. Gupta and N.K. Choudhry, ed. *Growth, equity and sustainability: studies in globalisation and development (volume one)*. University of Toronto, Canada: St Thomas University Press.

Desai, M., 1996. Hayek, Marx and the demise of official Keynesianism. In: M. Baranzini and A. Cencini, eds. *Inflation and unemployment*. London: Routledge.

Desai, M., 1997. Hayek, Marx and Keynes. In S.F. Frowen, ed. *Hayek the economist and social philosopher: a critical retrospect*. London: Macmillan.

Desai, M., 1997. It's profitability, stupid. In: G. Kelly, *et al.*, eds. *Stakeholder capitalism*. London: Macmillan, pp. 203–218.

Desai, M., 1997. Nice guys don't finish last; they are never finished (foreword). In: M. Sawyer, P. Arestis and G. Palma, eds. *Festschift volumes for Geoff Harcourt*. London: Routledge.

Desai, M., 1997. Why is India a low inflation country. In D. Nachane, and M.J.M. Rao, eds. *Macroeconomic challenges and development Issues*. Bombay: Himalaya Publishing House, pp. 31–38.

Desai, M., 1998. A basic income proposal. In: R. Skidelsky, ed. *The state of the future*. London: Centre for Post Collectivist Studies, Social Market Foundation, October, pp. 101–127.

Desai, M., 1998. Development perspectives: was there an alternative to Mahalanobis? In: I.M.D. Little and I.J. Ahluwalia, eds. *India's economic reforms and development: essays for Manmohan Singh*. Delhi and New York: Oxford University press, pp. 40–48.

Desai, M., 1998. Profitability and the persistence of capitalism. In: R. Bellofiore, ed. *Marxian economics: a reappraisal, vol 2: essays on volume III of capital profit, prices & dynamics*. London: Macmillan; USA: St Martin's Press, Inc, pp. 291–305.

Desai, M., 1998. Profitability, prices and values. In: R. Bellofiore, ed. *Marxian economics: a reappraisal, vol 2: essays on volume III of capital profit, prices & dynamics*. London: Macmillan; USA: St Martin's Press, Inc, pp. 3–14.

Desai, M., 1999. Foreign investment and economic development. In: K. Nikolov, ed. *Capital regulation: for and against*. London: Centre for Post Collectivist Studies, Social Market Foundation, February, pp. 43–53.

Desai, M., 1999. PRB: an appreciation of Brahmananda (foreword). In: A. Vasudevan, D. Nachane and A.V. Karnik, eds. *Fifty years of development economics; essays in honour of Professor P.R. Brahmananda*. New Delhi: Himalaya Publishing House.

Desai, M., 1999. The renaissance of LSE economics: a study of our times. In: S. Daniel, P. Arestis and J. Grahl, eds. *The history and practice of economics: essays in honour of Bernard Corry and Maurice Preston, volume two*. Cheltenham: Edward Elgar.

Desai, M. and Low, W., 2000. A characteristic analysis of financial innovations in short-term retail financial products. In: D. Blake, ed. *Finance: a characteristics approach*. London: Routledge.

Desai, M., 2000. British higher education: compacts or contracts. In: K.M. Gokulsing and C. DaCosta, eds. *A compact for higher education*. Aldershot: Ashgate.

Desai, M., 2000. Communalism, secularism and the dilemma of Indian nationhood. In: M. Leifer, ed. *Asian nationalism*. London: Routledge.

Desai, M., 2000. Quel developpement pour le XXXI siècle. In: J. Binde, ed. *Les cles du XXXIe siècle*. UNESCO publication, ISBN no. 2 02 04 1221, pp. 469–472.

Desai, M., 2000. Rejuvenated capitalism and no longer existing socialism: a classical Marxist explanation. In: J. Toporowski, ed. *Political economy and the new capitalism: essays in honour of Sam Aaronovitch*. London: Routledge.

Desai, M., 2000. Seattle: a tragi-comedy. In: B. Gunnell and D. Timms, eds. *After Seattle: globalisation and its discontents*. London: Catalyst, Aldgate Press.

Desai, M. and Said, Y., 2001. The new anti-capitalist movement: money and global civil society. In: H. Anheier, M. Glasius and M. Kaldor, eds. *Global civil society*. Oxford: Oxford University Press, pp. 51–79.

Desai, M., 2001. Well being or wel fare? In: N. Fraser and J. Hills, eds. *Public policy for the 21st century: social and economic essays in memory of Henry Neuberger*. London: Policy Press.

Desai, M., 2002. Defining a new vision for South Asia. In: K. Haq, ed. *The South Asian challenge*. Pakistan: Oxford University Press, pp. 1–33.

Desai, M., 2002. The possibility of deglobalisation. In: W. Dolfsma and C. Dennreuther, eds. *Globalisation, inequality and social capital*. Cheltenham: Edward Elgar.

Desai, M. and Said, Y., 2003. Trade and global civil society: the anti-capitalist movement revisited. In: M. Kaldor, H. Anheier and M. Glasius, eds. *Global civil society*. Oxford: Oxford University Press.

Desai, M., 2005. Hindutva's march halted? Choices for the BJP after the 2004 defeat. In: K. Adeney and L. Saez, eds. *Coalition politics and Hindu nationalism*. London: Rouledge.

Desai, M., 2005. India and China: an essay in comparative political economy. In W. Tseng and D. Cowan, eds. *India's and China's recent experience with reform and growth*. Basingstoke: Palgrave Macmillan.

Desai, M., 2006. A new measure of the poverty line in what is poverty: concepts and measures. Brazil: UNDP International Poverty Centre Brasilia. December.

Desai, M., 2006. Hayek and Marx. In: E. Feser, ed. *The Cambridge companion to Hayek*. Cambridge: Cambridge University Press, pp. 67–81.

Desai, M., 2009. Sita and some other women. In: N. Gokhaleand and M. Lal, eds. *In search of Sita: revisiting mythology*. Delhi: Penguin Books; Yatra Books.

Entries in reference books

Desai, M., 1983. Capitalism; Political economy; Underconsumption; Over production; and Vulgar economics. *The dictionary of Marxist thought*. Oxford: Blackwell.

Desai, M., 1987. Value and price; Schemes of reproduction; Lenin; Profit theory; Endogenous and exogenous money. *The New Palgrave Dictionary of Economics*. Basingstoke: Palgrave Macmillan.

Desai, M., 1992. Cash balances; Endogenous and exogenous money. *New Palgrave dictionary of money and finance*. Basingstoke: Palgrave Macmillan.

Desai, M., 1993. Capitalism. In: J. Krieger, ed. *The Oxford companion to politics of the world*. New York: Oxford University Press.

Desai, M., 1993. Neoclassical economics. In: W. Outhwaite and T. Bottomore, eds. *The Blackwell dictionary of twentieth century social thought*. Oxford: Blackwell.

Articles in academic journals

Desai, M., 1962. A comparison of consumer expenditure on foodgrains as estimated by national sample survey data and aggregate supply data. *Artha Vijnana* (Journal of the Gokhale Institute of Politics and Economics), December.

Desai, M., Bird, R., Enzler, G. and Taubman, P., 1965. 'Kuznets cycles' in growth rates: the meaning. *International Economic Review*, 6(2), pp. 229–239.

Desai, M., 1965. Stock prices, earnings and dividends in India: a quantitative analysis. *Indian Economic Journal*, 12(4), pp. 432–436.

Desai, M., 1968. Some issues in econometric history. *Economic History Review*, 21(1), pp. 1–16.

Desai, M. and Mazumdar, D., 1970. A test of the hypothesis of disguised unemployment. *Economica*, 37(145), pp. 39–53.

Desai, M., 1970. The vortex in India. *New Left Review*, 61, May–June.

Desai, M., 1971. Demand for cotton textiles in nineteenth century India. *Indian Economic and Social History Review*, 8(4), pp. 337–361.

Desai, M., 1972. An econometric model of the world in tin economy: reply to a comment by F.E. Banks. *Econometrica*, 40(4), pp. 753–755.

Desai, M., 1972. Environment and Underdevelopment. *Change or Decay: a Symposium on a Blueprint for Survival. Teilhard Review.*

Desai, M., 1972. Social science goes to war: economic theory and the Pentagon papers. *Survival*, 14(2), pp. 62–67.

Desai, M., 1973. Growth cycles and inflation in a model of the class struggle. *Journal of Economic Theory*, 6(6), pp. 527–545.

Desai, M., 1973. Macroeconomic models of the Indian Economy: a critical survey. *Sankhya*. Reprinted in *A survey of research in economics, vol. VII. Econometrics.* Indian Council for Social Science Research.

Desai, M., 1974. Pooling as a specification error: a note. *Econometrica*, 42(2), pp. 389–391.

Desai, M. and Henry, S.G.B., 1975. Fiscal policy and economic stabilisation. *Review of Economic Studies*, July.

Desai, M., 1975. The Phillips curve: a revisionist interpretation. *Economica*, 42(165), pp. 1–19.

Desai, M., 1976. The consolation of slavery. Review article of R. Fogel and S. Engerman's *Time on the cross: the economics of American negro slavery. Economic History Review*, 29(3), pp. 491–503.

Desai, M., 1976. The role of exchange and market relationships in the economics of the transition period: Lenin on the tax in kind. *Indian Economic Review*, April.

Desai, M., 1980. Ronald Meek's contribution to Marxian economics. *History of Economic Thought Newsletter*, Spring.

Desai, M. and Shah, A., 1981. Growth cycles with induced technical change. *Economic Journal*, 91, pp. 1006–1010.

Desai, M., 1981. Inflation, unemployment and monetary policy: the UK experience. *British Review of Economic Issues*, November.

Desai, M. and Blake, D., 1981. Modelling the ultimate absurdity: a comment on a quantitative study of the strategic arms race in the missile age. *Review of Economics and Statistics*, 63(4), pp. 629–632.

Desai, M., 1981. Testing monetarism: an econometric analysis of Professor Stein's model of monetarism. *Journal of Economic Dynamics and Control*, 3(1), pp. 141–156.

Desai, M. and Montes, D., 1982. A macroeconomic model of bankruptcies in the British economy. *British Review of Economic Issues*, Spring.

Desai, M. and Blake, D., 1982. Monetarism and the US experience. *Journal of Monetary Economics*, July.

Desai, M. and Shah, A., 1983. Bequest and inheritance in nuclear families and joint families. *Economica*, May.

Desai, M., 1985. Is state control necessary for economic development in the third world. *Arab Researcher.*

Desai, M., 1986. Is monetarism dead? De Rous lecture at the Free University of Amsterdam, November 1986. Nederlands Institut voor het Bank-en-Effectenbedrijf.

Desai, M., 1986. Men and things: an inaugural lecture. *Economica*, February.

Desai, M., 1987. A pioneering analysis of the core: Turgot's 'Essay on value'. *Recherches Economiques de Louvain*, 2.

Desai, M., 1987. Storytelling and formalism in economics: the instance of famine. *International Social Science Journal*, 39(3), pp. 387–400.

Desai, M. and Shah, A., 1988. An econometric approach to the measurement of poverty. *Oxford Economic Papers*, September.

Desai, M. and Weber, G., 1988. A Keynesian model of the UK economy. *Journal of Applied Econometrics*, January.

Desai, M. and Anderton, R., 1988. Modelling manufacturing imports. *National Institute Economic Review*, February.

Desai, M., Auerbach, P. and Shamsavari, A., 1988. The dialectics of plan and the market: on the transition from actually existing capitalism. *New Left Review*, 170, September–October.

Desai, M., 1988. The transformation problem. *Journal of Economic Surveys*, 2(4), pp. 295–333.

Desai, M., 1989. 1992: a market Europe or a social Europe? *Irish Business and Administrative Research*, 10(1).

Desai, M., 1989. Comments on S. Chakravarty's 'Marxian economics and contemporary developing economies'. *Cambridge Journal of Economics*, June.

Desai, M., 1989. Political/economic: crisis/reform. *Samizdat*.

Desai, M., 1989. Rice and fish: asymmetric preferences and entitlement failures in food growing economies with non-food producers. *European Journal of Political Economy*, 5.

Desai, M., 1990. Eastern Europe and the third world: rivals or collaborators? *Socialist Affairs*, 1.

Desai, M., 1991. The agrarian crisis in medieval England: a Malthusian tragedy or a failure in entitlements? *Bulletin of Economic Research*, 43(3), pp. 223–258.

Desai, M., 1992. Is socialism dead? V.S. Desai memorial lecture. H.L. College of Commerce, Ahmedabad, 15 December 1990. Indiana University Press.

Desai, M., 1992. Is there life after Mahalanobis? Political economy of India's new economic policy. *Indian Economic Review*, 27, pp. 155–156.

Desai, M., 1992. Make it BIG (basic income guarantee). *Basic Income Review*, September.

Desai, M., 1992. Population and poverty in Africa. *African Development Review*, 4(2), pp. 63–78.

Desai, M. and Estrin, S., 1992. Some simple dynamics of transition from command to market economy. *Centre For Economic Performance*, discussion paper no. 85, July.

Desai, M., 1993. The new international economic order: ideology or reality. *Journal of International Development*, 5(2).

Desai, M., 1994. Poverty and capability: toward an empirically implementable measure. *Frontera Norte*, Numero 1, La pobreza: aspectos teoricos, metodologicos y empiricos, 6, pp. 11–30.

Desai, M., 1994. Rice, fish and famine relief: comment. *European Journal of Political Economy*, 10, pp. 607–610.

Desai, M., 1994. The changing context of full employment. *The V.V. Giri memorial lecture*. New Delhi, January, 1993. *Indian Journal of Labour Economics*, 1994.

Desai, M., 1994. The measurement problem in economics. *Scottish Journal of Political Economy*, 41(1), pp. 34–42.

Desai, M., 1995. An endogenous growth cycle with vintage capital. *Economics of Planning*, pp. 87–91.

Desai, M., 1995. Europe: the next millennium. *Queen's Quarterly*, Summer, pp. 345–356.

Desai, M., 1996. India's triple bypass: economic liberalisation, the BJP and the 1996 elections. *Asian Studies Review*, 19(3).

Desai, M., Hendry, D.F. and Mizon, G.E., 1997. John Denis Sargan, 1924–1996. *The Economic Journal*, 107(443), pp. 1121–1125.

Desai, M. and Omerod, P., 1998. Richard Goodwin: a short appreciation. *The Economic Journal*, 108(450), pp. 1431–1436.

Desai, M., 2000. Globalisation: neither ideology nor utopia. *Cambridge Review of International Affairs*, volume XIV/1, autumn/winter.

Desai, M., 2001. Amartya Sen's contribution to development economics. *Oxford Development Studies*, 29(3), pp. 213–223.

Desai, M., 2002. Book review of *Growth, inequality and globalization: theory, history and policy* by P. Aghion and J. Williamson, Cambridge University Press, 1999. *Economica*, 69, pp. 173–174.

Desai, M., Fukuda-Parr, S., Johansson, C. and Sagasti, F., 2002. Measuring the technology achievement of nations and the capacity to participate in the network age. *Journal of Human Development*, 3(1).

Desai, M. and Holler, M.J., 2002. Why capital hires labour and why labour does not hire capital. *Homo Oeconomicus* XVIII(3/4), Munich: ACCEDO Verlagsgesellschaft.

Desai, M., 2004. Monetarism: a response to Minford and Mayer. *World Economics*, 5(3), pp. 165–170.

Desai, M., 2005. Will India ever catch up with China? *Journal of South Asian Studies*, August.

Desai, M., Henry, B., Mosley, A. and Pemberton, M., 2006. A clarification of Goodwin model of growth cycle. *Journal of Economic Dynamics and Control*, 12, pp. 2661–2670.

Desai, M., 2006. Michio Morishima, 1923–2004. *Proceedings of the British Academy*, 138, pp. 259–281.

Desai, M., 2007. Memories on Monroe? Econometric computing in the early 1960s. *Journal of Economic and Social Measurement*, 32, pp. 35–38.

Desai, M., 2007. Pobreza y governanza [Poverty and governance]. *Mundo Siglo*, XXI(9), pp. 5–30.

Other writings

Desai, M., 1968. Computer simulation of California dairy industry. [Monograph.] Department of Agricultural Economics, University of California, Berkeley.

Desai, M., 1973. The uneven development of nationalism among the Indian bourgeoisie: a comparative study of cotton textile and jute mill owners. *XXIXth International Congress of Orientalists*. (Abstract published in *Abstracts of Papers*, section 6–7, p. 105. Paris: Yves Hervoulet, Secretary-General ICO).

Desai, M., 1981. A nation of shopkeepers? Political economy of the British disease. Lecture at Kansai Economic Research Centre, Osaka, 17 March, 1981. Published in Japanese.

Desai, M., 1981. British economic crisis and Marxian alternative strategies; a dialogue between Meghnad Desai and Makoto Itoh. 15 March, 1981. Published in Japanese.

Desai, M., 1984. Foreword. *Time and the macroeconomic analysis of income* by Alvaro Cencini. London: Francis Pinter.

Desai, M., 1988. Dans six mois tout peut craquer. Interview with Beatrice Deavaus in *Le soir*. Brussels, 28 October 1988.

Desai, M., 1989. Foreword. *Dialectics and Social Theory, the Logic of Capital* by A. Shamsavari. Braunton Devon: Merlin Books.

Desai, M., 1989. Indian planning: techniques, perspectives and context. SOAS, *Conference on state and development planning in India*. London, April 1989.

Desai, M., 1993. Capitalism, socialism and the Indian economy. EXIM Bank lecture, Bombay, 4 January. Published, Bombay: EXIM Bank.

Desai, M., 1993. Economic prospects for India and Britain. *Handbook of the British Association of People of Indian Origin* (BAPIO). Festival edition, pp. 38–41.

Desai, M., 1994. The economic policy of the BJP. *NCSAS discussion paper no.1*. National Centre for South Asian Studies, Melbourne, Australia, January.

Desai, M., 1997. Fifty years: a balance sheet. *Handbook of the British Association of People of Indian Origin* (BAPIO). In: P. Flather and S. Mani, eds. LAAY World Features.

Desai, M. and Lord Kilmarnock, 1997. Destiny not defeat: Reforming the Lords'. *Labour in action*. Fabian Society.

Desai, M., 1998. Globalisation: for and against. E.P. Thompson memorial lecture. Worcester Trades Union Council & Friends of E.P. Thompson.

Desai, M., 1999. Does India need new politics? Indian Council for Research on International Economic Relations & The Associated Chambers of Commerce and Industry of India, November.

Desai, M., 1999. What should be India's economic priorities in a globalising world. Indian Council for Research on International Economic Relations & The Associated Chambers of Commerce and Industry of India, 6 January.

Desai, M., 2000. Amartya Sen. Prospect, 54. [online]. Available at: https://www.prospectmagazine.co.uk/2000/07/amartyasen/ [accessed 30 June 2011].

Desai, M., 2001. The debt of development: beyond the question of price. Nigerian Institute of International Affairs, Lecture series No. 80, November.

Desai, M., 2002. Death, democracy and decline. *Britannica India book of the year*. pp. viii–xvi. Encyclopaedia Britannica India.

Desai, M., 2006. Counting the costs: the effects of diversity for the British community. *Catalyst*, May–June.

Desai, M., 2006. The poverty of politics and the politics of poverty. Ramkrishna Hegde Lecture Delhi, January.

Desai, M. and W. Hutton, 2007. Does the future really belong to China? *Prospect*, 130. [online]. Available at: http://www.prospectmagazine.co.uk/2007/01/doesthefuturereallybelongtochina/ [accessed 30 June 2011].

Desai, M., 2007. Gandhi & Gandhi. *India International Centre Quarterly*, 34(2).

Desai, M., 2008. Southern engines of global growth: very long cycles or short spurts? *WIDER*, February.

Desai, M., 2009. The great Dalit hope. *Prospect*, 158. [online]. Available at: https://www.prospectmagazine.co.uk/2009/05/thegreatdalithope/ [accessed 30 June 2011].

Desai, M., 2009. Rama: the God that divides. *The Little Magazine*.

Index

Page numbers with 'n' are notes; with 't' are tables; 'b' boxes.